D0342722

Praise for

WHERE A MAN STANDS

"An inspirational must-read, *Where a Man Stands* is about human connection, rising above barriers, and seeing beyond the surface. It's an uplifting tale that shows us what is possible when we take a stand."

—T.D. Jakes, *New York Times* bestselling author

"*Where a Man Stands* will inspire by example and bring tears of happiness to those who honor and admire achieving great success out of the mouth of adversity."

—Suzanne Somers, actress, *New York Times* bestselling author

"*Where a Man Stands* is one of those books that is impossible to put down! The only way I can try to understand Carter's experience is to reminisce about a championship fight in 1981 against Tommy Hearns when my left eye was closed shut and the temperature in the ring in Las Vegas was 100 degrees. It's during those moments in our lives that we question, do we proceed and reach for respect and equality or do we quit? Carter answered, and it's a victory for all of us!"

—Sugar Ray Leonard

"If you believe that a single person can change the course of your life, this book is for you. Carter and Steven's friendship and their willingness to put everything on the line for one another is remarkable. *Where a Man Stands* is a winner."

—Bill Rancic, *New York Times* bestselling author, star of *Giuliana and Bill*, winner of NBC's *The Apprentice*

"I have known Carter and Steven for over four decades. Their inspirational story proves that the measure of a man lies in where he stands when circumstances are far from ideal."

—Josh Berger, CBE, President of Warner Brothers UK, Spain, and Ireland

"*Where a Man Stands* provides a powerful and heartwarming story of race, class, and friendship in Beverly Hills, California, where character triumphs over prejudice and hope for a post-racial society remains eternal. Readers will enthusiastically stand with Paysinger and Fenton as they break down racial barriers and implement educational reforms at Beverly Hills High School."

—F. Michael Higginbotham, Joseph Curtis Professor of Law at the University of Baltimore, author of *Ghosts of Jim Crow*

"When someone's life is at a crossroad, you can be the blessing that puts them on the correct path. At a pivotal point in my life, Carter was this blessing for me. Providing me with genuine love, guidance, and a sense of belonging—family."

—Adam Kennybrew, head football coach, Willamette High School

"*Where a Man Stands* is an inspiring story of friendship and the challenges in life. Carter and Steven prove that if given a chance you can accomplish your dreams with hard work, perseverance, courage, and faith."

—Marianna and Roger Staubach,
Heisman Trophy winner, Super Bowl MVP

WHERE A MAN STANDS

Two Different Worlds, an Impossible Situation,
and the Unexpected Friendship that Changed Everything

CARTER PAYSINGER *and* STEVEN FENTON

HOWARD BOOKS
A Division of Simon & Schuster, Inc.
New York   Nashville   London   Toronto   Sydney   New Delhi

Howard Books
A Division of Simon & Schuster, Inc.
1230 Avenue of the Americas
New York, NY 10020

Copyright © 2014 by Carter Paysinger and Steven Fenton

Scripture quotations are from The Holy Bible, English Standard Version, copyright © 2001 by Crossway Bibles, a division of Good News Publishers. Used by permission. All rights reserved.

All rights reserved, including the right to reproduce this book or portions thereof in any form whatsoever. For information address Howard Books Subsidiary Rights Department, 1230 Avenue of the Americas, New York, NY 10020.

First Howard Books hardcover edition November 2014

HOWARD and colophon are trademarks of Simon & Schuster, Inc.

For information about special discounts for bulk purchases, please contact Simon & Schuster Special Sales at 1-866-506-1949 or business@simonandschuster.com

The Simon & Schuster Speakers Bureau can bring authors to your live event. For more information or to book an event, contact the Simon & Schuster Speakers Bureau at 1-866-248-3049 or visit our website at www.simonspeakers.com.

Interior design by Davina Mock-Maniscalco
Jacket design by Gearbox Design
Jacket art by Brandon Hill

Manufactured in the United States of America

10 9 8 7 6 5 4 3 2 1

Library of Congress Cataloging-in-Publication Data

Paysinger, Carter.
    Where a man stands : two different worlds, an impossible situation, and the unexpected friendship that changed everything / Carter Paysinger and Steven Fenton.
        pages   cm
    1. Paysinger, Carter. 2. Fenton, Steven. 3. African American school principals—California—Beverly Hills—Biography. 4. Beverly Hills High School (Beverly Hills, Calif.)—Biography. 5. Friendship—Case studies. 6. Beverly Hills (Calif.)—Biography. 7. Beverly Hills (Calif.)—Race relations. I. Fenton, Steven. II. Title.
    LA2317.P39A3 2014
    370.92—dc23
    [B]
                                                                    2013050132

ISBN 978-1-4767-1140-9
ISBN 978-1-4767-1141-6 (ebook)

CARTER:

To my heroes:
Lessie and Carter Paysinger Sr.
and to the love of my life: Karen

STEVEN:

To the three men who changed my life:
Frank Fenton, Carter Paysinger & Al Silvera
and . . . to the woman who saved it:
Leeza Gibbons

*The ultimate measure of a man is not where he stands
in moments of comfort and convenience,
but where he stands at times of challenge and controversy.*

—MARTIN LUTHER KING JR.

INTRODUCTION

South Los Angeles, California
August 11, 1965

C ARTER, COME HERE quick. You need to see this."
   I was eight years old when I heard my momma call out for my father, her voice loud and urgent. Something was wrong. My father, Carter Sr., dropped what he was doing and ran into the living room. I followed him there.

For the next few minutes we stood silently and stared at our small black-and-white TV. Instinctively, I leaned against my mother's leg and held on to her dress. From what I could tell, there was a war movie on TV—buildings on fire, people fighting in the streets, stores with shattered windows. It reminded me of the newsreels they showed us in history class.

"Shootings are being reported all over the city," I heard an announcer say.

Then the strangest thing happened.

I heard gunshots coming not from the screen but from somewhere outside my house. Police sirens sounded on our street. I caught the strong smell of smoke and fire. What I was seeing on TV was suddenly happening all around me. But why?

"What's wrong, Momma?" asked Vonzie, my youngest brother, in a desperate little voice.

"I don't know, baby," my mother said. "I don't know."

My father went to the front of the house to see what was going on. I followed and peered out from behind him. Across the street, people ran in and out of the Better Foods Supermarket, where we did our shopping. They were lugging away bags and boxes of food. All the store's windows were smashed into pieces.

I had a sudden, terrible thought: *They're going to burn down Better Foods. Then they're going to burn down our house.*

A day later soldiers with guns stormed our neighborhood. An army truck blocked off our street. We weren't allowed to leave our house, and the sound of sirens and the smell of smoke got worse. Once or twice I mustered the courage to peek out the bottom of our living room window, beneath the drawn shades. I was terrified but I didn't know of what, and I wanted to put a face on my fear. Who was going to come in and hurt my family? The police? The soldiers? The angry people on TV? My own neighbors?

My mother and father had taught me how to pray, so I prayed no one would kill us or burn down our home.

It would be a few days before I heard people use the term "Watts Riots." All I knew back when it happened was that the streets I used to play on, where my brothers and I tossed baseballs and footballs for hours on carefree summer days, no longer belonged to me.

I guess you could say that was the day my education began.

———

NEARLY HALF A CENTURY LATER, on another hot day in 2010, I sat in a crowded conference room in an office building in Beverly Hills. I was fifty-three and in a suit and tie. Beverly Hills is only twelve miles from where I grew up in South Central, Los Angeles—from where the Watts Riots tore apart my neighborhood—yet I might as well have been on another planet.

Beverly Hills—mythical land of cream-white mansions, towering palms, swimming pools, and movie stars. Home to Rodeo Drive, the swankiest street in the world, where the cheapest socks at a store called Bijan will cost you $25 to $50 a sock! A place that exists as much in the American imagination as it does in California.

A place where only 2 percent of residents are black—the mirror image of South Central, where only 2 percent of residents are white.

What was I doing in Beverly Hills?

I was there for a meeting of the local board of education, which was holding a controversial vote to elect the next principal of the city's most famous school:

Beverly Hills High School.

If you've ever watched the popular '90s TV series *Beverly Hills 90210*, about a high school full of rich kids in BMWs and designer jeans, you should know that show was based on Beverly Hills High. It's been around for a hundred years, and it's catered to some of the richest sons and daughters of Hollywood—people like Rob Reiner and Angelina Jolie and Richard Dreyfuss and Jamie Lee Curtis and Lenny Kravitz and even Betty White.

Maybe you caught a glimpse of the school in the movie *Clueless*, or in the classic *It's a Wonderful Life*. Remember that scene where Jimmy Stewart and Donna Reed are dancing in the gym and the floor splits open and they fall into a swimming pool? That was filmed in Beverly High's famous Swim Gym, which, as far as I know, is the only gym in the country that has a basketball court built right over a functional pool.

Judging from all that, your first impression of Beverly Hills

High—or simply Beverly, as people who went there call it—might be that it's some kind of gilded fortress where the famous and privileged park their kids for four cushy years. And I guess there is a bit of truth to that. But it is not the whole truth, not by a long shot. Sometimes things aren't what they seem to be at first glance.

You see, Beverly also embraced a skinny black kid from beleaguered South Central and gave him the chance to change the course of his future. As unlikely as it may sound, I, too, went to Beverly.

And the board of education vote that day was controversial because of the man being voted on. If he was elected principal, he would upend a century of tradition and break through barriers that were thought to be unbreakable.

You know how in movies it's always the white guy who goes into the run-down black school and saves the underprivileged kids?

Well, this would have been the opposite of that.

This man would become the first African-American principal of one of the country's most privileged schools.

The man they were voting on was me.

——————

I NEVER WANTED TO BE a principal. I was going to be a professional baseball player. After that I was going to be a real estate mogul—the black Donald Trump. I believed these things were my destiny.

But sometimes destiny isn't ours to understand.

I wound up coming back to Beverly and becoming a coach and teacher there. I spent much of my life on a playing field—not with professional athletes but with a bunch of kids. Time after time I tried to leave that field and escape those kids—to get on with my real life— but something kept pulling me back.

Maybe it was the beautiful fairness of the playing field, which is flat and doesn't play favorites. On a field it doesn't matter if you wear the latest fashions from Halston, as many of my Beverly classmates did, or your cousin's hand-me-downs. Doesn't matter if you drive a Jaguar to school or have to walk ten extra blocks to take your little brother to class before morning practice.

Doesn't matter if your mom and dad are rich and famous or if you're the son of a cafeteria worker and a custodian.

On a playing field all that matters is what you can achieve.

Or maybe it was the Beverly kids who kept pulling me back.

You see, at first glance the students at Beverly might seem far luckier in life than me. But who's to say living in a mansion with four wings is better than sharing a tiny room with four brothers? Who's to say every parent in Beverly Hills is as fierce a champion of her children as my mother was of hers? A home is nothing but an empty house if it has no leader, and if your parents are absent it doesn't matter if they're crack addicts or CEOs. Dysfunction doesn't discriminate.

In the end, kids are kids, no matter where they come from. And *all* kids can lose their way without someone to believe in them.

Maybe once I learned that, there was no way I could leave them.

My reward for staying was better than any trophy or title—I've been told I have made a difference in the lives of hundreds of kids. "*My* kids," I like to call them. In this way Beverly became like a second family to me—a place where I was accepted, nourished, valued, and loved.

But even so there came a time when everything I believed to be true about the school—everything I thought was true about *me*—came crumbling down. When the Beverly Hills High I loved so much seemed likely to vanish forever. When all the dreams I had for my life seemed out of reach.

Had the sacrifices I'd made been worth it? Had I really made a difference? Had I truly been accepted at Beverly, or would I always be no more than the black kid from South Central?

Had I somehow wasted my life?

That is when, in my darkest hour, something amazing happened.

Just when I found I could no longer help my Beverly kids, that's when one of those kids came back and *saved me*.

Like I said, sometimes destiny isn't ours to know.

―――――――――

THIS BOOK IS ABOUT JOURNEYS—NOT just mine from the streets of South Central to that conference room in Beverly Hills but the ones we all take in our lives, toward our best and brightest selves. "Don't just strive to be good," my momma always told me. "Strive to be great." Those words, embedded in my mind now, are at the heart of this story.

This book is also about character—about reaching to help your neighbor when your neighbor is down. It's about race and class and facing obstacles rooted in fear and stereotypes. It's about how the truth never lies on the surface, but somewhere deeper—somewhere we have to dig to get to.

But most of all, this story is about taking a stand.

Because, as I found out in that conference room, where you stand, and with whom, and for what, matters as much as anything in life.

PART

1

CHAPTER

1

Beverly Hills, California
1972

I PRESSED MY FACE against the car window and watched my world
disappear.

We were rolling down Santa Monica Boulevard in Los Angeles. I
was buckled in the passenger seat of my family's big powder-blue Mercury Montclair, next to my mother, Lessie Paysinger, who was driving.
My mother sat bolt straight, same as she always did, both hands firmly
on the deep-dish steering wheel and eyes never leaving the road, even
when she talked to me. She was still wearing the blue floral dress and
white shoes from her job as a school cafeteria worker. Her hairnet was
tucked inside her purse.

"You know, Carter," she said, "Beverly Hills High is a very special
place. This is your chance to get a great education."

"I know, Momma."

"I have no idea what they're going to ask you. But you just answer
them as honestly as you can, you hear?"

"I will, Momma."

I was fourteen years old, and this was the most important day of my life.

Where I lived, in South Central, Los Angeles, we had low-slung houses and chain-link fences and lots of giant billboards. But as we drove down Santa Monica, those gave way to spacious homes, majestic lawns, and men with rakes and hoses fussing over sidewalks. Where I lived, we had more electrical poles than trees, but now the poles became swaying palms and stately eucalyptus. Block after block I saw exotic, unfamiliar sights—flowering vines spilling over wooden fences, rows of elegant Tudor homes, birds prancing on privet hedges.

In South Central the sun is unblocked and merciless, beating down on the asphalt all day long. But in Beverly Hills the sunlight flickers gently through leaves and fronds.

I felt like my childhood was receding in the rearview mirror.

We were driving to Beverly Hills because, just three weeks earlier, my mom had a talk with the mother of one of my Little League teammates.

"Lessie, do you know about the multicultural permit?"

The multicultural permit allowed a few minority kids from less privileged parts of Los Angeles to attend the exclusive and predominantly white Beverly Hills High—which normally was only open to kids who lived in Beverly Hills. Each year several hundred students applied for the permit, and only a couple of handfuls got one. If you won a permit, it was like winning the lottery. It was the golden ticket.

Back then my options for high school were limited. Most likely I'd wind up where nearly all my friends were going: Crenshaw High School in South Central or University High in West Los Angeles. These were not terrible schools, at least not then. But my mother wasn't the type to settle for "not terrible."

So, one day after speaking with my friend's mother, Momma sat me down at the kitchen table and spread a bunch of papers in front of me.

"We're going to apply for a permit for you to go to Beverly Hills High," she announced.

I was confused. Me? In Beverly Hills? It didn't make sense. If all my friends were going to Crenshaw or Uni, why weren't those schools good enough for me? Why did I have to go somewhere I didn't know and didn't belong?

Of course, it didn't much matter what I wanted. Issues like these weren't open for debate in my family. Once my mom decided I was going to Beverly, good luck to anyone who got in her way. And that included a neatly dressed, perfectly groomed man named Mr. Hoag—Beverly's acceptance officer.

The man my mother was driving me to see.

———

AFTER JUST A FEW MINUTES my mother pulled the Mercury onto the campus of Beverly. It sat on some nineteen rolling acres on the west side of Beverly Hills, on the border of Century City and around the corner from the LA Country Club. I saw gently sloping hills and classical white buildings, and behind them the awesome high-rises of Century City. It all looked like a movie set to me.

"Now remember, Carter, it isn't certain you'll be able to go to this school," my mother said. "It all comes down to this interview. So don't say anything we'll both regret later."

"I won't, Momma."

"I know you won't."

A security guard pointed us toward the school's garage. I will never forget what I saw next. Rows and rows of Porsches and Mercedes and

BMWs and other sleek, shiny machines lined up in orderly parking spaces separated by crisp white lines.

I'd never seen so much luxury in my life, and certainly not all in one place. It was just breathtaking. My mother found a spot and parked the Mercury, and for the first time I felt nervous—like someone had kicked me in the stomach. My legs were rubber as I got out of the car.

"Carter," my mother said, sensing my nerves.

"Yes, Momma?"

"No matter what happens, I'm proud of you and I love you. You know that, don't you?"

"Yes, Momma," I said. "I love you, too."

WE WALKED DOWN A WIDE hallway and entered a room with creamy white walls and red carpets. There were shelves crowded with plaques and trophies and walls plastered with posters for school productions of *42nd Street* and *Singin' in the Rain*. I thought of the only posters I'd ever seen on the walls of Emerson and how they all began with the same two words: "DO NOT."

My mother and I sat down and waited. Before long a nice woman came over and nodded at me.

"Hello, Carter," she said. "Mr. Hoag will see you now."

I stood up slowly and looked over at my mother. She got up, too, and together we walked toward a closed door in the back of the office.

"Only Carter, Mrs. Paysinger," the nice woman said.

I looked up pleadingly at my mother, who smiled and narrowed her eyes and gave me a tiny nod. I'm not sure anyone else would have noticed that nod, but I did, and I knew just what it meant. My mother and I had our own language made up of looks, smiles, frowns, and nods, and this particular nod meant a lot.

My mother was saying, *Carter, it's all up to you now. This is your moment. This is your future we're talking about. You have to find a way to make this work.*

Carter, you can do this.

Slowly I walked toward Mr. Hoag's office. Picture a thin, lanky kid in tan pants and a tucked-in, button-down shirt, trying not to trip over himself. The nice woman opened the door and motioned to me.

I leaned forward and peered in. The office was filled with framed photos of Mr. Hoag and his radiantly blond wife and their two blond sons smiling on sunny beaches and snowy slopes and silvery boats. And there, behind a huge mahogany desk, sat Mr. Hoag himself.

"Come on in, Carter," he said, standing up. We shook hands, and he settled back behind his desk. He had a deep tan and styled hair. I sat in a chair that was too big for me and so plush I felt myself sink.

"So, Carter, you'd like to attend our school," Mr. Hoag began. "What is the most important reason you want to come here?"

My mouth felt dry. I gripped the arm handles of my plush chair. Mr. Hoag waited for an answer.

Carter, this is your moment.

"HOP ON UP IN THIS chair, son."

I was seven when my father took me for my first haircut at Tolliver's Barber Shop. It was a small, square store on Western Avenue just a couple of blocks from our house. Lawrence Tolliver, the shop's owner, motioned me up into one of the big white barber's chairs. I slid in and stared at my nervous face in the mirror.

Tolliver's was crowded, noisy, and alive. I don't remember it ever not being packed. There were men everywhere, in the chairs, on benches and stools, standing in corners, gathered outside. Pastors, cops, businessmen, construction workers—everyone went to Tolli-ver's. There was a television blasting, but the sound of men joking and arguing and shouting all but drowned it out. The real music of the place was laughter, raised voices, and the clip-clip of scissors, and that music never shut off.

These men, I soon learned, weren't at Tolliver's just to get a hair-cut. Some of them didn't come for haircuts at all. They were there to be in each other's company—and to solve the problems of the world.

"That boy Jack Kennedy needs the black vote, and he knows it."

"Then he better do something about discrimination!"

"Who's gonna win the Clay-Liston fight?"

"No way Liston can beat him. Cassius is just too quick."

"I heard Elvis is coming to town to shoot a movie."

"Who cares about Elvis? Boy can't hold a candle to Sam Cooke."

Most of the stuff I heard at Tolliver's went straight over my head, but that didn't matter. Sitting in that big barber's chair, I got my first glimpse at what it meant to be a man. I learned how men stood, how they talked, how they gestured, what they valued. I learned what friendship and community meant to them. I learned how they didn't back down from what they believed in.

The haircuts were always secondary.

Eventually all three of my younger brothers—Carlton, Donald, and Vonzie—got their hair cut at Tolliver's, too. My father worked out a pretty good deal: normally a haircut was $2.50, but Mr. Tolliver cut all four of our heads plus my father's for an even ten bucks. Tolliver's on Saturdays became one of our many childhood rituals, like having delicious chicken sausage burgers at Mama's Chicken and playing football and basketball and baseball on the street outside our sin-gle-story, two-bedroom house on Manhattan Place, near the intersec-tion of Slauson and Western, in the neighborhood of South Central.

Today, when people hear the words "South Central," they think of guns, drugs, and violence. But the image they conjure up is only a tiny snapshot of a much more complex place. It says nothing of the people who live there, or the struggles they endure, or the texture of their lives, or the deep rich history of the community. It doesn't show you what's beneath the surface. When I was growing up in South Central—which back then was known as South Los Angeles—that snapshot was *not* the reality.

Back then, South Central was just about the best place in the world to be a boy.

I may have grown up without a lot of money, but I certainly didn't know it. I felt like we had everything a family could ever need. As far as I could tell, the six of us—my mother, Lessie; my father, Carter Sr.; and us four boys—never wanted for anything. My brothers and I shared two bunk beds in one small bedroom, an arrangement that, to some, might not sound ideal. But to us it was a blessing. It meant we could spend our days playing and hanging out, then come home and joke around some more right before bedtime. We didn't need more space—why would we? The last thing we wanted was to be split up.

Both my parents worked, my father gassing up and washing and later fixing cars in Paul Brooks Garage on Fairfax and Third (that was his main job, though he had two others) and my mother as a cafeteria worker, and later an administrator, for the Los Angeles Unified School District. My brothers and I occasionally got new clothes to wear, but we mainly wore hand-me-downs and constantly shared outfits. We had a backyard with trees and grass, which my father and his staff— and by that I mean his sons—kept mown. We sat together for dinner every night, and we went to Sunday school every week, and we looked out for one another, as people who love each other do.

On top of all that, we had a second family—South Central itself.

Where I grew up, the word "community" meant more than just a place to live. It meant a place to be raised. Your neighbors, local shopkeepers, the corner barber—everyone in the community was part of the same extended family. Everyone looked out for each other's kids. Everyone believed they were part of the same *team*. It wasn't just your parents who were raising you; it was the whole of South Central.

That is how my childhood passed—the pleasant rituals of family life, the endless summer days playing ball with my friends, the noisy afternoons at Tolliver's, the familiar sound of my mother calling, "Carter, you guys come in now. Time to eat!", the wonderful sameness and dependability of it all. If we were missing something, I sure didn't know what it was.

Then came August 11, 1965—the day the riots began.

———

AT FIRST MY PARENTS DIDN'T try to explain to us what was happening. I'm sure they didn't understand it themselves. My father told us to sit down in the back of the house and stay low. At one point I heard him say, "The whole city's on fire." I heard people yelling and running up and down our street and police cars and fire trucks racing by every few minutes. I don't remember going to sleep that first night.

Things only got worse in the next two days. I heard my parents talking about a citywide curfew, and we weren't allowed to leave our house, or even play in the backyard. We felt like prisoners. When I peeked out a window, I'd see army trucks and armed soldiers sealing off our street. I later learned the National Guard had rolled into South Central.

The presence of soldiers with weapons didn't make me feel any safer. From what I could see on TV, this was a war between police and citizens, specifically black citizens. Were these soldiers on our side or against us? I had no way of knowing. Some of them stood sentry outside of Better Foods, while others went door-to-door, asking about the looting. Some people in our neighborhood were arrested and taken away in handcuffs. The shock of it all, the sheer terror of being under siege like that, is something I can hardly exaggerate.

After three long days things began to calm down. The National Guard went away. Better Foods boarded up their windows, and the curfew was lifted. Slowly life in South Central went back to normal.

Except, of course, it never did.

After the riots a lot of white residents and business owners abandoned southern Los Angeles. Lots of middle-class black families left, too. Over time great swaths of southern LA became predominantly black and poor. Whole generations of young black men were swallowed up by the culture of gangs and drugs and violence that soon took root in South Central. The place I'd known as the best place in the world became a much darker, more fearsome place.

And over time the civic institutions in South Central deteriorated, too. The one thing my parents talked about most—the one essential thing that could save us from being swallowed up like so many South Central boys—became all but impossible to achieve in our hometown.

Getting a good education.

"SO, CARTER, YOU'D LIKE TO attend our school," Mr. Hoag said. "What is the most important reason you want to come here?" He fixed his eyes squarely on mine and waited for my answer.

When you're young, you don't have a lot of serious conversations. Once in a while your parents sit you down and tell you what's what, but most of the time you're under no obligation to form a serious thought. You're just a kid, after all. Your words don't carry weight.

But suddenly I felt like my words carried all the weight in the world. I felt like what I said next would determine my future.

"I would like to get the best education possible, sir," I finally answered. Obviously, I left out the part about wanting to go to Uni or Crenshaw with my friends.

Mr. Hoag nodded and made a notation on his pad of paper.

"What's your favorite subject in school?"

"History."

"Why history?"

"Well, I like studying the problems we've had in the past and figuring out how we should solve them."

Another notation.

"What interests do you have outside of school?" Mr. Hoag asked.

"Sports, sir," I answered. "I like to play sports."

"Oh yeah? What's your favorite sport?"

"Baseball. I like basketball and football, but baseball is my favorite."

"Carter," Mr. Hoag asked, "do you think you could make our high school baseball team?"

Something happened when I heard that question. Somehow my nervousness went away. I may not have been raised in Beverly Hills, and I may not have been driven there in a Rolls-Royce or a BMW. But no matter where I was or who I was talking to, there was something I was absolutely sure of.

And that was sports.

Carter, this is your moment.

"Yes," I told Mr. Hoag, "I think I could make your baseball team."

He looked up from his pad.

"You sound pretty confident about that."

"Yes, I am. I am confident I could make the team."

Mr. Hoag made one last notation and looked up again. All the jitters I'd felt before were gone now, drained away. I sat up straight in my chair, and I held Mr. Hoag's gaze.

"Any last comments, Carter?"

"Yes, sir," I said. "This is the most beautiful school I've ever seen. And the reason I want to come to this school is because I want to be somebody someday. I hope you'll give me the chance to be somebody."

Mr. Hoag smiled, stood up, and shook my hand.

"All right, Carter," he said. "We'll let you know."

I CAME BACK INTO THE main office, but my mother wasn't there. I waited for a few minutes, then wandered outside and onto the main campus. When I turned a corner, the sun blinded me, and I had to squint to be able to see. As soon as I could, something remarkable came into view.

A vast, glorious, endless field, with a baseball diamond at one end and the greenest grass infield you could imagine.

Not a single infield in South Central had a blade of grass on it. They were all dirt and rocks. From the top of the hill I looked down at the sprawling field, and I was sure I was looking at the most beautiful thing I'd ever seen.

I was looking at the Beverly Hills High athletic field.

It may have been precisely then that I realized the meaning of what my mother always told me about good versus great.

There were plenty of schools in Los Angeles that were good. But this place was *great*. I finally understood the difference and the importance of striving for one, not the other. And all at once I was filled with an undeniable urge.

I want to play on that field, I thought. *I want to go to this school.*

"Carter!"

It was my mother, calling from just outside the administrative building. I ran to her, and we went down to the garage and got back in the Mercury to drive home to South Central.

Two weeks later, on a Wednesday evening in April, I came home from school and saw my mother standing in the living room. She had a white envelope in her hand.

"Guess what I have here in this envelope, Carter?" she said.

"I don't know, Momma, what?"

But I already knew what it was from the big smile on her face.

CHAPTER

2

IT WAS OFFICIAL: I was going to Beverly Hills High. "You're going to be a Norman!" my mother announced, invoking the school's team mascot, before wrapping me up in a big hug.

On the one hand, the news made me feel pretty good. I'd impressed Mr. Hoag enough to get in, and I'd made my mother proud.

On the other hand, I wasn't completely sure I *wanted* to go to Beverly.

Much as I loved the baseball field, I didn't really want to hear what my friends in South Central would have to say about me going there. Three years earlier I'd attended an elementary school that was mostly white, and my friends had had a lot to say about that.

Because both my parents worked long hours, they'd had to devise an elaborate system to get all four of us kids to school and back every day. My mother got up early, roused us from sleep, fed us breakfast, got us ready for school, and handed us over to my father, who was just coming home from his graveyard shift at the garage. My dad then drove us the one mile to school, rushed home to get some sleep, picked us up after school, and handed us back to my mother—who was just coming home from work—before setting out for his second job.

There was no margin for error in our system.

But then, out of the blue, officials at our elementary school in South Central switched Vonzie and Donald onto different schedules, throwing my parents' system into chaos. There was no way they could get us all to school on time now. My mother went and pleaded with the officials.

"I'm sorry, Mrs. Paysinger, there's nothing we can do," they told her.

"Well, thank you very much, but there's something *I* can do."

With that my mother yanked us right out of school.

She found another school for us in West Los Angeles—a top school with a great reputation, Overland Elementary. They had room for my brothers and me to enroll in the fall, so that was no problem. The only hitch was that Overland was much farther away from our home.

"Carter," she said to my dad, "you can drive them every morning, and I'll pick 'em up when they finish the after-school program."

"Lessie, you gonna want to drive all that way every day?"

"I'd rather do that than deal with those trifling old folks up at their old school," she said. "Besides, my boys weren't learning anything there anyway."

My father didn't seem convinced, but he knew enough not to argue. He could see my mother was on a mission—and that mission was getting her children the best education possible. Scheduling issues and inconvenience were no match for a mother on a mission. "You don't have to see the whole staircase," she told my father, quoting Martin Luther King Jr. "You just need to take the first step."

I spent the sixth grade at Overland, and it was unlike any school I had known. It was immaculate, the playground was huge, and the students all got along. For the first time in my life I was in an atmosphere that was all about learning.

And that long commute? Somehow, my mother organized the parents of some other kids who were also coming from South Central to rent a yellow bus that would come through our neighborhood and take us to school.

She took the first step, and the staircase came into view.

The next year, I had to find a new junior high, and my mother enrolled me at a school in South Los Angeles. I was back in my own neighborhood. One afternoon, though, I was hanging out with some friends after class when a couple of them turned on me.

"What's the matter, the white folks kicked you out of their school already?" one student said.

"What's your name?" asked another. "Oh yeah, Uncle Tom."

My friends had a pretty good laugh over that. After a few weeks things calmed down, and the kids left me alone.

But then, a few days after I got my acceptance letter from Beverly, I was playing ball with some friends in South Central.

"Hey, Carter," one of my buddies said, "how many times you going to have those white people kick you out before you come back to the neighborhood?"

I hated the feeling of having somehow betrayed my friends. At the same time I understood what my mother was telling me about not settling. But going for great, I was realizing, came with a cost. And sometimes, that cost was losing friends.

And so in the weeks before my first day at Beverly I spent a lot of time wondering if I belonged there. My greatest fear was that, no matter how hard I tried, I would never really be a Norman.

TO GET TO BEVERLY I had to take two buses—one all the way up Western Avenue to Olympic, and another west all the way to Beverly Hills. It took about an hour each way. But on my first day, my parents drove me to school in the Mercury.

On the ride over I was nervous as heck. My only goal was to not stand out in any way. I know that's the goal most kids have on their first day of high school, but I felt the extra pressure of being a black kid at a mostly white school. In any case, it was too late to do anything about my doubts and fears. Whether or not I belonged, I was there.

My dad, ready for work in his dark-blue factory overalls and white shirt, drove up to the Moreno Drive entrance, and we all got out. To the left I could see the building that housed the gym and swimming pool, and to the right was the main campus building sitting atop a big sloping hill. Kids were milling around in clusters, waving and yelling happily at one another.

The first thing I noticed was the clothes.

There was no uniform at Beverly, so you could wear anything you wanted. On my first day I wore khaki pants and a white button-down shirt my mother had ironed the night before. I wasn't trying to dress any certain way. I didn't have an image. All I wanted was an outfit that would make me invisible.

I could see that many of the other students, though, were done up head to toe in the latest fashions. My parents bought me new clothes exactly twice a year: during Easter vacation and in August before the new semester. But some kids at Beverly went shopping for new clothes *every week*. They always had the best designer jeans, the best tops and sweaters, the best shoes and sneakers, the best everything. For some of them, it was hugely important to be the first to wear any hot new style or trendy outfit. I'd never known people who devoted so much thought and energy to their clothes; for my friends and me, clothes were functional. But not here—at Beverly, clothes were a statement. A statement I couldn't hope to make in my khakis and button-down shirts.

I hesitated before walking away from my mother and father. I squeezed my little notebook in my hand and felt a pang of homesickness.

"Don't be nervous, Carter," my mother said.

"I'm not nervous," I lied.

"Just pay attention and keep your head down, and you'll be fine," my father told me.

"I know, Pops. I'll be okay."

My parents hugged me and, with a final wave, left me to my new world. I watched as they drove away and nearly got sideswiped by a silver Porsche.

———

TAKING A DEEP BREATH, I trundled up the hill to the main building. "Look like you belong," I kept telling myself. But I had yet to see another face that looked like mine.

A big banner above the front entrance read:

WELCOME BEVERLY HILLS HIGH SCHOOL CLASS OF '72!

Inside the main building I found my freshly painted locker and tried the combination lock. To my surprise, it worked. Functioning locks were a rarity in the schools I knew.

I was early, so the first place I went was the library. I figured I could always hide in there if things didn't work out.

The library was astonishing.

It was a huge, sprawling room with giant shelves of books and rows of cubicles for students to study in. Some of the cubicles even had little TV screens attached. There were also conference rooms for kids to work together in study groups. It was like the Disneyland of schools, just so perfect, so complete, as if nothing in this world mattered more than helping students succeed.

For the rest of the day, as I walked around, I had to be careful to keep my mouth closed so no one would see how awestruck I was.

I had a math class to lead off the morning, and I strolled in and sat in the first open seat I could find, toward the back. Most of the students obviously knew each other and were busy catching up on their summers. I was relieved to see there were three or four other black kids in the class, but even so it dawned on me that I was in a room filled predominantly with white people.

Back in South Central I was practically always around people who looked and talked and acted like me. The people who cooked us meals in restaurants and read us sermons in church and sold us shoes and cut our hair—they were all black. All my friends were black, and all their friends, and all our cousins, and pretty much everyone we knew. Certainly we came across white people in our lives—a teacher, a police officer, a cashier—but the truth is I could go months at a time without interacting with someone who wasn't black. In South Central we had our own little world, and we were happy with that world and didn't need much, if anything, that we couldn't find there.

And so everywhere I went—a store, a church, a baseball field—I always fit right in. But now, all of a sudden, I stood out. I was outnumbered. I was the stranger in someone else's world. A million thoughts raced through my mind as I sat in the back by myself. *Are all these kids rich? Are the few black students rich, too? Do they all know each other? What in the world am I doing here? Will I ever fit in?*

No one spoke to me that first class, but I did overhear one student tell another, "You have to try the cinnamon rolls in the cafeteria. The cinnamon rolls are *amazing*." I'm not sure I even knew what a cinnamon roll was, but I vowed to try one just as soon as lunch—or Nutrition, as they called it at Beverly—rolled around.

The cafeteria, it turned out, was even more astonishing than the library.

I walked into a cavernous room on the second floor of the main building, framed on one end by a giant set of windows overlooking the city of Beverly Hills and the Hollywood Hills. The serving area was like a huge open food court, with different stations set up and cash registers at one end. Every Easter our parents took us to Clifton's Cafeteria in downtown Los Angeles, a cafeteria-style eatery we all thought was the height of fine dining.

This cafeteria was even better.

I walked around the serving area in a daze and piled a few dishes on my tray. It was pretty hard to choose, considering the selection— mounds of chicken and steak and mashed potatoes and fresh pasta and vegetables and a million fixings before you even came to the desserts. I paid at the cash register—my parents started me out with a few dollars—then walked toward the dining area. This was my first moment of truth at Beverly—where would I sit for lunch? Would I make new friends and be part of a group? Or was I going to be one of those guys who always ate alone?

I walked slowly, tray in hand, past tables full of white kids. No one paid much attention to me, except maybe to look at me sideways, then get back to their conversations. I saw an empty chair here and there, but they were all in the middle of clusters of happy, laughing white students. I didn't have the nerve to plop myself in the middle of a group—not on my first day, anyway—so I kept walking. And, I wondered, did I even *want* to sit at a table full of white kids who didn't really want me as a part of their group? So what if I ate lunch by myself? Food would taste the same, wouldn't it? If everyone was going to ignore me, well, I was more than happy to ignore them right back. I kept walking and hoped I'd figure out where to sit before I ran out of tables.

But before I had a chance to sit anywhere, I heard the most welcome sound in the world: someone calling my name.

"Hey, Carter, over here!"

I turned and recognized a boy named Michael Greene who had gone to Emerson with me. He was at a table with eight or nine other black kids, a few of whom I also recognized from the neighborhood. This was Michael's first day at Beverly, too, but his brother and sister went there, so he felt a lot more comfortable and confident than I did. I walked over and sat next to him. I guess he could tell how anxious I was.

"What's wrong, blood?" he said, using common slang that long predated any gang reference. "You act like you never been in Beverly Hills before. You look like a tourist in New York City."

All the kids had a good laugh, and it actually made me feel better. Michael introduced me to everyone as his buddy Carter. Minutes later, another group of black kids walked into the cafeteria, including several more who had been at Emerson with me. There were the Garrison twins, Marilynne and Carolynne, and this kid named Howard Lewis, and Michael's older brother, Lincoln. Soon, the whole group was laughing and joking, and for the first time that day I relaxed. For the first time I felt like I might belong after all.

But it was not lost on me, even then, that I was sitting at a table with only black students while the other tables were filled with white kids.

It made me wonder if this was the way things were going to be at

Beverly. And it reminded me of something I'd seen in Louisiana on one of my family vacations, when I first experienced what I later learned was called segregation.

———————

I SAY THEY WERE VACATIONS, but really they were reunions. Most summers we'd pack up the Mercury and drive to Louisiana and Michigan to meet up with relatives and explore our family history. The first stop was where my dad grew up—the tiny town of Plain Dealing, Louisiana. Honestly, the town is so small it's only about five minutes from the "Welcome to Plain Dealing" sign to the one that says, "Come Again."

But it was there, a step or two from the Arkansas border, that my father's grandparents staked their title to 160 acres in the 1800s, forever claiming the fertile land as Paysinger land. My father and his seven siblings helped their father sharecrop the land, working fifteen-hour days and harvesting corn, cotton, and wheat.

When my dad turned eighteen, he left Plain Dealing to live with an aunt in Muskegon, Michigan, where he went to work making auto parts in the Campbell factory. My father found a girlfriend, too, but when she went away on vacation, he asked a buddy to help find him another girlfriend for the two weeks she was away.

The friend introduced him to a pretty young lady who lived a few streets down from his aunt's house—a young lady named Lessie.

For two weeks my father and Lessie had a lovely time together—until Lessie saw him sitting on a park bench with his old girlfriend, now back from vacation. Lessie stormed right over.

"Who's it gonna be, Carter, her or me?" she demanded.

"Now wait a minute, Lessie . . ."

"No, you have to choose right now. *Right now.* Who's it gonna be?"

My father was a big strong man with muscled forearms and broad shoulders. Still, he was no match for Lessie. He bid his old girlfriend good-bye, married Lessie out of high school, and one year later they had me. I may be partial, but I think my father chose wisely. Eventually, my parents moved their new family to California and onto a little street in South Central called Manhattan Place—the street where I grew up.

The drive from South Central back to Plain Dealing was a good 1,600 miles, and my folks took turns driving. They'd drive twenty-four hours straight and make it in one shot. They had to because finding hotels in the South that welcomed blacks wasn't easy. And we weren't alone; behind us in their own cars were my uncle Cal Bennet—we called him Uncle CB—with his wife, Lurene, and their kids, and Uncle John and Aunt Bessie and their kids. A bunch of other relatives were driving or flying in from other places as well.

We all descended on my grandmomma's one-story, wood-framed, two-bedroom white house, with its towering pecan tree and backyard swing big enough for three people. My family slept in one bedroom, while Uncle CB and his clan took the other. Grandmomma slept in the living room. Grandmomma's house had no running water, so we had to pump buckets up from the well and dump them in a tub out back. That tub was hauled inside, and the water was boiled in the kitchen and dumped back into a separate tub. The kids all took turns bathing in this tub.

All told, there were probably fifty Paysinger relatives scattered all over Plain Dealing for the reunion. For us kids, the next few days were simply magical. They were filled with games and swimming and playing and eating. In the evenings we'd light firecrackers until it got dark. Firecrackers were legal in Louisiana, and you could hear the sound of them echoing through the swampland. One of my cousins showed us a special way of flicking a firecracker from his hand, but when my brother Vonzie tried it, the firecracker went inside his shirt, where it exploded. He ran screaming to the house, and we had to put our firecrackers away.

One night we watched my father and one of our uncles shoot a hog right between the eyes. They skinned it, dug a big pit in the backyard, and barbecued the hog for two days. They did the same thing with a goat the next day. Watching my father shoot those animals made me realize I didn't know everything there was to know about him, or the world, like I thought I did.

The Paysinger feast went on all week, and the meals were something to behold. Barbecued beef, pork, goat, and chicken. Mounds of collard greens, corn on the cob, macaroni and cheese, and potato salad. And for dessert, big slices of peach cobbler and watermelon. Then afterward, when your stomach was bursting, a trip to the creek, where you'd play with the frogs and listen to their calls sounding through the trees under the bright light of the moon.

It seemed like heaven.

Then, one evening, my father and Uncle CB and Uncle John drove some of us kids to a local family restaurant on the Louisiana-Arkansas border. I absently walked up to the front door, but before I could go through, my father grabbed me by the shoulder and stopped me.

"Boy, pay attention," he said. "You can't go in that door."

I looked up and saw the front door was marked, "White People." Another door a few feet away said, "Colored People."

I was confused. I followed my family in through the "Colored People" door, and inside I noticed all the white people on one side of the restaurant and all the black people on the other. But what confounded me most of all was that the two doors led into the *very same room*. How could it be that you needed two doors to get people into the exact same space? The reality of segregation in Louisiana hit me like a kick in the teeth. I'd learned about things like racism in school, but I never dreamed it was still happening to this degree. My black cousins who lived in Plain Dealing didn't think anything of it. But when I got back to Grandmomma's and told my cousins from South Central about the two doors, they were as shocked as I was.

"Boy, you just keep living," my father told me. "There's gonna be a lot of things you're not gonna believe."

———

THERE WEREN'T TWO SEPARATELY MARKED doors leading into the cafeteria at Beverly, but once we all got in the same room, the white kids went one way and the black kids went the other. This wasn't like the segregation I'd seen in Louisiana. But was it segregation just the same?

Over time I'd learn few things in life are cut-and-dried—few things are either this or that. Most things are shaded and complex and far deeper than meets the eye. After all, that's precisely why my mother enrolled me at Beverly. I was there to experience the world that existed outside the bubble of my youth. I was there to try and *bridge* the gap between those two sets of kids in the cafeteria.

But that wasn't always easy to do.

On one of my first days at Beverly I was standing by my locker in the first-floor hallway when I felt someone run by me and rub my head.

"Thanks for the good luck!" he yelled out.

When I turned around, I saw four or five white students running away, laughing. I couldn't tell which one had rubbed my head. But I knew why he'd done it. It was some old tradition I didn't understand, based on the idea that rubbing a black person's head allowed you to steal their good luck. Usually only people who don't spend a lot of time around black people—and don't realize how offensive it is—dare do it.

A few days later I felt someone rub my head again in the hallway outside science class. This time I spun around and saw only one student running away. I knew who it was. He was a big white kid who was on the basketball team and thought of himself as the life of the party—the guy who could make everyone laugh. Later that day I saw him again outside the gym. He was by himself.

I took a deep breath and walked over.

"Don't touch my head again," I said.

"Hey, I was just playing."

"I don't care; it's not cool. Don't do it again."

"I'm sorry, man," he said. "I didn't mean any harm."

Then he walked away.

At the time I didn't believe he was genuinely sorry, and looking back on it now, I still don't. I believe he knew exactly how insulting it was. He never rubbed my head when I was with any of my friends, only when I was alone. And he never did it to my face, only when I had my back turned. He did it for laughs, and he didn't care how I felt about it.

But still, that doesn't mean he hated me or harbored any ill will. Maybe he was just repeating something he'd seen someone else do. Maybe he was acting on something he'd learned at home. Maybe he was just a stupid kid who still had a lot to learn. I had no way of knowing what was in his heart. Like I said, few things in life are cut-and-dried.

The truth is, I had my own secrets. I wasn't exactly who anyone thought I was, either. That's because at Beverly I had to live a kind of secret double life.

CHAPTER

3

ONE OF THE students I befriended my first year at Beverly was a black kid named Calvin. Calvin lived in Baldwin Hills, an upscale suburb only about a ten-minute drive from South Central, and he got into Beverly on a permit, same as I did. Calvin also had his own car, so every once in a while I'd ask him for a ride home after school. He didn't seem to mind, and we drove home together a few times.

One day after my last class I was hanging around in front of the school with Calvin and a bunch of other students. I asked Calvin for a ride home, expecting he'd say yes. But this time, he took two big steps away from me as if he was shocked.

"What?" he said loudly. "Give you a ride home? I'm not going to Watts today."

Everyone burst out laughing. I was embarrassed but tried not to show it. Never mind that I didn't live in Watts, which everyone had heard about because of the riots. As far as most Beverly students were concerned, Watts and South Central were the same place: a ghetto. I didn't bother explaining the difference because I knew it only would have made matters worse.

But inside I didn't like being lumped in with the people at the center of the riots. I was still too young to fully comprehend the history of racism that contributed to the riots; instead, I took comfort from the fact that I didn't actually live in Watts. Yes, the riot spilled over into my neighborhood, but the riot wasn't really *my* problem. Certainly it wasn't my doing. Looking back, that was such a meaningless distinction for my young self to make, but at the time—when all I wanted was to fit in—it seemed like an important distinction. Even within the black community, I was realizing, there were issues of class and perception that separated people. Even I was capable of judging a book by its cover—or a town by its name.

What surprised and hurt me most at the time, though, was how my friend Calvin turned on me. He'd driven me home many times without ever making a disparaging remark. I wondered if he was having his own problems fitting in as a black kid at Beverly and saw an opportunity to get in good with the crowd by making a joke at my expense. I guess that happens in high schools everywhere. But even so, his joke made me more reluctant to share my background with anyone at school.

In general, most students had no idea where I lived, and I tried to keep it that way. Occasionally someone would ask where I was from, and I'd tell them the truth, but then I'd quickly change the subject. It's not that I was ashamed of where I grew up—far from it. It's that I didn't need anything else—beyond the color of my skin—setting me apart from the rest of the students at Beverly.

———

EARLY IN MY FIRST YEAR at Beverly, the football team trounced our rival high school Culver City by a score of 23 to 7. When the final gun sounded, the Beverly players celebrated on the field while the fans in the stands went crazy.

Suddenly, and without warning, a gleaming, brand-new red BMW drove right onto the field.

I watched with my mouth open as the car came closer and closer to where the players were. It was the most beautiful car I'd ever seen, so red and so shiny, and the sight of it on the football field was surreal. It stopped just in front of one of my friends on the team, and right on cue the crowd began singing "Happy Birthday." My friend's father was a big shot in show business, and he'd arranged to have his son's sixteenth birthday present driven onto the field so he could get it with everyone watching. My friend was so excited he jumped into the BMW and honked the horn over and over. The rest of us all piled in to share the moment.

I played it cool, but inside I was in shock. What amazed me most was how all the parents and teachers and coaches just stood around and applauded—as if someone had handed my friend a blue ribbon or a trophy. He'd been given a BMW! And everyone was acting like it was no big deal!

That was my life at Beverly—one foot in a fairy tale and one foot in the hood.

Most of the people I was meeting there came from wealthy families in town. Their parents were lawyers, doctors, agents, and movie stars. They lived lives I could only dream about. I'll never forget being invited to the home of one of my classmates for his birthday party. His father was in show business and rich beyond any measure I understood. I showed up at his mansion and was given the grand tour, eventually finding myself in what was called the Pillow Room. It was an entire room—and a huge room at that—filled with big, fluffy pillows. No furniture, just pillows! The whimsical extravagance of that just floored me. I grew up in a small room filled with brothers, not pillows. The closest my family ever came to that level of indulgence was when my mother put out four or five different kinds of pies for Christmas dinner.

While some of my new friends came from staggering wealth, all of my childhood friends still lived in South Central, and their parents, like mine, were hardworking middle-class folks. Part of me was tempted to tell my old friends about the Pillow Room, to share the experience with someone who would understand my disbelief, but I never did. I knew they already felt I'd betrayed them by going to Beverly, and I didn't want them to think I was rubbing it in.

As a result, I constantly floated between two separate worlds.

Only on the rarest occasions would I mix the two. I might bring a friend from South Central to a party in Beverly Hills, but I was very careful to pick my moments—I needed to know how the party host would react to having him there, *and* I had to be sure my friend would feel comfortable in whoever's fancy home we were in. I was constantly monitoring situations and reading people's reactions. What's more, straddling these two worlds meant none of my friends ever got the chance to know the whole me—they only got to see the parts of me I was willing to share. Different friends knew different Carters, but no one could see the whole person. At times this made me feel lonely and tired, and looking back, I wish I hadn't felt the need to constantly keep up this charade. But honestly, I didn't know how else to handle the tension between my two worlds.

———————

"YO, CARTER, LET'S GO FOR a drive."

I was walking on the sidewalk outside my house when I looked up and saw my cousin Freddy in his black Dodge Challenger. Freddy was seven or eight years older than me, and everyone in South Central knew who he was. He'd show up at some of our family events, but even if he wasn't there, I noticed people were always talking about him. Sometimes they whispered when they said his name.

I knew my cousin was a gangster before I knew what that word meant; I'd hear my relatives use it when telling stories about him. I learned its meaning one day when I was ten. I was walking home from Harvard Park in South Central after Little League practice with my friends Jimmy and Chris when we ran into a group of older boys. At first they were across the street, but in a flash they had us surrounded. A few of them stood behind us so we couldn't run away.

We were trapped.

"Where you guys going?" one of them asked.

"Whose baseball gloves are those?" asked another.

"Those your shoes?"

"Got any money?"

"You lying to us? These cats are lying to us."

We were terrified. When one of the boys said, "We should kick their asses right now," I balled up my fists and waited for the inevitable.

Just then, the oldest boy came right up to me and stared at my face. It was like he somehow recognized me, though I didn't think that was possible, seeing as I had no idea who he was.

"Aren't you a brother of Freddy Paysinger?" he finally asked.

"He's my cousin," I answered.

And that was that. The boys looked at each other and, without another word, rode off just as quickly as they'd surrounded us. The three of us stood there in disbelief, shaking in our cleats. Jimmy and Chris looked at me like I was Superman.

"Carter, what did you do?" Jimmy asked.

"I don't know," I said. "Let's just get out of here."

That was how I learned that being a gangster carried some kind of weight in our neighborhood. Being a gangster meant something.

I'd later learn Freddy ran away from home when he was twelve and might have vanished from our lives altogether had not my father gone looking for him and dragged him back home. Even so, Freddy grew up mainly on the streets. As a teenager he joined the Black Panther Party, and as far as I could tell he never held a traditional job. I didn't know how he lived or how he made money; I just knew he did those things on the streets.

For whatever reason, perhaps because I was his uncle's oldest son, Freddy took a liking to me. I didn't have the benefit of a big brother to look out for me, so Freddy took that role. Some days we just drove around Los Angeles for hours, talking. I loved hopping in his car and hearing his stories, and my parents didn't seem to mind.

One day, Freddy called me over to his car and said, "Let's go for a drive." We drove to one of his friend's homes, and the three of us sat around talking the afternoon away. One of the things we talked about was how easy it was for someone to get sucked into the street lifestyle, especially if you were hanging out with the wrong people. Suddenly Freddy got up.

"Come with me," he said.

I followed him into the kitchen.

"Open the refrigerator," Freddy said.

I swung open the door and looked inside.

There were dozens, maybe hundreds, of clear plastic packets filled with white powder.

"Do you know what that stuff is?" Freddy asked.

"Yeah, I think so," I said.

"Good. Now here's what you need to know about this stuff—*don't ever touch it.*"

It wasn't what you'd expect a gangster to say. But what I didn't know then was that Freddy had made a pact with my mother. He promised her he'd never put me in any danger or trouble, and he promised he'd always watch out for me in the neighborhood. Freddy never broke that promise. Instead, in our long drives and talks, Freddy tried to teach me things.

And the biggest lesson of all was *don't be like me*.

"Don't buy this stuff, don't sell it, don't use it, don't get near it," Freddy went on. "There is nothing good about this stuff, okay? *Nothing*."

I nodded.

"Just being with the wrong people in this neighborhood can get you killed," Freddy explained. "You gotta be careful who you talk to, who you hang out with, who you trust." The fridge filled with coke drove his point home. Freddy wasn't just telling me how easy it was to find myself in the wrong place with the wrong people—he was showing me.

His words reminded me of something my mother always told us: "Be careful not to hitch your wagon to the wrong horse."

Same lesson, different teaching method. But both were effective.

While some kids I knew from the neighborhood wound up getting sucked into a life of drugs, my brothers and I never did—never even came close. My mother and father had a lot to do with that, for sure. My father made it clear he'd have no mercy if we were ever stupid enough to get on the wrong side of the police. "If you get in trouble, don't waste your dime calling me, 'cause I ain't comin' to get you," he'd say. And my mother—well, the last thing in the world we'd ever want to do was get her mad at us. Together my parents made a pretty good case for staying on the straight and narrow.

On top of that, our coaches at Beverly constantly told us to stay away from drugs and alcohol, and we might have even had a formal antidrug lecture or presentation, though, honestly, I can't remember.

But it was Freddy's warning that made the deepest impression on me. Looking back on that day now, I'm pretty sure the whole afternoon was a setup, just so Freddy could show me the fridge filled with drugs. I don't think anyone at Beverly Hills High would have approved of his approach. I can only imagine how parents in Beverly Hills would react to a South Central gangbanger like Freddy being allowed to lecture their sons and daughters about the perils of drug use—and to use bags of cocaine as props.

But the fact is, at least with me, Freddy's results are hard to argue.

———

JUST A FEW WEEKS INTO my first semester at Beverly something called Freshman Friday rolled around. It's a tradition in many high schools, the one day out of the year when upperclassmen get to mess with freshmen by duct-taping them to flagpoles or tossing them in dumpsters—and not get in trouble for it. Good, clean fun. At Beverly, though, there was a twist: the freshmen and seniors teamed up to mess with the sophomores and juniors. If you were a sophomore or junior who got caught walking alone, something would definitely happen to you.

Even though this was my first year at Beverly, I started in the tenth grade, so I was a sophomore. I was one of the hunted.

That morning I walked to my first class with a friend so I wouldn't be caught alone. After class I disappeared inside a group of students heading to our next class. At lunch I was careful never to stray too far from my friends. But after history class, my luck ran out. I stood in the doorway, watching my friends head one way while I had to go the other way for my next class. I waited for the heavy hallway traffic to dissipate, then made a break for the stairwell. I crept down the stairs slowly, peering around corners, listening for footsteps. I knew this was only a game, but still it felt so real. I swear I could hear my heart thumping in my chest.

I got to within a hundred feet of my classroom. *Better make a run for it*, I figured. All I had to do was go through a hallway door, keep my head down, and I'd be home free. Stealthily inching forward, I suddenly sensed someone leaping out from behind the door. Before I could even react, a senior named Gary Belstrom took a swing at me. He was a big white kid, and when he popped me in the chest, I felt it pretty good. I don't know if you've ever been punched in the chest, but it can knock the wind out of you. As Gary ran off, laughing and victorious, I leaned against a wall and tried to catch my breath.

"Oh man," I said, smiling slightly despite the knot in my chest, "he got me."

Believe it or not, that's one of my fondest memories of Beverly.

You see, Freshman Friday was an all-day, campus-wide, super-competitive event, and everyone got in the spirit of the game. I wasn't the only one creeping around, checking corners and trying to avoid getting "tagged"—*all* the sophomores and juniors were. That's why I didn't mind getting punched by Gary Belstrom. To me, it meant so much more than just a prank. It meant I was just like any other student at Beverly.

Gary and I went on to become good friends.

MAKING FRIENDS AT BEVERLY, JUST like at any other high school, is a complicated process fraught with missteps and drama. Fitting in and finding your niche is a challenge wherever you go, but at Beverly there was an extra layer of complications. There was a class structure in place that could ruin your life if you didn't learn how to deal with it. There were the extremely rich white kids who lived in mansions in north Beverly Hills, the slightly less rich kids in south Beverly Hills, the fairly rich black kids who lived in upscale black suburbs like Baldwin Hills—and the kids like me who lived in middle-class neighborhoods, or worse.

The temptation was to pretend to be someone you weren't just to be accepted. For instance, if you were with a group of kids talking about their fancy summer homes, you might feel tempted to talk about your family's beachside bungalow, even if they didn't own one. Or you might want to lie about the kind of car your parents drove. But I learned early on that pretending to have money would inevitably backfire. Eventually you'd get caught in your lie, and when you got caught, you faced a long, long road of ridicule and despair.

One girl in my class, Angela, stood out because she was pretty, stylish, and always wore the very latest fashions. She gave the impression of coming from wealth, and she cultivated that image. It's what made her part of the popular crowd. A few weeks into her first semester, one of her friends got hold of her address and drove out with a few buddies to see where she lived. It turned out Angela lived in a tiny house just two blocks inside the border of Beverly Hills, in the far less fashionable south side of town. What's more, the grass on her front lawn was badly overgrown; it was clear her family did not employ a gardener. When her friends at Beverly found out about her house, Angela became the butt of jokes for months.

"Hey, Angela, I heard you live in a jungle."

"Hey, Angela, your front lawn is a forest."

"Hey, Angela, your house is so small you have to step outside to change your mind."

It didn't matter that she wore the newest jeans and the nicest heels, or that she acted like she was rich—all that mattered was that she *didn't* come from money. In Beverly Hills, you can't hide a shabby front yard.

For that reason I was careful never to pretend to be someone I wasn't. And, luckily, I made friends anyway. I even started branching out from my original group in the segregated lunchroom as I began to get to know different kinds of kids. Some of them were even from north Beverly Hills. Chico Ross, Diana Ross's younger brother, was in one of my classes and became a really good pal. Berry Gordy—son of the founder of Motown Records—and his brother Terry also became friends. Sandy Hackett, whose dad was legendary comedian Buddy Hackett, was really cool and easy to hang out with. None of these guys cared where I was from or what my parents were worth. They just liked hanging out with me, and I liked hanging out with them.

In my second semester at Beverly, one of my friends was given an assignment in English class. I don't remember exactly what the assignment was, but I do remember my friend decided to make a short movie as his project. He enlisted the help of a bunch of his friends—me, Chico, Berry, maybe twenty-five kids in all. He told us his movie was called "The Informer," and it was about a gang of guys who robbed banks. I was cast as the leader of the gang, which I didn't mind at all. At least I was the guy in charge.

Over the next few weeks we filmed "The Informer" on campus and around Los Angeles every chance we got. We'd run from location to location, setting up shots and quickly filming before anyone shooed us away. In a way it reminded me of the adventures my brothers and I would go on in South Central. When the movie was finally finished, we all got together at my friend's house in Beverly Hills and screened his masterpiece. I don't think I ever laughed so hard in my life. As I sat there watching the movie, I felt the satisfaction that comes with being part of a group—with being *accepted*. In high school there are few better feelings than that.

Nearly forty years later a bunch of us from that group of twenty-five friends *still* get together every now and then to watch "The Informer" and have a good laugh.

———

THE VERY FIRST FRIEND I ever made at Beverly, though, was a small white Jewish kid named Jon Cohen.

Jon and I both played football, me as a quarterback, Jon as a center—the guy who snapped the ball to me. Because of that we ran a lot of practice drills together, and we often found ourselves waiting for rides home at the same time. Jon's brother was the quarterback of the varsity football team, and on Fridays Jon and I would sit together in the stands and watch his brother play.

One Friday, after the game, Jon asked me a question.

"Have you ever been to a Shabbat?"

"A what?" I said.

Jon explained a Shabbat was the traditional Jewish meal honoring the creation of the world in six days. It was a happy and festive occasion his family marked every Friday a few minutes before sunset.

"Do you want to come to Shabbat tonight?" he asked.

"Let me call my parents."

My mother agreed to pick me up after dinner, and Jon and I walked to his home in Beverly Hills. On the way over he told me all about Jewish foods, preparing me for what lay ahead. Jon wasn't one of the mansion kids; his home was lovely but modest. When we got there, an array of foods was already set out on the dining room table. I don't think I recognized a single dish. Jon, his brother, his mother, and I sat at the table, and his mother lit two candles and recited a blessing:

Barukh atah Adonai, Eloheinu, melekh ha'olam
Asher kidishanu b'mitz'votav v'tzivanu
L'had'lik near shel Shabbat. Amein.

That means, "Blessed are you, Lord, our God, sovereign of the universe, Who has sanctified us with His commandments and commanded us to light the lights of Shabbat. Amen." I didn't understand what Jon's mother was saying, but at the same time I kind of knew what she meant. At my house, my mother or father recited a blessing before every meal: "The Lord is my shepherd; I shall not want. He makes me lie down in green pastures. He leads me besides still waters. He restores my soul." I figured the two blessings couldn't be all that different.

Then it was time to eat, and Jon's mother explained all the dishes to me: the *challah* (delicious bread), *tzimmes* (a stew made with carrots), main courses of *of* (chicken) and *basar* (red meat). All of it was amazing.

Neither Jon nor I thought much about our dinner that Friday, but looking back on it now, I'm struck by the idea that this is precisely what Beverly officials had in mind when they created the multicultural permit. There was no chance I'd ever have made a friend like Jon had I not gone to Beverly. Yet there we were, two kids from different faiths and worlds, happily sharing a Shabbat meal.

My friendship with Jon and with guys like Chico, Berry, and Sandy made my first year at Beverly more fun than I'd ever hoped it could be. Those friendships even allowed me to disregard, if only for the moment, the single most important thing I would come to know about my new school. It was something that was true back when I was a student there and something that would endure for decades to come. And it was simply this—if you didn't come from Beverly Hills, you would *always* be an outsider.

That was a lesson I had to learn and relearn more than once in the years to come.

CHAPTER

4

TWO WEEKS INTO my first semester the athletic department held tryouts for junior varsity baseball.

This was the day I'd been waiting for.

A few months earlier in my interview with Mr. Hoag, I'd told him I felt confident I could make the baseball team. I wasn't trying to be cocky; it's what I truly believed. You see, back then, I didn't just feel confident I could make the team at Beverly.

I felt confident I could make the major leagues.

It's a dream a lot of boys share, and for me it was a powerful driving force. That's because sports in general, and baseball in particular, weren't just another part of my life.

They were my *whole* life.

Tryouts for the JV team were held on a typically bright, beautiful day in September. I brought my worn baseball glove, and I stood in the infield, waiting for a coach to hit ground balls in my direction. I felt butterflies in my stomach, but once I fielded my first ground ball and whipped it to first base, the butterflies went away. After that I shagged fly balls in the outfield and took my turn in the batting cage. When try-outs were over, the JV baseball coach had us sit in the infield and wait to hear our names called. If you heard your name, you'd made the team. I listened as kid after kid got his name called and watched them jump up and high-five one another. I waited patiently, and anxiously, for my turn.

And then it came.

"Paysinger!"

Finally, I was on my way to the big leagues.

"CARTER, DO YOU KNOW WHAT Josh Gibson's fans used to call Babe Ruth?" my father asked me as we sat at the kitchen table late one night, listening to the Dodgers on the radio.

"I don't know, Dad, what?"

"They called him the white Josh Gibson!"

My father laughed when he told me this, and I laughed, too. Not because I understood what he was saying—not completely, anyway—but because I liked seeing my father laugh. I was five or six, and my father had just started letting me stay up late to listen to Dodger games with him. He'd come to Los Angeles in the summer of 1957, and exactly one year later the Dodgers showed up from Brooklyn. My father felt an immediate kinship with this exiled team, maybe because they were both the new kids in town. On game nights he'd pull the transistor radio out of a kitchen drawer and sit at the table and listen to the scratchy sound of Dodgers announcer Vin Scully calling the games.

I sat there with him, happy as could be.

Long before I jogged onto the field for tryouts at Beverly, I'd fallen madly in love with baseball. It was my father's deep affection for the game that did it. So many fathers and sons first bond over a love of baseball, and my father and I were no different. The first language we both shared was that of strikeouts, base hits, and home runs. But that language lent itself to an exploration of something far more significant than just sports.

In our time together listening to games—my dad relishing the chance to share his passion, me determined not to miss a word but fighting to stay awake—my father talked a lot about all the great black ballplayers who never got the chance to play in the majors. "Those major league records are not completely true," he'd say, "because Negroes couldn't play in the majors and their statistics don't count." He told me about the great athletes who were stuck in the Negro leagues—prodigious talents like the legendary slugger Josh Gibson.

"Babe Ruth only hit seven hundred fourteen home runs," my father bragged. "Josh Gibson hit over eight hundred!"

But what impressed me most about Gibson was his background. My father explained how Gibson trained to be an electrician and worked as an elevator operator at Gimbels department store in Pittsburgh before getting discovered while playing on an amateur team sponsored by the store. He was, my father said, an ordinary man who had something extraordinary in him, and he went on to become one of the greatest hitters the game has ever known.

Gibson, in other words, was a regular, humble black man who, despite enormous obstacles, became a hero. Not surprisingly, black athletes like Gibson—and Jackie Robinson and Satchel Paige and Buck Leonard—became my role models in a way no white major leaguer ever could. Precisely because they were ordinary and came from backgrounds just like mine, they were a *huge* inspiration to me.

When my father spoke of these great players, he did so without an ounce of resentment. He wasn't bitter about how black athletes had been banned from the major leagues. He simply believed his baseball heroes were better than the best major leaguers there were, and he was quietly confident about that. He showed nothing but a fierce pride in what they had accomplished.

I surely didn't realize it then, but my father's quiet confidence in his heroes would one day become *my* quiet confidence in myself.

Sitting in our kitchen late on summer nights even after my father had gone to bed and let me stay up by myself, I listened to the games with my chin resting on my folded arms, letting baseball seep into my blood. In that quiet kitchen lit softly by a single lamp, with the crack of bats rising above the hum of the fridge, a dream was born. I knew then and there what I wanted to do and who I wanted to be.

I was going to be a major league baseball player.

———————

SOCKBALL, KICKBALL, TETHERBALL, STICKBALL, CAROMS, pickle-in-the-middle—you name it, my brothers and I played it growing up. Before school, after school, after dinner, on the streets, in the house, the backyard, the front yard, we played ball. We had a basketball rim in our backyard, and every year we staged the Block Games, a ferocious contest between the kids on block 5700—our block—and the kids on 5500. When we weren't playing baseball or basketball, we held touch football games spanning two front lawns—get it past the farthest driveway and you had a touchdown.

You might think all the games I played in my youth were just frivolous kid stuff, but to me they were anything but. No matter what game I was playing, no matter how small the stakes, I wanted to win. I *needed* to win. Who could skip a stone the most times on a lake? That had to be me. Who could throw a football and hit a far-off garbage can? I had to hit it first. I was fiercely competitive—and the longer the odds against me, the more determined I was to win. Some kids didn't care if they won or lost. But I cared, and deeply. It wasn't something I could control. It was just my nature.

I didn't get that competitive drive from my father. My refusal to ever be bested or outsmarted came from someone else—my mother.

When I was ten or so, my brothers and I were playing catch on the street outside our house. At one point Don threw the baseball over my head, and it landed in our neighbor Mrs. Ford's front yard. Now, in any other circumstance we'd have scooped up our ball and continued to play. But this wasn't any other circumstance.

This was mean old Mrs. Ford.

Mrs. Ford lived in the prettiest house on the block, and she had the best-looking lawn for miles. That lawn was her pride and joy, and she spent her days making sure every blade of grass was perfect. Not surprisingly, she didn't want us kids anywhere near it.

"You boys stay away from my yard!" she'd bark if we came within twenty feet of her house. "Take your noise to your own backyard!"

We did our best to avoid Mrs. Ford, but then Don went and threw the ball onto her property. Mrs. Ford happened to be sitting just inside in a beach chair, looking out through the screen door and guarding her precious yard.

"Don't even think about gettin' that ball," she snarled. "It belongs to me now."

We stood there meekly while Mrs. Ford came out of her house and took our ball; then we slunk back home. Don and I had no plans to mention what had happened to my mother—that's how afraid we were of Mrs. Ford—but Carlton came right out and told her.

"What do you mean, Mrs. Ford took your baseball?"

I explained the situation.

"Where's the ball now?" she asked.

"Mrs. Ford has it."

My mother marched us right out of the house and over to Mrs. Ford's. It wasn't often I saw her this worked up, so I knew a showdown was coming. She walked up to the front stoop where the old lady was still sitting in her chair.

"Mrs. Ford, did you take my sons' baseball?"

"They were playing in my yard, and I told them not to—"

"Mrs. Ford, I know that's not true because my boys do their best to stay off your grass," Momma interrupted. "Now, I want my boys' baseball back right now."

Mrs. Ford pulled the ball out of her apron pocket, handed it to my mother, and threw in a warning: "You just keep your boys off my lawn!"

"You don't have to worry about that," my mother snapped back. "But any time their baseball lands in your yard, they're gonna come get it, and I *dare* you to take it again."

With that my mother marched us back home, and our irrational fear of Mrs. Ford subsided. Not only that, but my mother and Mrs. Ford wound up becoming good friends.

And we got our baseball back.

No one ever got the best of my mother or her sons. Not school officials, not ornery neighbors—no one. When it came to her family, my mother was fiercely protective—and fiercely competitive. She insisted we never get cheated out of anything, and she wanted our childhoods to be as rich and full as possible. Even though we never had much money, she made sure we always had plenty of Christmas and birthday presents. Every holiday meant festive decorations and heaping plates of food. When there wasn't much extra money, my folks would drive us to LAX airport so we could park near a runway and watch the planes fly in over our heads—a simple, cheap, but memorable outing we absolutely loved.

My mother never settled for "good enough" or "just okay"; that's why she pushed so hard to get me into Beverly. When it came to her family, my mother simply never quit.

Some of that drive got passed down to me. My mother was a fighter by nature, and so was I. Of all the Paysinger boys, I took after her the most. But the rest of that gift was bestowed on me through lectures and by example.

My mother was my very first coach, and my first team was my family.

———————

WHEN I WAS YOUNG, MY mother drafted all four of us boys to be in something called a Tom Thumb wedding.

Long a tradition in black churches and communities, Tom Thumb weddings are planned and held like regular weddings— except the participants are all kids. This particular Tom Thumb wedding took place on the Sunday before Easter—and smack in the middle of the Block Games, our epic battle against the boys from 5500. We weren't crazy about postponing the games to be in the wedding, but we had no choice. Like I said, you didn't argue with my mother.

My brother Vonzie, whom we often called Ray, was chosen to be the groom, and I was the best man. Our neighbor Mrs. Williams organized the wedding, and her daughter Janeen was the bride. Carlton and Donald were groomsmen. Several families on our block spent weeks sewing wedding gowns and bridesmaids dresses, making bridal bouquets and decorations, and cooking up endless platters of food. Someone baked an enormous wedding cake. The ceremony was held in Mrs. Williams's backyard with rows of white seats set up for all the grown-ups.

When Ray and Janeen were pronounced man and wife, I noticed nearly all of the mothers crying.

Afterward we cut the cake, and we posed for a thousand photos. At the time all my brothers and I could think of was getting home to our Block Games. But looking back on it now, I can see why my mother and all the ladies in the neighborhood were so keen on the Tom Thumb wedding and why they staged it with so much love.

It was to prepare their children for what lay ahead.

Everything my parents did was meant to teach us something and help get us ready for adulthood. The Tom Thumb wedding is a perfect example. It may have struck me as a silly party back then, but I realize now there were valuable lessons to be absorbed—the importance of community, the power of ritual and tradition, the strength of families, and the virtue of comporting yourself in the proper way.

"Train up a child in the way he should go," it says in Proverbs 22:6, and "even when he is old he will not depart from it."

My mother believed that was true.

She also liked to quote Martin Luther King Jr., who said, "It is always the right time to do the right thing."

My mother never missed a chance to show us what the right thing was.

"Pay close attention when you're spoken to."

"Don't talk. Listen and you just might learn something."

"Act like you got sense, boy; it might come true."

My mother was our champion, but she was also our harshest critic. I believe that's why she encouraged my crazy love of sports. Because she saw it as a chance to teach me even more lessons, to show me the importance of how I chose to live life. And her words always added up to the same basic lesson.

In a white world, it wasn't enough for me to be as good as everyone else. I had to be *better* than everyone else. I had to work harder, try more, aim higher, and never quit.

"I don't care if you're a street sweeper," my mother would tell me. "You be the best street sweeper you can possibly be." The things that mattered—integrity, honesty, character—were nonnegotiable. Regardless of circumstances, we were expected to handle ourselves the proper way. No excuses, only results. Do the right thing.

In this way my mother's lessons were the sound track of my childhood. And while I'm sure my classmates at Beverly learned many of the same lessons from their parents, neighbors, and cousins—or at least some of them did—I believe what I learned about life in South Central, from my parents and from the community, gave me something many of my Beverly classmates lacked.

A strong sense of who I was.

"You are a Paysinger," my mother told me time and again, "and being a Paysinger *means* something."

––––––

"PAYSINGER! KEEP UP THE PACE! We're only running laps because of you!"

Beverly's head football coach, Ben Bushman, shouted this at me as I ran hundred-yard sprints across the football field in what felt like 180-degree heat. My teammates, gasping for air same as I was, threw me dirty looks as we staggered back and forth. I'd tried out for the junior varsity football team my first year at Beverly partly to keep myself in top shape for when baseball rolled around again, but now I was starting to regret that decision.

Football practices were, in a word, brutal. Most of the time we had two each day, one more awful than the next. We ran a *lot*, in full uniform and at full speed, and often in sweltering heat. When my mother told me I'd have to miss a couple of two-a-day practices because we were going to Louisiana on vacation, I didn't mind all that much. Until I returned to Beverly, that is.

At my first practice back Coach Bushman made the whole team run *twenty* hundred-yard sprints in my honor.

"While all of you were here working your butts off, Carter was in Louisiana sipping lemonade," Coach called out as we ran. "So make sure to thank Carter for this little workout."

I got the message loud and clear: *Don't miss practice. No excuses. Just show up.*

Coach Bushman was an old-school, no-nonsense kind of coach. He was six foot one and in great shape. When he came to Beverly, the school's football program was in disarray. Beverly was pretty much the doormat in its league. Coach Bushman changed all that. His goal was to have Beverly respected in the world of high school football. And as I soon learned, Coach Bushman was passionate about his goals.

One afternoon Coach ran blocking drills at practice. A player from the offense ran at a player from the defense, and the defensive player had to make sure he didn't get past him. Apparently Coach didn't like the way the drill was going because he stopped it and started screaming at us to be tougher.

"You gotta block your man like your life depends on it!" he hollered. "All of you, get in a line and come at me one at a time!"

One by one all twelve of us charged our coach. We were in full pads, while he was in shirtsleeves. But that didn't matter. When we charged him, Coach Bushman blocked us with his big forearms, brushing us away and yelling at us to keep charging.

"Come on, harder, harder! You gotta be tough to win!"

After a while I noticed Coach Bushman's forearms were bleeding.

Still, he kept yelling at us to charge him hard as we could.

My first thought was, *That guy must be losing his mind.* But pretty quickly I responded to Coach's intense focus and passion. He brought the same level of dedication to every drill, every practice, every play. I could relate to that. If I thought I was tough and driven heading into Beverly, Coach Bushman took me to a whole other level. He taught me how to push myself past what I thought was my breaking point. He taught me that's the place where champions live.

And, just like my parents, he taught me to tackle every challenge with passion and persistence—even if it means getting a little bloodied.

Nothing worthwhile in life comes without a cost.

CHAPTER

5

WHEN I WAS sixteen, my parents scrimped and saved and bought me my own car.

It wasn't a sports car, like a lot of my Beverly friends tooled around in. And it certainly wasn't a brand-new red BMW.

It was a used 1956 bright-green Buick.

I couldn't have been more thankful to my parents for getting me a car because it sure beat having to take four buses every day. At the same time I was worried about all the ribbing I was sure to get for driving such an old car. Beverly was all about status, and the kind of car you drove did not go unnoticed. That's when I had a really brilliant idea.

Instead of waiting around meekly for nasty comments about my car, I decided to create a mystique around it.

"Hey, my parents bought me a car!" I announced to my friends the first day I got to drive it to Beverly.

"Oh yeah? What kind?"

"Exactly what I wanted—a 1956 Buick."

"What? An old Buick?"

"It might look like any old Buick on the outside. But inside, it's very special. I call it the Green Machine."

My friends liked the sound of that, and pretty soon they were telling everyone else about the Green Machine. Instead of being ridiculed I had a lot of students asking me for rides.

The Green Machine faced its first real test, though, when one of the cuter girls at Beverly asked for a ride.

Her name was Iona Morris, and she was the daughter of Greg Morris, star of *Mission: Impossible*. After a home basketball game, she came up and asked if I could drive her home, and I said sure. The only problem was, I'd also promised to drive a couple of my friends home after the game. The last thing I wanted was my knucklehead buddies ruining my romantic little ride with Iona. So I asked them to stay behind at Beverly and I'd come back for them after I dropped her off.

"Not a chance," my pal Tony said. "You want to leave a couple of black kids standing around in Beverly Hills on a Friday night? What am I going to tell the police? 'Hello, Officer, I'm just waiting here in the dark for my friend to pick me up.' No way, Carter."

He had a point. My two friends clambered into the back as I held the door open for Iona to slip into the passenger seat.

"So, this is the Green Machine," she said, looking up and down at the Buick and trying to figure out what was so special about it.

"What, you've never been in the Green Machine?" Tony asked from the back, as if such a thing was impossible to believe.

Then we were off to one of the most prestigious neighborhoods in Beverly Hills: Trousdale Estates, nestled up high in the Hollywood Hills. The Green Machine cruised on Sunset toward Hollywood and handled beautifully all the way up Doheny. *So far, so good.*

Then we came to the hill.

It wasn't just any hill—it was the steepest hill I'd ever seen.

"It's straight up there," Iona said casually while I surveyed the imposing mountain. Suddenly, I was struck with terror that the Green Machine would break down somewhere on the way up. It might even stall and roll back down. I honestly feared that if the Green Machine didn't make it, I might end up killing all of us—or at the very least become the laughingstock of Beverly. But what could I do but give it a go? I held my breath and gunned the Green Machine up the hill.

It felt like the slowest drive ever. While my friends laughed it up in the back and Iona flashed me a warm smile, I sat there white-knuckling the steering wheel and worrying that every second of forward progress would be the last.

And all the while I knew very well what was at stake. I was already an outsider. I was already the guy who got in on a permit. And now, if the Green Machine stalled, my image would forever be sealed. I would always be the poor black kid with the crappy car from South Central.

Then I heard something clang in the Green Machine's engine.

———————

"CARTER, JUST KEEP YOUR COMPOSURE, and hang in there. You're going to be okay."

It was halftime of a big football game against Palm Springs High School, and the Normans were losing. I was playing wide receiver, but I hadn't done much to be proud of in the first half. In fact, the whole team was stinking it up. In the locker room Coach Bushman and his assistants really let us have it, telling us we had to play harder, be smarter, get tougher. We just sat there, shell-shocked. I, for one, wasn't used to losing like this. All through my childhood I had found a way to win just about every game I played. I couldn't tolerate losing, so I rarely lost. But now there were a whole bunch of kids who were just as competitive as I was, and most of them were on the other team. I sat in the somber locker room completely dejected because I didn't know how to handle losing any other way.

Then, right before we ran back on the field for the second half, one of the assistant coaches, Chuck Kloes, pulled me aside. He didn't yell at me or tell me to play tougher; he calmly and quietly gave me advice.

"Just keep your composure, and hang in there," he said. "You're going to be okay." Then he patted my helmet and sent me out to play.

Coach Kloes's words helped me to focus on what I needed to do. His message, which went beyond that night and took root over the course of my whole time at Beverly, was simple—when the going gets tough, when things get chaotic, stay calm and stick to the game plan. Don't let the emotion of the situation distract you from your purpose. Don't let anyone rattle you.

We didn't win the game that day, but we did come back and play a great second half. The reason I remember that game, though, is because of Coach Kloes's halftime message. He was one of the most popular people at Beverly, a blond surfer type who coached and taught history. He was the kind of teacher who would delay a test for a day to make sure his students had a good enough grip on the subject matter. His job, as he saw it, wasn't just to teach; it was to make sure his students were successful. He took a special interest in me, I believe, because he appreciated my work ethic and competitiveness. That's why he pulled me over at halftime.

On the two-hour bus ride back from Palm Springs I couldn't help but notice that the bus was nearly empty. Most of the other players either had second homes in the Palm Springs area, or their parents had made a weekend of the trip. But Coach Kloes was on the bus, and he and I had the chance to talk further about sports and strategy and how to handle yourself. He became one of the most important mentors I ever had at Beverly, and his words have stayed with me ever since: *Keep your composure. Stick to the game plan. You will be okay.*

———————

IGNORING THE CLANGING IN THE Green Machine's engine, I calmly kept my foot on the gas. I turned and smiled serenely at Iona, not letting her see how nervous I was. The Green Machine sputtered some more but kept going. Unfortunately, so did the hill. Turn after turn, higher and higher, it wouldn't end. After what seemed like an hour—but was probably just five minutes—we reached a crest and leveled out.

The Green Machine had made it.

I breathed the biggest sigh of relief and walked Iona to the front door of her home. As we said good-bye, I could see straight through the spacious living room of her home to a big, beautiful pool out back. I was still unaccustomed to lavish displays of wealth and luxury, and a glimpse of a shimmering in-ground swimming pool in someone's backyard could still take my breath away. I wasn't part of this world; I knew that.

But neither did I have to apologize for being there.

And I certainly didn't have to apologize for my 1956 Buick. After that heroic climb up an endless LA mountain, the legend of the Green Machine was born.

———————

OVER TIME I CAME TO realize the elitism I had sensed on my first day at Beverly wasn't really going to be a problem. There were plenty of jerks at Beverly, to be sure, but the kids I hung out with were down-to-earth and unpretentious—even the kids whose parents were celebrities. One of my best friends was a guy named Walter Kahn, the grandson of the former chief justice of the US Supreme Court. He was a pitcher on the baseball team, and he had a killer curveball. I'd watch and marvel as Walter set batters up with his mediocre fastball, then struck them out with a curve they never saw coming. After the games we'd talk strategy, and before long we were buddies. Didn't matter that he was white and I was black, or that his grandfather once had led the Supreme Court and mine was a sharecropper. On and off the field, we treated each other like brothers.

Looking back, there was something beautifully egalitarian about it all. I truly began to believe I was being given the chance to become who I wanted to be, not who other people said I was. And in life, that chance is all you can ever expect to get.

In my first year at Beverly, during a football game against our archrival, Inglewood High, I caught a huge pass late in the game that led to the winning score. This was the school's most important win in a long time. On the bus ride back to Beverly the whole team yelled and laughed and slapped high fives and savored our victory. Even Coach Bushman was having fun. After showering and changing in the locker room, we walked out onto the campus. What we saw there amazed me.

Hundreds of people—students, parents, cheerleaders, teachers— were waiting there to greet us.

When they saw us, they erupted in cheers and applause that went on for several minutes. What a feeling that was! We were treated like conquering heroes, and we basked in every sweet moment of it.

Something clicked for me that night. I may not have been raised in Beverly Hills, and I might always be thought of as somewhat of an out- sider there, but on that one wonderful night, I was a school hero. I not only belonged at Beverly; I *was* Beverly—the fleet-footed, shoul- der-padded embodiment of everything the school stood for.

I was a Norman.

That game and that night showed me that being an outsider doesn't have to be a defining characteristic. Like the great Negro league players, the ultimate baseball outsiders, you can make your mark through what you achieve. You can be good enough to break down barriers and win on your own terms. It doesn't have to be about where you come from or what you look like.

It can be about what you achieve, and who you are *inside*.

AS THE YEARS PASSED, I was no longer the only Paysinger at Beverly— my brother Carlton enrolled one year behind me. My other brothers, Donald and Vonzie, soon followed. I tried to help them adjust to life at Beverly in any way I could. I remember taking all my brothers out to our backyard and teaching them everything I was learning about sports at Beverly before they got there. I pretty much taught Vonzie, the youngest, how to throw a baseball and football.

"Hold it like this," I'd say. "Throw it with your whole body, not just your arm."

The closer they got to coming to Beverly, the more specific my instructions became.

"The coaches are going to expect you to do it this way," I'd tell them. "So when you get to Beverly, this is how it works."

Unfortunately Carlton, the first of my brothers to follow me to Beverly, wasn't really an athlete like I was. Growing up, he liked to swim and he had competed in a couple of meets, but that was about it. The summer before he enrolled at Beverly, I sat him down for a talk.

"You have to go out for the football team," I said.

"But I don't like football."

"Doesn't matter. You have to play football, and maybe try out for wrestling, too."

I knew how hard it was to make friends at Beverly, particularly for kids like Carlton and me, who had so little in common with most of the other students. I also knew that being on a team was a shortcut to making friends. Carlton was a quiet, introverted kid, and I'd seen how kids like that could become outcasts, always eating alone and missing out on all the fun. I wanted to make sure that never happened to Carlton. He took my advice and played football for all three of his years at Beverly. He was never all that good of a player, but that wasn't important. What mattered was that he made friends and fit in.

Other times Carlton was less receptive to my advice.

One morning, as we were getting ready to take the bus to Beverly, I noticed Carlton wearing a colorful shirt that was popular in South Central but not in Beverly Hills.

"You wearing that today?" I asked.

"Yeah. What of it?"

"Hmmm. I don't think you should wear that," I said, reaching for a less colorful shirt. "Wear this instead."

"No way," Carlton said. "This is who I am."

There was a reason I advised Carlton against wearing the shirt. In my second year at the school I was invited to a friend's party in Beverly Hills. Up until then I'd had to miss most after-school events and parties because, unlike my friends who lived in Beverly Hills, I had no way to get back out there once I took the bus home. I remember being on the outside of a lot of Monday conversations about how great a certain party had been. So when I got my own car, I was most excited about being able to go to parties.

Maybe because I was so excited, I chose to wear my beloved black leather jacket and black leather cap to the party. Leather jackets and caps were hugely popular in South Central, and my friends and I wore them not to make any statement but because we felt we looked cool in them. If you went to a party in my neighborhood, you'd see a dozen kids in leather jackets and caps. That's just what we wore.

But as soon as I walked into my friend's house in Beverly Hills, I knew I'd made a mistake.

"Hey, look," one student said, "it's Carter the gangster!"

"Hey, Carter," said another, "I didn't know you were in the Black Panthers."

I laughed off those jokes and the many more that came that night and for weeks afterward. But I never wore my leather jacket to Beverly Hills again.

I don't know what happened to Carlton the day he wore his colorful shirt to Beverly. But the next time I gave him advice about what to wear, he took it.

It's not that I was against Carlton being himself at Beverly. Like I said, I never pretended to be someone I wasn't just to fit in, and I would never have advised my brothers to do that. But what I learned was that there's a way to stay true to who you are without drawing unnecessary attention to yourself.

Many years later I'd learn an even more important lesson: There comes a time in life when you *do* have to draw attention to yourself. When you have to stand up in front of the world and declare, come hell or high water, "This is who I am."

———

MY SENIOR YEAR AT BEVERLY was the best year of them all. I led our high school baseball league in fielding percentage, I batted over .500, and at one point I had an eleven-game hitting streak. Yet these accomplishments were bittersweet because as baseball season wound down, so, too, did my time at Beverly. All that remained of my long, unlikely adventure was graduation itself.

The ceremony was held on the bright-green grass of Beverly's rolling front lawn, and it was scheduled for midmorning because, I'd heard, students were less likely to get antsy and do something stupid to ruin the ceremony. My parents bought me a sharp, three-piece white suit, and my whole family was there to see me accept my diploma. I went up onstage and shook the principal's hand and immediately scanned the crowd for my mother's face. In a sea of proud parents, most of them white, it was easy to spot her near the front. My mother was crying. I thought of how, three years earlier, she'd proudly held up my acceptance letter as if it were written on gold parchment. And now I was holding an even more precious slip of paper. One dream for my mother had come full circle. Another was just beginning.

I walked back to my seat fully aware I was no longer a student at Beverly Hills High.

After the ceremony, my family had planned a huge luncheon at our home, with relatives from all over and tons of great food. At the time, I had a part-time job as a box boy at Ralphs supermarket on the corner of Slauson and Crenshaw, which was great because it earned me a little spending money, but not so great because the manager, a grumpy, middle-aged white man named Mr. Sullivan, was not the nicest guy. One day not too long before my graduation, I was working my usual day shift when Mr. Sullivan walked up to me.

"Carter, I need you to report to the deli clerk," he said. "She has the perfect job for you."

I couldn't wait to see what job he considered "perfect" for me, so I hustled over to the deli section. The clerk told me to get a broom and a box and pointed me behind the counter.

When I got there, all I saw was a big dead rat.

My first reaction was anger. I stormed off to find Mr. Sullivan, who was up front.

"Mr. Sullivan, how is cleaning up a dead rat the perfect job for me?"

"Don't ask questions," he responded. "Just do what you're told."

Something about his voice set me off, and I said, "Sorry, I'm not cleaning up that rat."

"Ace," he said, using his pet name for me, "I am writing you up for that."

Two days later, Mr. Sullivan called me into his office and pushed a letter across his desk. It was a reprimand for refusing to keep the store sanitary.

"Sign it," he said.

His tone made me feel cornered, and I didn't like how that felt. My mother was the same way; she didn't like anyone telling her what she should or shouldn't do. "I'm not signing that," I found myself saying, "not until you put in how I refused to clean up a rat."

Mr. Sullivan stared me down for a few long moments, then told me to leave. After that our relationship was, to say the least, strained.

Then came graduation, which fell on one of my usual shift days. Well in advance, I'd put in for the day off, and Mr. Sullivan was fine with it. But back in my home, during the luncheon, the phone rang. It was Mr. Sullivan calling for me.

"Carter, we need you to come in today as soon as possible," he said.

"Mr. Sullivan, you know today is my high school graduation," I said. "I have a lot of friends and family over at my house."

"Ace," he said, "you're digging a hole for yourself you will not be able to get out of."

Then he hung up on me.

I was shocked. To my family my graduation was a monumental event, and yet it meant nothing to Mr. Sullivan. Maybe all he saw when he looked at me was a kid whose only future was as a box boy. I was so upset I went to my father and told him what had happened.

"Tell your friends you'll be right back," my father said. Then he hustled me into the car with him.

We drove to Ralphs, and my father found Mr. Sullivan in his office.

"My name is Carter Paysinger, and I'd like to know about this hole my son has dug for himself," he said.

Mr. Sullivan's usual bluster was nowhere to be seen.

"Mr. Paysinger, I just called to ask your son to come to work today."

"He told you he was graduating today, and I understand you gave him the day off."

"That's true, Mr. Paysinger, but we had some people call in sick today and I'm short on help."

"How is that my son's problem?" my father asked.

"I guess it's not," Mr. Sullivan said. "I was just calling to see—"

"Well, he can't. He has a house full of guests who are celebrating his graduation. And cleaning up rats is not the perfect job for my son."

Mr. Sullivan had nothing to say, so he said nothing.

"And his name isn't Ace," my father called back just before we left.

At the moment I felt about ten feet tall. My father had stood up for me, but more importantly, he had just drilled home another invaluable lesson:

The best way to deal with any problem is *head-on*.

ON MY VERY FIRST DAY at Beverly, after finally getting to try one of those fabled cinnamon rolls in the cafeteria (it lived up to its billing), I went to my first English class. A smart and friendly woman named Ms. Georgadous was our teacher. Ms. Georgadous didn't talk too much about what we'd be studying that day; instead, she gave a long speech about what we needed to do to succeed at Beverly.

"Every teacher believes his or her class is the most important class in the school," she told us. "So you can't afford to fall behind in any of your classes. You have to take your homework seriously and do it every night. If you don't, it could be disastrous.

"You have to learn to manage your time," she went on, "because the coursework can be overwhelming. Plan out your days.

"The best way to survive as a new student at Beverly is to find an interest outside academics," she explained. "Beverly has so, so much to offer you, and you're doing yourself a disservice if you don't take advantage of that. *Find your niche.*"

The blueprint Ms. Georgadous gave me that first day turned out to be incredibly accurate—and incredibly helpful. And now, as I look back on my three years at Beverly, her words ring truer than ever.

I was given an extraordinary chance when I won a permit to attend Beverly, but that's all I was given—the rest was up to me. I had to make my own way there; no one was going to carve a path for me. Whatever burden I shouldered as a black student at a largely white school, I had to get out from under it entirely on my own. Beverly taught me to be responsible for myself. It verified everything my mother and father taught me by demonstrating that hard work, strong values, and perseverance pay off.

The motto of Beverly Hills High School is just three words taken from an old Sanskrit proverb—"Today Well Lived." To live well today, the proverb goes, "makes every yesterday a dream of happiness, and every tomorrow a vision of hope." So it was that I left Beverly a wiser, more confident person, a dream of happiness behind me, a vision of hope ahead.

What I couldn't possibly have known back then was that my past and future were intertwined, and that hope and happiness are fragile, fleeting things.

What I didn't know was that Beverly was far from done with me.

PART
2

CHAPTER

6

JUST A FEW years after graduating Beverly I came back on a Friday night to watch my brother Vonzie play in a football game.

I saw my old baseball coach, Coach Friedman, waving and heading toward me in the stands. He sat down next to me, and we caught up on each other's lives. Then he said something that floored me.

"Carter, would you be interested in coming back here in the spring as a baseball coach?"

I didn't answer right away because I didn't know what to say. So Coach Friedman kept talking.

"Your brother is probably the best player on the baseball team, and he could have a really phenomenal year. I figure you're going to be here anyway watching him play, so you might as well get paid for it. What do you say?"

I'd never thought of being a coach. My dream all along had been to play pro ball. But then, when I was a junior at California State University, Los Angeles, I faced one of our very best pitchers, a big, strong six-foot-two kid named Freddy Martinez, in a preseason intrasquad game. The word on Freddy was that he was good enough to probably get drafted by some major league team but perhaps not good enough to actually make the majors.

Well, the first pitch Freddy threw me was a fastball I hardly saw. I mean, it was *invisible*. The second pitch was another fastball I somehow managed to foul off. His third pitch was an honest-to-goodness major league curveball. It started like it was going to end up behind me, then began breaking right at my head. Out of instinct I jumped away from the plate to save my skin. But the ball kept breaking, crossed home plate, and hit the heart of the strike zone. Strike three. I was out.

I walked meekly back to the dugout and—for the first time in my young life—experienced doubt about my dream of playing pro ball.

If Freddy was that good and only had a 50-50 chance of making it, what chance did I have? Baseball can be a very cruel sport—it can string a player along for years before ultimately deciding he hasn't got what it takes. I'd heard horror stories about players suffering years of agony in the minor leagues, trying to please this guy or that guy or any guy they think might give them their big break. You could literally waste a decade of your life before finally realizing your dream had long since died.

I didn't want to be one of those guys.

This was not a decision I made quickly or took lightly. After all, the dream to play in the majors had sustained me ever since I was a tyke sitting in our kitchen, listening to Dodger games. It had become an integral part of my identity. Plus, I'd been raised to aim high and settle for nothing less than greatness. Would I be betraying my mother's lofty ambitions for me by abandoning my dream?

At the same time, I knew deep inside I didn't want to be someone who wasn't good enough to make it but hung on for years anyway. If I couldn't be great at baseball, then I should put all my energy into being great at something else. It wasn't so much about the specific dream. It was about *having* a dream, striving to be great, and pushing yourself to be the best person you could possibly be. *That* was the lesson my parents tried so hard to teach me. And so, over the course of my last two seasons at Cal State, I slowly began to loosen my grip on the dream that had nourished me for so long. Slowly, I started devising plan B.

That's when Coach Friedman asked me if I wanted to coach.

The words came out of my mouth without me even realizing I was saying them.

"I would love to coach," I said.

Just like that I was part of the Beverly family again.

———

THERE WAS ANOTHER REASON I was able to let go of my dream to play pro ball. And her name was Karen.

I'd dated a few girls at Beverly, none seriously, but in college my social life took off. That's the thing with being twenty years old—you fall in love pretty much every day. In my first year at Cal State I met three different gorgeous women on the same day and took a liking to all three. I didn't see any reason why I had to choose one over the others, so I didn't. I met the first girl on my way to baseball practice. She was walking toward me and I only had a few seconds to size up her beauty, but that was all I needed.

"Excuse me," I said, stopping her, "do you go to school here?"

"Uh, yeah, that's why I'm here, on campus."

"Oh, I'm sorry, I just hadn't seen you before, and I thought I knew all the pretty girls here."

That smooth line earned me date number one.

Just a while later I ran into another girl I knew from sociology class. In that class the teacher had us break up into groups, and I walked clear across the classroom so I could be in her group. Afterward, when I saw her in the hall, I stopped and chatted her up.

Date number two.

I met the third girl, Karen, in the bookstore at the student union. She was with a friend toward the back, flipping through a textbook. I picked up a book and pretended to read it while keeping my eye on her. As I circled closer, she looked up and caught me staring, so I quickly looked away. A few minutes later she caught me staring again.

Suddenly she was walking toward me. I pretended not to notice until she was right next to me. Finally I looked up, and we both smiled. Up close, she was even more beautiful.

"Didn't you throw a party at the Universal Sheraton last week?" she asked.

"Yeah, I did."

My friends and I had started our own little party business, throwing events in ballrooms and clubs all over town.

"So do you remember me?" she said.

I searched her pretty face. Her eyes were bright and happy, and there was so much warmth in her smile. For some reason, I felt like I already knew her. But for the life of me I couldn't remember meeting her.

"Of course I remember you!" I lied. "How are you?"

"Sure you do." She laughed, seeing right through me. Luckily, she stuck around, and we talked for a while. I only grew more and more enamored. You know the feeling—that little extra spark that's there when the chemistry between two people is real. We eventually exchanged phone numbers and agreed to hang out in the future.

Date number three.

A few days later I was at a fraternity party when I saw Karen across the floor, talking to some other guy. I felt an instant pang in my gut. Jealousy? How could it be? I'd only just met her. Whatever it was, my instinct was to do something and do it quick.

I asked the DJ to play "Hello It's Me," a slow love song by the Isley Brothers, and I asked him to dedicate it to Karen, from Carter. Just as the DJ announced the song and dedication, I strolled up to Karen and asked her to dance. I don't know what I'd have done if she said no, but happily she said yes. We went out on the floor and slipped into an easy embrace, my right hand on her back, her left hand on my shoulder, as if we'd been dancing together for years. Then we swayed slowly to the music.

All too soon the song ended, and Karen and I went back to our own friends. Later on we all headed to the same after-party, which, I soon discovered, was being hosted by the very same guy Karen was talking to before our dance. When I saw them together again, I felt that same twinge in my gut. Without thinking I walked right over to them.

"Hi, Karen," I said.

"Hi, Carter."

"Want to go for a walk?"

Karen hesitated for a moment, but only for a moment. She excused herself, and we slipped out of the party. We walked side by side on the street near the frat house, talking and laughing. It wasn't like I knew instantly she was the one or anything like that, but there was something about Karen I just couldn't shake. We walked and talked for about a half hour without a single awkward silence. Just before we headed back in, I stopped and leaned in and kissed her.

That's when I knew she was the one.

I'd later learn the guy Karen had been talking to was a good friend who was *very* interested in dating her. Had I not so rudely interrupted them, who knows how their conversation might have gone? Another five minutes and they might have fallen head over heels in love, forever dooming my chances to be with her. That's how life works. Sometimes you only get a tiny little window of time. Fortunately, my parents taught me the value of taking decisive action. Thank God they did, because that slow dance—and that first kiss—changed my life.

———————

MY MOTHER WAS THE FIRST person I told I wanted to marry Karen. I can't remember an exact moment when I made that decision—I don't think there was one. It was just one of those truths that makes itself obvious. My mother was ecstatic. She adored Karen, and after four boys she was more than ready to have a daughter-in-law. When I told her the news, she hugged me tight, then, as usual, told me how I should act.

"Carter, now you know you have to ask her parents for their blessing before you ask her," she said.

"Momma, people don't do that stuff anymore."

"Well, if you want to do this the right way, you have to ask her parents."

Once my mother said "the right way," I knew I had no choice. Paysingers only did things the right way. I went over to Phil's Market, a store on Compton Avenue in South Central owned by Karen's father, Joe, and found him there. Joe was something of a curmudgeon. The first time I met him was at his home, when Vonzie and I dropped by for a visit. When Joe walked into the living room and saw us there, he didn't say a word. Instead he looked up at the ceiling and stared at something none of us could see.

"Daddy, what are you looking at?" Karen asked.

"What does it look like I'm looking at? I'm looking at the ceiling. These two jokers have their hats on in the house, so it must be raining."

True enough, Vonzie and I had our baseball caps on, and apparently that was impolite in Joe's household. I guess he could have just told us to take them off, but his way was more dramatic. Then it was time for him to introduce himself.

"My name is Cut-and-Shoot Joe," he declared. "If you mess with any of my daughters, I will either cut you or shoot you."

When I walked into Phil's Market to ask Joe if I could marry Karen, my heart was in my throat. But in my mind I could hear my own father's words, clear as ever: "Son, the best way to deal with this is head-on. Get it over with. Just do it." I approached Joe and asked if I could speak with him in his office.

"I would like your permission to ask your daughter for her hand in marriage," I said.

Joe looked at me for a while before answering.

"That's up to her," he finally said. "I don't know what she sees in you, but if she wants to marry you, that's up to her."

Not exactly a ringing endorsement, but I took it.

"But, boy," Joe added, "I do appreciate that you asked me first."

As always, my mother had been right.

The next day, I went to Karen's home, dropped to one knee, and asked her to marry me.

Karen said, "Yes."

We knew our engagement would be long because I still had coursework to finish up at Cal State. In the meantime Karen and I began to chart our future. Now that I wasn't going to play pro ball, I turned my attention to real estate. I believed the focus and drive that made me a successful athlete could also make me a successful real estate mogul, maybe even the next Donald Trump. At Beverly

I'd been exposed to truly wealthy and powerful people for the first time, and that had broadened my view of what was possible for someone like me. I saw no reason why I couldn't be just as successful as them.

"I already have some great connections through Beverly," I reasoned to Karen as we discussed our future. "And this is something we can do together. We can get our real estate licenses and open our own company. We can learn and grow together."

"I'm in," Karen said.

Those days were some of the happiest times of my life.

———

AT BEVERLY I STARTED OUT coaching the infielders on the varsity baseball team, while my good friend Emery came back and coached the outfielders. Honestly, I probably would have paid the school to do it. The same competitiveness that drove me as a player was still there as a coach, and I found I really enjoyed imparting whatever lessons I'd learned in my time at Beverly to younger kids like my brother.

Sometime during that baseball season Beverly's head football coach asked if I would consider working as an assistant football coach the next year. Naturally, I jumped at the chance.

I guess I did a pretty decent job because at the end of football season Coach Friedman and Coach Stansbury cornered me and asked if I'd like to keep coaching the following season.

They didn't have to ask twice.

The year after I graduated Cal State, Coach Stansbury offered another interesting suggestion.

"You know, as long as you're working at Beverly, you might want to go ahead and get your teaching credentials. You never know."

I hadn't considered that, but it made perfect sense. Why not get a license that allowed me to pinch-hit for teachers at Beverly since I was spending so much time there anyway? I started pursuing a California Life Single Subject Teaching Credential, and suddenly I was signed up as a substitute teacher in Beverly Hills, Culver City, and other school districts in LA.

Before I even knew it, I'd become a teacher and a coach.

Then on a hot July day in 1981, in a Lutheran church in the San Fernando Valley, Karen and I got married. By then we'd already been dating for five years and engaged for a year and a half. Karen swept down the aisle in a gorgeous white dress, while I nervously waited for her in an all-white tuxedo. After the ceremony and reception Karen and I drove down to San Diego, spent the night, then flew to Hawaii for our honeymoon. My old Beverly baseball coach, Hank Friedman, had helped me put my honeymoon together. His parents, who lived in Beverly Hills, had a connection to a travel agency, and they arranged a lavish fourteen-day trip to four different islands. Without his help there was no way I could have afforded it.

Coach Friedman didn't have to do that for me, but he did.

We humans have an innate ability to create a family wherever we are. Bonding is in our nature. By the time I got to Beverly as a student, I already had two families: my parents and brothers and cousins and aunts and uncles and all my other relatives, and everyone in my neighborhood in South Central—shop owners, Little League coaches, the gang at Tolliver's.

Then I became part of another family at Beverly Hills High. And when I went back as a teacher and coach, I met a lot of my students' parents and became part of a family I never expected to be a part of: the family that is Beverly Hills itself.

That is why Coach Friedman helped me with my honeymoon. I was part of the family, and family members look out for their own.

THE NATURAL NEXT STEP FOR me was applying for a permanent teaching job. I could teach, coach sports, and still build my real estate business with Karen on the side. I called Beverly's principal and told him I was interested in teaching. He let me know there was going to be a job opening in the history department. I had a degree in social science, and I'd taught history as a substitute, so I went in for an interview, which I thought went well.

But a few days later Principal Levine told me I didn't get the job.

At the same time he made it clear Beverly wanted to keep me around. He offered me the job of running the school's detention program, as well as coaching football and baseball. I said yes.

Only three months later a position opened up in the physical education department, and I moved there. Our PE department was full of amazing and dedicated educators, and I soaked up their insights. When they gave me evaluations, I hung on every word. I understood going in I had the least experience of anyone in the department, and in a way my job was not to be the weak link. And I wasn't.

In my time in Beverly's PE department our program was recognized as *the* top physical education department in California.

In the spring of 1985 I was also named head coach of Beverly's freshman baseball team. I set up tryouts and put the forty or so kids who showed up through infield drills and batting practice. I kept my eye out for the ones who showed that little special something—that extra inner gear. At that time Beverly wasn't attracting the nation's best young athletes like other high schools with more money and bigger profiles were. We were a small school, and people saw our athletes as "soft"—after all, how tough could kids from Beverly Hills be? My chances of finding one of the special ones weren't great. Still, I was hopeful.

Early on in the workout, one of the youngsters trying out came running over to me.

He wasn't big, maybe five foot one and south of a hundred pounds. He might have been the smallest kid on the field. He had tousled blond hair and a sunny, slightly crooked smile. I could tell he had a ton of energy just from the way he bounded toward me. Stopping in front of me, he stuck out his little hand, more confident than any kid his age had a right to be.

"Hello," he said. "I'm Steven Fenton."

I shook his hand, and I knew right then I'd found a special one.

CHAPTER

7

THE SUMMER BEFORE Steven Fenton's first semester at Beverly he took a bus to campus so he could try out for freshman football. A coach handed him a Beverly football jersey and a set of shoulder pads. Steven had never worn shoulder pads in his life. At the end of the practice, when the other kids took off their pads and jerseys to go home, Steven refused to take his off. He kept them on, marched off the field, walked up to the bus, and stepped through the door.

And got stuck.

Steven's shoulder pads were too wide. The driver and the other people on the bus looked at him like he was crazy. But Steven just wiggled his way through the door and walked down the aisle—though he had to walk sideways because his pads barely fit. He stood in the back for the whole ride home because he was too excited to sit—and because he probably wouldn't have fit in a seat.

If anybody was laughing at him, Steven didn't notice.

When the bus stopped on the corner of his neighborhood, Steven tumbled out. He walked the entire block home, proud as he could be, and saw his father waiting for him on the front lawn.

"Look, Dad!" Steven yelled, running up to his father. "Look at my uniform!"

Mr. Fenton smiled and scooped up his son.

"I'm proud of you, Steve-o," he said.

That's why Steven wore the pads and jersey home. He couldn't wait for his father to see him in them. He couldn't wait to make his father proud.

AFTER SHAKING STEVEN'S HAND AND introducing myself, I watched him field ground balls and take his cuts at the plate. After a couple of hours I sat the kids down on the bleachers and called off the names of those I wanted to see on the field. I read one name. Then another. Then a third and fourth.

Then came the fifth name.

"Fenton!" I called out. "Get over to second base!"

Steven got up and ran to second base as fast as he could. Then he planted himself there, as if to say, "I'm never leaving."

He never did.

What did I see in Steven that day? Well, for one thing, he was good. He could play. He understood the game, he took it seriously, and he never stopped hustling. Over time I'd find he played sports with more focus and intensity than any other kid I knew—and even many grown-ups. It was like making the team was the most important thing in the world to him. No kid who played for me ever had a dirtier uniform.

But even before I saw Steven play, I could tell there was something special about him. I saw it when he came up and shook my hand. He was poised, direct, determined. It was almost as if he introduced himself because he knew he was good enough to make the team and wanted to move things along.

I guess he reminded me of another kid who'd been confident he could make the team.

When he was in Little League, one of Steven's baseball coaches taught him to bang his bat on home plate before facing the pitcher. The idea was to do it in a way that would intimidate pitchers. So every time Steven came up to hit, he noisily banged his bat on home plate two or three times. Never mind that he was usually the smallest kid playing. In his mind, he was Babe Ruth, and he meant business.

During one game an opposing player saw Steven bang his bat and yelled out, "Look, it's Bam Bam!"—a reference to the little blond boy on *The Flintstones* who banged his big club everywhere. Predictably, the nickname stuck.

But the joke was on the other players—at eleven Steven was named a Little League All-Star, and in his first season at Beverly, as the team's starting second baseman, he batted over .300. Considering some of the pitchers he faced were nearly a foot taller than he, that was exceptional.

At the end of his freshman year Steven asked me to sign his copy of the yearbook, the *Watchtower*. I grabbed a pen:

Bam Bam,
    You're an excellent lead-off hitter even if you can't hit (smile). I enjoyed having you on the team, and I look forward to teasing you next year about your inability to hit.
                              Have a good summer.
                              Coach Paysinger

DURING BASEBALL SEASON STEVEN LIKED hanging around after practices and games and spending time with the coaches. While his friends were fooling around in the cafeteria or going off campus for burgers, Steven was in my office, having lunch and joking around with the coaching staff. My office in the athletic building was tiny—just big enough for two chairs and a desk. It wasn't really even a desk, more like a shelf built into the wall. I guess it was closer to being a closet than an office, but that didn't bother me. And it didn't bother Steven. Effortlessly taking in all he could from his coaches, this kid with that crooked smile turned my tiny office into an inner sanctum.

At first, Steven would stick his head in to say hello on his way to the weight room or the batting cage. Before long he was pulling up a chair. Eventually, it was Steven who brought lunch. His family had an account at a popular sandwich spot called Giuliano's, just three blocks from Steven's house. All he had to do was walk in and tell them his account number—029140—and he'd walk out with as many sandwiches as he wanted. He brought so many sandwiches for us over the years those six numbers are now seared into my brain.

What did we talk about during those lunches? Anything and everything. Mainly sports, at first—the ins and outs of baseball, the trick to turning a double play, the proper way to slide, stuff like that. Eventually, though, Steven began opening up to me about his life.

I already knew his father, Frank Fenton, from around Beverly. Frank was the president of the board of education and was involved in all kinds of things around Beverly Hills. He may have been the most powerful political figure in town. He was also a big supporter of sports at Beverly, and he liked coming to games and meeting me afterward to talk about the team. Frank was smart and friendly and charming, and we hit it off right away.

But because of his status in politics and his slick suits and easy demeanor, I came to think of him as a typical Beverly Hills big shot—another rich white guy who grew up and still lived in the lap of luxury. Considering what I'd gone through at Beverly, I should have known better than to assume such a thing. But, to be honest, that was my first impression of Frank. I typecast him as Mr. Beverly Hills.

I was wrong.

It turned out Steven's family had come to Beverly Hills with nothing. Literally nothing.

One of the first stories Steven told me during our lunches was the remarkable one of his grandparents, Rose and Karl Freudenthal, who lived in Berlin, Germany, during the rise of the Nazi Party.

One night the Gestapo knocked on their front door and hauled Karl away to the Sachsenhausen concentration camp. Rose tried for weeks to get him released and finally managed to bribe the Gestapo clerks to free him. They were able to fly out of Berlin to Amsterdam, then board a Dutch ocean liner called the *Simon Bolivar* headed for North America.

But just one day out to sea, off the English coast near Harwich, the *Simon Bolivar* struck two mines and began to break apart.

As the giant ocean liner sank, Rose and Karl jumped in a lifeboat, clutching their young son—Steven's father, Frank. Then another explosion rocked the liner, and Karl dove into the water, still holding tight to his boy. Rose jumped in after them.

They clung to a tiny piece of wood in the freezing, oily ocean, Rose and Karl's legs intertwined so they wouldn't drift away from each other. They had no idea how long they held on; all they remembered was waking up on a minesweeper, wrapped in blankets. Rose, Karl, and Frank survived. Rose's mother, and eighty-three other people, did not.

After weeks in a hospital they finally made it to Cuba, and from there to Los Angeles. All the valuables they'd packed were lost at sea, so they showed up with just the tattered clothes on their backs. With a friend's help they moved into a tiny apartment off Melrose and La Brea Avenue, on the nondescript edge of West Hollywood. For a while Karl tended bar at the Hillcrest Country Club, then tried his hand at a dry cleaning business that failed. He finally found steady work with an Italian family that made and sold shoes.

Spared from the Nazis and a cruel death in the Atlantic, Karl slowly made a life for his family in America. There, young Frankie grew up as American as any other kid. He played baseball with his friends and rode his bike around town and did all the stuff most kids do. When Frank was twenty, he met a pretty young woman named Judie, then a seventeen-year-old taking a nursing class at Cedars-Sinai Hospital in LA. A year later they got married, and some years after that Steven was born.

The family settled into a new home on a pretty street called Wetherly Drive in a beautiful place called Beverly Hills.

ONE OF THE MOST SURPRISING discoveries I made in the course of my lunches with Steven was how similar our childhoods had been. I hadn't really believed that was possible because in my mind Beverly Hills was the exclusive paradise of wealthy, famous people.

Once again, I shouldn't have been so quick to make that assumption. So many of my classmates at Beverly wrote off South Central as a ghetto when I knew it was much more than that. Yet for some reason I did the same thing to Beverly Hills. I wrote it off as one-dimensional. I soon learned that wasn't the case at all.

Steven Fenton is the one who showed me that.

Originally an untouched wilderness of oak and eucalyptus trees, freshwater streams, and bunchgrass, Beverly Hills was settled at the turn of the twentieth century. In 1919, silent movie stars Douglas Fairbanks and Mary Pickford remodeled a hunting lodge on fifty-six acres in Beverly Hills's San Ysidro Canyon and turned it into a lavish twenty-five-room mansion they called Pickfair. More celebrities followed: Harold Lloyd, Rudolph Valentino, Gloria Swanson, Buster Keaton, Charlie Chaplin. And Hollywood's biggest stars still haven't stopped moving in.

Since it was incorporated in 1914, exactly one hundred years ago, Beverly Hills has become one of the most celebrated and iconic cities in the world, as well as one of the wealthiest.

But all that wealth and all those movie stars don't tell the whole story. You might find this hard to believe, but Beverly Hills, in its own way, is like any other small town in America.

You see, there isn't just *one* Beverly Hills. It's roughly divided into two distinct parts—the northern part, which includes Rodeo Drive and most of the fancy mansions, and the southern part, which is where Steven Fenton; his brother, Gary; and his sisters, Jenny and Mindy, grew up. People talk about this divide as the divide between the "haves" and the "have-mores."

The Fentons were "haves."

If you take a drive through their neighborhood, you'll see what I mean. The homes are certainly pretty, and there are plenty of maple and ash and juniper trees, but it looks more like an ordinary suburb than it does the mansion-strewn northern part of town. On Steven's street, South Wetherly, the homes are bunched together on snug lots, and there aren't any towering privet hedges or giant circle driveways in sight.

In fact, it doesn't look all that different from the street I grew up on in South Central.

What's more, Steven spent his childhood doing much the same thing I did—playing sports from sunup to sunset. He and Gary competed at everything—Strat-O-Matic baseball games, basketball and football on their street and in their yard, youth soccer matches at Beverly Hills's Roxbury Park. And when the sun began creeping below the mountains, their mother hollered for them to come in for supper, same as mine used to do.

In the same way I was more than just another black kid from South Central, Steven was more than just another white kid from Beverly Hills. The broad strokes I used to define him were as useless as the ones people used to define me.

During one of our lunches Steven told me a story that sounded strangely familiar.

When he was young, he and his friends tried hard not to throw a ball in the backyard of one of their neighbors, the Taylors. The Taylors were an older couple who had no kids of their own and no use for boys yelling outside their window all day long.

"If we happened to throw a ball in their yard, the first thing we did was check their driveway," Steven told me. "If a car was there, it meant one of them was home, and we forgot about the ball. But if there was no car, one of us would hop their fence, get the ball, and scramble back as fast as possible."

One day, Steven explained, something got stuck in Mr. Taylor's chimney. When it rained, the clogged chimney caused Mr. Taylor's bedroom to flood. He turned around and sued Steven's father for damages in small claims court, claiming it was a ball that Steven and his friends had thrown up there. Steven wasn't allowed to go to the courthouse when the case was heard, but in his mind it all played out just like in *To Kill a Mockingbird*, with his dad as the noble attorney Atticus Finch. After all, Steven knew he was innocent—he and his friends had never lost a ball in the Taylors' chimney.

"So my dad comes home and tells me he won the case," Steven explained. "I ran up to him and said, 'Dad, Dad, what did you say? How did you win?' And my father said, 'I told the judge I'm the president of the Beverly Hills Little League, and I know a hundred boys who can throw a baseball far enough to get it in that chimney. So how are you going to prove it was my son?' "

At that point in the trial Mr. Taylor reached under the plaintiff's table and pulled out a cardboard box packed with baseballs and basketballs and footballs and soccer balls he claimed belonged to Steven and his friends. And in fact some of them *did*. But Mr. Taylor couldn't prove Steven threw a ball in the chimney, so he had to drop the suit.

The bad news was that Steven and his friends never got all their balls back.

It's true Steven's father told off Mr. Taylor in a courtroom and not on a front porch like my mother did with old Mrs. Ford. But basically, these two stories are the same. Young boys playing sports all day long. Parents standing up for their children. Ornery next-door neighbors hoarding errant balls. It's a universal childhood scenario, and it's the kind of story that binds us all as humans.

During our lunches I slowly discovered that—even though I was raised in South Central and Steven was raised in Beverly Hills—we were a lot more alike than we were different.

But I also learned that, in South Central, I grew up with certain blessings and advantages Steven never had in Beverly Hills.

STEVEN WAS IN THE EIGHTH grade when Frank Fenton won his first election—a seat on the Beverly Hills Board of Education. Steven went with his father to many of his board meetings, soaking up the back-office dealings and watching board members cast their votes with the same awe and delight he once had reserved for Dodgers games. It might seem an odd passion for a kid, but in Steven's case it wasn't. Because politics was the Fenton family business.

During our lunches Steven talked a lot about his parents. His pride in them was obvious. He told me how Frank worked as a stockbroker—how he got up every weekday morning precisely at 5:30 a.m. and had breakfast in his dapper business suit, his crisp white shirt freshly starched by the Wong Wing dry cleaners, his conservative tie from Carroll & Co., and his polished black Bally loafers. He described how his father was the picture of elegance, always so calm and in charge. Steven loved the way people were drawn to Frank, and he loved how Frank made everyone around him feel like a friend. He also loved their father-son tradition of watching Dallas Cowboys football together every Sunday. As a Raiders fan myself, I used to tease him all the time about the Cowboys.

From what I could tell, Steven's mother, Judie Fenton, was a great match for Frank. She was smart, feisty, and driven, and Steven got his competitive fire from her—just like I got mine from my mother. Judie got married at eighteen and had three children by the time she was twenty-seven. She loved her children dearly, but she also yearned to be more than just a stay-at-home mom. A nurse by trade but a businesswoman at heart, she went on to run several successful enterprises, including the popular Beverly Hills Sports Camp. Together, Frank and

Judie Fenton became one of the most visible and highly regarded couples in Beverly Hills.

Over time I'd learn their stature and success was both a blessing and a curse for Steven.

The year his father won his first election, Steven decided to run for office himself—eighth-grade student council president. "I went into it thinking there was no way I could lose," Steven told me in one of our lunches. "Then I found out who I was running against." His opponent, it turned out, was a student named Kristin—his elementary school ex-girlfriend and the first girl Steven had ever kissed. Kristin was smart and outgoing and extremely popular, and she had the female vote sewn up. And as Steven discovered, she had a good share of the male vote sewn up, too.

"My best friend, Josh, had a huge crush on her . . . and he was my campaign manager!" Steven told me with a laugh. "I knew I was in trouble."

Steven explained how, on the heels of his father's stirring election—a victory that filled him with so much pride—he couldn't bear the thought of losing his own election. He knew his parents worked hard to uphold a certain image in the community, and he didn't want to be the first one in his family to fail to live up to that image.

"I knew it was going to be a tough campaign, and I couldn't even count on my guy friends a hundred percent," he told me. "So at the last minute, I got scared and pulled out of the race."

When he shared that story, Steven made a joke out of it. But to me, it was a much more powerful story than he realized. It told me a lot about who he was. I knew his parents, and I knew what imposing figures they were in Beverly Hills. Now I could see their success, and particularly Frank's, was daunting to their son. Rather than step out of their shadow and risk failure, Steven quit.

After that story, it occurred to me the lessons my parents taught me—never give up, believe in yourself, don't back down from any challenge, work twice as hard as everyone else—could help Steven develop a sense of his own worth, independent of his parents' successes. I believed I could teach him how to better focus his energy and realize more of his potential. I believed I could bring out the best in him.

Imagine that—the guy from South Central teaching life lessons to the kid from Beverly Hills.

Steven knew full well he was comparatively lucky and blessed in life. He didn't see himself as a victim in any way. But at the same time, as he sat across from me in my office, I could still see the vulnerable little boy in him. Without knowing everything that was going on in his life, I could sense a void, a missing piece.

In Beverly Hills he was known as "Frank's kid" or "Judie's son." Maybe that's the way most people in town treated him—not as his own person but as the son of one of Beverly Hills's most powerful men, the "heir" to his father's legacy. And maybe Steven was already struggling under the pressure of being "the son of . . ." or "the heir to . . ." and was just trying to discover who he was. Maybe he just wanted to be Stevie—a regular kid without anyone else's expectations to live up to besides his own.

From that point on I made it a point to never address or even think of Steven as Frank and Judie Fenton's son. To me, he was just Stevie. Like so many kids under my watch, he needed someone to believe in him and encourage him no matter what happened, win or lose. He needed the space and the support to blossom into his own person, whoever that would be. So when Steven came to my office, he found a place where his parents' long shadow didn't reach. A place where he could create his *own* shadow.

The time I spent with Steven taught me something valuable, too. It taught me that, just as anyone can achieve great things, no matter where they came from, anyone can have a part that needs fixing, no matter how easy their life may seem.

STEVEN WAS THE FIRST STUDENT at Beverly I took a special interest in as a coach.

Something clicked in my lunches with him. Something was activated. I remembered how Coach Bushman and Coach Kloes had taken me under their wings, and now I felt compelled to do the same with Steven. In his four years at Beverly, he and I had lunch together probably a hundred times, maybe more. We talked a lot about sports, but we talked a lot more about life. We spoke a lot about something I'll call comportment—about how a champion carries himself. Steven was particularly interested in this topic. I could see him hanging on every word.

"Once you plan your work, work your plan," I told him. "Once you have a clear vision of what you want to achieve, you don't let anyone or anything stand in your way. The only way you can achieve it is to be a hundred percent determined. Your mentality has to be that *nothing* can stop you. That is how champions think.

"*Plan your work, work your plan.*"

I made sure that, at Beverly, Steven had continuity in his life. He knew he could come see me whenever he wanted; my door was always open. He knew he could count on me to be the same way every day, at every practice and every game. He understood my demands on him as a player and a person were nonnegotiable, just as my mother's had been on me. He knew the lessons I taught him one day would be the same lessons I would drive home the next.

Steven knew that, at Beverly at least, he always had someone who believed in him.

Yet Steven wasn't the only one learning something.

Steven was teaching me how to bring out the best in a kid, that the more you believe in someone, the better they become.

Steven's junior and senior years were remarkable. By then I was co-manager of the varsity team, which had incredible chemistry. Steven hadn't shown up to Beverly alone. He'd arrived as part of a group of boys who'd been playing Little League baseball together for years and were something of a legend in Beverly Hills. Besides Steven there were Albert Silvera and Mike Sutton, two talented players whose fathers, Big Al Silvera and Joe Sutton, were also beloved Little League coaches. These three boys—the Three Musketeers—took their great success in Little League and transferred it straight to Beverly. I was just the lucky coach who was there when they did.

Largely because of those three kids and their parents, the baseball team at Beverly became like one big family—and I was part of that family. They were the nucleus of a really special team, and I got pulled into that nucleus. Very quickly I went from having few adult relationships in the community to being friends with some of the most respected people in Beverly Hills. For someone who felt saddled with an "outsider" label, this was a wonderful change. It was during Steven's four years at the school that I truly found my place in Beverly Hills.

In Steven's time at Beverly the baseball team won two league titles and nearly won a third. We came within a game of winning the Southern California High School Championship; only one other team in the history of Beverly had ever made it that far. In his senior year, Steven's batting average for the year was .423, and he hit for an even higher average in the play-offs. He was named a First Team League All-Star, as well as a First Team All-Star for the whole Westside school district. Ultimately, this meant that very few kids anywhere had a better season than Steven.

Steven had one more honor his senior year, and fortunately for me, I got to be a part of it.

Beverly Hills High has an Athletic Hall of Fame; after every season the coaches get together to figure out who to nominate. The day of the ceremony several hundred kids packed into the Swim Gym. I went up to the podium to present the first award.

"We call him our Charlie Hustle," I said, invoking the nickname of baseball's fiercest warrior, Pete Rose. "He doesn't stroll to first base when he gets a walk; he runs at full speed. He doesn't jog after fly balls; he goes all out. That's just who he is. He'll always give you one hundred percent. So join me in congratulating our newest inductee into the Beverly Hills High School Athletic Hall of Fame, Steven Fenton."

I looked over and watched Steven get up from his seat. There was a four-foot railing between his row of seats and the middle of the gym where the podium was. Steven jumped right over it. I handed him his plaque, and we shook hands. He cracked a sheepish half smile.

After the ceremony he rushed home to show the plaque to his father—just like he'd rushed home with his shoulder pads and jersey after that first tryout.

The very next day, Steven graduated from Beverly. His parents threw a big luncheon in Steven's honor, and I was happy to be invited. Once again, Steven came over with his copy of the *Watchtower* and asked me to sign it one last time. I spent a little more time thinking about my final message, before I finally wrote this:

> *Stevie, it's been absolutely fantastic working with you the past four years.*

You know how I feel about you, so I won't repeat everything or all of the things I've been saying for years about you. If you don't know, you should know when I rag a person it's because I care about and truly like that person, and I probably ragged you more than anyone ever!

You also gave me a lot to rag about!!

Just because you're graduating doesn't mean we should end our friendship.

Stay in touch, and good luck always.

Your coach and good friend, C. Paysinger

Not long ago, I got the chance to go through Steven's senior yearbook again and look over what I'd written. There's a lot there that I find meaningful today.

The affection, for one thing. Because we were so alike, because we both drove ourselves so hard, because we saw something in the other that we well understood in ourselves. And the endless ragging—it still makes me laugh to think of all the good-natured joking that went on and how that really did reflect how much we cared for each other.

But what affects me most of all is the tone of what I wrote near the end. *Just because you're graduating doesn't mean we should end our friendship*, I wrote. *Stay in touch.*

There's something touching about this to me now. It reads like a kind of hopeful plea—as if we both understood our friendship would never really be the same as it'd been at Beverly. Steven was moving on, and while I knew he would never turn his back on Beverly, I also knew his big, bright future was destined to take him elsewhere. And so I wrote down my fondest hope.

Sadly, that was not to be.

I lost track of Steven after he left Beverly, but I never forgot what he meant to me and what I had meant to him. I was already a coach and a teacher when I met him. But Steven taught me how to be a true mentor.

I didn't know it at the time, but because of that little blond kid with the crooked half smile, I had found my calling.

THE COLD, HARD FACT, HOWEVER, is that there's a difference between your calling and your dream. My dream had long been to be a pro baseball player, and when that didn't happen, my new dream was to be a real estate tycoon. I did not spend any time dreaming of what it would be like to sit in a small office on a high school campus and counsel confused young kids. But I guess that's why it's known as a calling—because it calls out to you, not the other way around. And sometimes your calling takes a little getting used to. Sometimes it has to call you more than once.

Just one year after Steven graduated Beverly, I made an appointment to see the school's principal—my old blood-and-guts football coach, Ben Bushman. I was delighted when Coach Bushman was named principal. He didn't have much of an academic background, but he was clearly someone who loved Beverly and had the trust and respect of everyone there. We became even better friends once he got the top job, and he helped show me the teaching and coaching ropes.

But this visit to his office was something I was dreading.

I walked in, said hello, and put a signed letter on his desk. Then I pushed it toward him.

"What's this?" he asked.

"Ben," I said in a voice barely above a whisper, "I'm submitting my resignation from Beverly Hills High School."

CHAPTER

8

WHY WAS I resigning? How did I get to that point? Let me roll things back just a bit.

From the day I sat across from Mr. Hoag in his office to the day I signed Steven's senior yearbook at Beverly, sixteen years of my life had passed. I was fourteen when I first set foot on campus, and I was thirty when Steven left. That means that for more than half my life I'd been involved with Beverly Hills High in one way or another. South Central may have been where I lived, but in a very real way Beverly had become my home.

Even so, when I took the job of assistant coach after college in 1979, I really thought I'd be staying at Beverly for maybe just a year or two. The plan was always to get back to real estate, which was the dream.

Not that it was hard to figure out why I never left.

Beverly kept pulling me back in.

In my first few years as a teacher and coach I was finding out just how much many of my students—and even many of their parents—

needed the kind of guidance I myself had received growing up. I'd been on the other end of that equation; I'd seen how important the mentorship of Coach Bushman and Coach Kloes had been to me. Now I was the guy kids were turning to for help.

All sorts of issues and problems—academic, athletic, *and* personal—wound up at my feet. On my very first Back to School Night—an annual gathering of teachers and parents before the start of the school year—an elegant, middle-aged, blond-haired woman came up and introduced herself to me. She was the mother of one of the linebackers on our football team, Paul. Her son was talented, but he often seemed off in his own world. His mother and I talked about that for a bit before she told me Paul's father was a successful night-club owner on Hollywood's Sunset Strip. Because his father wasn't often around, Paul's home life was chaotic.

"He's becoming more and more rebellious," his mother told me. "And I know he's snorting cocaine."

I was shocked to hear her say this so casually.

"How do you know he's doing coke?" I asked.

"Well, because I'm buying it for him."

I'm pretty sure my mouth fell open at that point. Paul's mother went on to explain that she felt it was important for kids to stay off the streets—the streets are where all the bad things happen.

"Kids are going to do things they shouldn't do," she reasoned, "so if I buy him the cocaine, at least it's incentive for him to do it at home."

And then she asked, "Do you think there's anything else I can do to keep my son safe?"

"Well," I said, "you can start by not buying him coke."

My position as assistant football coach allowed me to spend more time with Paul as time went on, and eventually he straightened himself out. But meeting his mother was a real eye-opener for me, and I realized some of my students weren't getting quality guidance at home—if they were getting any guidance at all. For a moment I imagined my own mother concluding that her best option was to buy me drugs. I couldn't even fathom a world where such a thing would happen.

Another parent came by to see me in my office one day. His son Derek was on the football team, and because of that Derek's father and I had become friends. Now, the coaching staff had a strong suspicion Derek was smoking pot, but we couldn't prove it. I thought it better not to mention anything to his father until we knew for sure.

Then Derek's dad dropped by to see me.

"Carter, I found this pipe in Derek's car, and I asked him about it," he said. "Derek told me it wasn't his, that he was holding it for a friend. He said his friend is afraid to take it into his house, so he kept it for him."

That seemed far-fetched to me, but Derek's father wasn't done.

"Last night I went through his drawers, and I found a bag of weed," he said. "I asked if it was his, and he said he was holding it for the same friend."

Derek's father told me the friend's name—another kid on the team—and said I should be aware that one of my players had a drug problem.

I thought about what I'd just heard before I spoke. A father finds a drug pipe in his son's car. Then he finds a bag of weed in his son's drawer. His son tells him they're not his.

And the father doesn't question it?

It seemed to me Derek's father was in deep denial. But his quick acceptance of his son's story didn't surprise me. I was beginning to see that was how a lot of Beverly parents dealt with their children—with kid gloves. They never pushed them too hard or did anything that might set them off. The parents didn't have the power. They'd willingly handed it over to their kids. Once again I imagined myself trying to squirm out of some wrongdoing by lying to my mother. She would have cut me off at "But Mom . . ."

"You know," I said to Derek's father, "it's possible those drugs don't belong to your son's friends."

"What do you mean?" he said.

"My advice is, sit down with your son and have a good, long talk with him about why he is holding these drugs and paraphernalia. Have the drug talk."

We had no more problems with Derek after that, but I never knew if his father got tougher with him—or if he was still willing to believe whatever story his son told him.

I was constantly amazed at the lengths parents went to to bail their kids out of trouble rather than discipline them. One of the boys in my summer school health class, Bobby, was the son of an incredibly wealthy Beverly Hills businessman. Bobby was a nice kid, but he, too, lacked motivation. He was really struggling academically, barely scoring Ds. A few different teachers worked with him, but his grades never seemed to come up. In my class, he was flirting with an F.

One afternoon, shortly after class ended, a man in a suit knocked on the door of my classroom. He introduced himself as Bobby's private tutor. I told him to have a seat and asked how I could help.

"Mr. Paysinger, I need to know what Bobby needs to do to get a B in your class," he said.

"Well, his highest score so far has been a D, and he really had to struggle to get that," I said. "So he'll have to work really hard and get a couple of As."

The tutor paused and leaned forward.

"Mr. Paysinger, do you know who Bobby's father is?"

"Yes, I do."

"Okay. Then I will ask you again. What does Bobby have to do to get a B?"

I half expected that's where he was heading, but I didn't much like his threatening tone.

"Then I will tell you again," I said. "Get a bunch of As."

I never saw that tutor again or heard from Bobby's father directly. In the end I gave Bobby a D for my class because that was the grade he deserved.

What happened with Bobby wasn't an isolated event. More than once I was approached by parents or surrogates and asked to cut a kid some slack. "What can we do to make this go away?" was a typical approach. Some parents would appeal to me as a friend; some would suggest that as a coach I should have my players' backs.

But the last thing in the world I would ever want to do is have my players start thinking, *Hey, I play for Coach Paysinger; he will take care of me. Thanks to Coach, I'm immune.*

Instead, I followed the very same principle my mother used to raise my brothers and me.

As long as we stayed on the straight and narrow, my mother was our greatest champion. We understood our mother had an imaginary line we could never cross, and we knew that she would support us all the way up to that line. But if we ever went over it, boy, look out. We knew our mother wasn't going to bend the rules just to protect us.

"What you did is wrong, and wrong is wrong," she would say.

That was exactly my policy as a coach and teacher.

But at Beverly, leniency and indulgence seemed to be the preferred method of way too many parents. I began to see myself as a last wall of defense for some of my kids. If I didn't draw a line in the sand for them, who would?

At first glance many of these wayward kids seemed to have everything a kid could want. They lived in Beverly Hills; they drove pricey cars; they never lacked for money. But I was discovering that, in fact, these kids didn't have everything—they had *nothing*. Because if you don't have parents who believe in you and champion you—who set a standard of conduct and hold you to it and teach you how to be decent and strong—then what, really, do you have?

I realized these Beverly kids needed the lessons I had learned from my parents and from my community. And I saw how those lessons could have an immediate impact. Many of the kids just needed to know someone was holding them accountable. I became that person.

Understanding that filled me with a profound sense of responsibility. It's the reason I stayed at Beverly for more than a decade and not just a couple of years. I was good at helping these kids, and I loved doing it. Walking away from them wasn't an easy thing to do.

AS MUCH AS I LOVED my life at Beverly, something was nagging at me, and I couldn't make it go away.

When Karen and I got married, we had agreed to go into real estate together. Even when I got hired as an assistant coach at Beverly, the idea was to stay there only as long as it took me to transition to real estate full-time.

Somehow, that transition never happened.

For a long time I'd teach and coach at Beverly during the day, then, right after the last practice, rush to the office Karen and I were renting to help with our real estate deals. This wasn't an ideal setup. A good coach always hangs around after practices in case players or other coaches need to see him. A lot of coaching happens after the final whistle. But I had no choice but to disappear as soon as practice ended. It got to the point where I dreaded having to leave Beverly to go to our office. It seemed like I was dealing with issues and making decisions every hour of every day, sunup to sundown. I was exhausted.

But it was even worse for Karen. You see, I actually liked the real estate business; I enjoyed making sales calls and dealing with prospective buyers and closing deals. I guess that was the competitive side of me. But Karen never had that same love for the business. She only got into it because we'd agreed to work at it together. Then she wound up working alone in our office all day, keeping everything afloat, while I was off at school. As much as I loved coaching I could never shake the feeling I was letting Karen down.

Then things began to change at Beverly.

For the first time since I'd started there, Beverly entered a period of instability. I can't say exactly how or when it started, but I guess it would be naïve to think that anything could stay the same as it's always been forever. Things, by their nature, fall apart. In schools, people leave and new people come in. Values change. Priorities change. Compromises happen. Beverly, for all its grand history, was not immune to this. Even a place as wonderful as Beverly would eventually have to redefine itself in a changing world.

If there was a single event that started the instability, I'd have to say it was a labor strike. In 1990 the teachers at Beverly threatened to go on strike, which led to acrimony between students, teachers, and administrators. Accusations were leveled at city officials—including Steven's father, Frank Fenton—as different factions fought over the school budget. At one point, the teachers even picketed the Fentons' house. I hated to see the way the whole messy situation affected everyone. We even had to cancel football games, which meant some kids missed their final games at Beverly. They got cheated out of what should have been their crowning high school moments. Many of their parents held that against the school for a long, long time.

In the middle of all the turmoil I decided to put the brakes on my life at Beverly. It was time to reevaluate. In 1990 I asked the principal if I could take a leave of absence for the spring semester. My plan was to spend the next twenty weeks working full-time on real estate, and if things went well, I'd leave Beverly altogether. It wasn't an easy decision to make, trust me. But at the time it felt like the right choice.

During those twenty weeks Karen and I spent every day building our business. As I'd expected, the passion I felt for sports and coaching transferred right over to real estate. On top of that, Karen and I made a really good team, and we loved being together more than just a couple of hours a day. Things seemed to be falling into place.

So at the end of my leave of absence I faced the toughest decision of my life. Should I go back to Beverly as a teacher and coach and work real estate part-time again? Or should I quit and keep building our business?

I no longer wanted to halfheartedly chase my dream. I had to practice what I preached—100 percent commitment. I realized if there was ever a time for me to make a change, now was that time.

And so I made an appointment to see Ben Bushman.

I EXPLAINED ALL MY REASONS for leaving to Ben, and while he was sad to see me go, he shook my hand and wished me the best. Just like that, my long association with Beverly was over. To be honest, leaving hit me like a punch in the gut. Coaching there had become a big part of my identity. But I understood that change is never easy and that just because it's rough going doesn't mean it's not the right thing to do.

Only when I searched the very deepest parts of my soul—when I allowed myself to truly examine my innermost feelings—did I brush against one irrefutable fact.

My heart was still at Beverly.

Six weeks after I resigned, I got an unexpected phone call. I figured Ben was calling to catch up and see how I was doing, and indeed that's what we talked about the first few minutes. But then everything changed.

"Carter, I'm happy to hear that you're doing so well," he said. "But the reason I'm calling is that, as you may know, Coach Stansbury and Coach Billingsley have both left."

I'd been sad to hear about Beverly's co-head football coaches leaving the school. They were two of the nicest, most solid guys I'd ever met, and they'd both taught me a lot. And then, perhaps for the same reasons I did—to see if their dreams lay elsewhere—they packed up and left, leaving Beverly's football program leaderless.

"Carter," Ben went on, "I was wondering if you would like to be our new head football coach."

I really wasn't sure if I'd heard him right. "You want me to be the head football coach?" I said.

"Carter, you were an assistant here for ten years, and you know our system, and you know our kids. If you don't do it, we'll have to hire from the outside, and the kids will be at a great disadvantage. We'd be throwing away another whole season."

My mind was racing. I didn't know what to say.

"Look, Carter," Ben went on, "we want you back at Beverly. We need you back here. *You are one of us.*"

A million thoughts raced through my mind.

"What about my resignation?" I asked. "The board isn't going to hire someone who just resigned."

Ben Bushman chuckled.

"Carter," he said, "I never turned it in."

CHAPTER

9

I DON'T KNOW WHY my old coach held onto my resignation. Maybe he realized long before I did that I belonged at Beverly.

Principal Bushman told me that on top of being head coach I could come back to my old teaching position and continue to work part-time in real estate if I wanted. I told him I'd have to talk it over with Karen and get back to him. The conversation with Karen wasn't something I was looking forward to. Our business was going really well, and I could tell she was feeling a lot less pressure these days. Still—head football coach?

That night, I approached Karen in the kitchen.

"I spoke with Ben Bushman today," I said.

"Oh yeah? What about?"

"He offered me the job of head football coach."

I wouldn't have been surprised if Karen had chewed me out right then and there. It's what I deserved. Instead, she looked at me thoughtfully for a moment or two, then smiled.

"I don't know why you didn't just say yes on the spot," she said.

"We both know this is something you have to do. You have no choice."

My wife is a wonderful, remarkable person, and she has never been less than 100 percent behind me no matter what journey I take. She saw the gleam in my eye when I mentioned the head coaching offer, and she understood I really needed to do it—even if I didn't yet realize it myself.

"Karen, I will not do this unless we both agree it's the right thing to do. Let's talk about it."

"What is there to talk about? We have our whole lives to work in real estate, and we can still do it while you're coaching. But we both know this is what you need to do."

It would not be the best arrangement for Karen. She would have to go back to working long hours by herself. But never, not for a moment, did she make me feel like I was letting her down.

God blessed me when he put Karen in my path.

The next day I called my old colleagues Dick Billingsley and Bill Stansbury. I didn't want them to think I'd left Beverly because I didn't like working with them and that, now that they were gone, I was jumping back in and taking their jobs. Before I could say yes to Principal Bushman, I needed to know Dick and Bill were okay with it.

Both of them said, "If you really want to be a coach, then do it." At the same time they both warned me that being a coach at Beverly was like being a small fish in a very big pond. We were in a league with a bunch of powerhouse programs—schools that routinely attracted the big six-foot-four, three-hundred-pound recruits and dumped bunches of money into sports. Beverly wasn't like that. We were always going to be the scrappy underdog.

I thanked them for being such generous friends, and I sat down to think about what they'd said. Why was I interested in coaching, after all? Why would I drop my career dreams to coach a bunch of under-sized, overachieving kids?

And what about my family—my wife and her parents and every-one else who had a stake in our real estate business? How could I just walk away from them? But was this connection I felt to Beverly not important? What if it was my destiny to be at Beverly? I was truly, truly torn.

In the end, it all came down to that one irrefutable fact.

My heart was at Beverly.

I called Principal Bushman back and accepted the job.

———————

MY LUNCHES WITH STEVEN FENTON had opened my eyes to how much influence I could have in steering a kid onto the right path. They also showed me how much I enjoyed that role. And now, as head foot-ball coach, I would have even more opportunities with the kids.

I loved the strategic side of coaching—the Xs and Os, designing plays, drawing up game plans. I loved the camaraderie of being part of a team. Certainly I loved winning games. But for me, none of those things were what coaching at Beverly was really about.

One of the first things I did as head football coach was call a meet-ing of our coaching staff. I wanted to lay out our plan for the year.

"We're going to have one central goal this season," I told everyone, "and it's not 'Improve the Offense.' It's not 'Win More Games.' It's not 'Score More Points.'

"Our goal for the season is simple: '*Be the Best.*'"

The most satisfying part of coaching for me was helping kids expe-rience success and get a sense of accomplishment. Teaching them to be tough and resilient, the way my parents taught me. Encouraging them to reach heights they never thought they could reach.

Pointing them in the direction of their best selves.

I had a student named Jamie Marks in one of my PE classes. Jamie was shy and withdrawn, and she didn't appear to be very athletic. In class we played games of two-hand touch football, an activity that was popular with a lot of the girls because they liked the idea of playing football with the boys. But I could tell Jamie didn't feel comfortable in class at all. She wasn't fitting in or making friends. Sometimes it seemed like torture for her to be there.

I could see Jamie was a smart, lovely person, but I could also see she might not have much confidence. I felt it was my job to find a way to change the way Jamie perceived herself.

For our touch football games I'd always put myself on one team and a lot of the better players on the other. When it came time to pick sides, I made sure Jamie was on my side. I knew the boys wouldn't take Jamie seriously as a player—heck, they wouldn't take *any* of the girls seriously. That's just the way boys are. So, as quarterback, I picked four receivers—three boys and one girl, Jamie. Just as I figured, the boys on the other team only guarded the boys on my squad, leaving Jamie wide open. On our very first play, I threw Jamie the ball.

She caught it. First down.

On the next play, Jamie was wide open again, so I threw her the ball again. Another first down. This went on all game and into the next couple of games until I started hearing boys yell, "Will somebody please guard Jamie?!"

Pretty soon, all the kids wanted Jamie to be on their team.

Slowly, Jamie came out of her shell. It didn't happen overnight, but it happened. And before long she was one of the most popular kids at Beverly.

Jamie went on to become a football manager for the varsity team and later enrolled at USC and managed their team, too. After graduating she went to work for the Avengers, a team in the professional Arena Football League. Today, she is a happy, successful, thriving adult.

A lot of factors went into shaping the person Jamie Marks became. I like to believe one of them was catching that first football pass. There were no leaping cheerleaders or crazed fans when she caught it, and we didn't win any trophy or title.

But to me, that was as big a victory as any I ever earned at Beverly.

———

I WAS IN MY OFFICE at Beverly one day when a student, I will call Gordon, came to see me. Gordon was one of Beverly's best athletes and a funny, smart, caring kid. I knew Gordon's mother, Florence, was a very popular elementary school teacher in our district, and his father was well known in the community as well. Gordon asked if he could talk to me about something, and I said sure. He sat down and took a deep breath.

"Coach," he finally said, "did you know I was adopted?"

So this wasn't going to be about Friday's game.

"No, I didn't know that, Gordon."

"Yep, I'm adopted. Don't get me wrong, I love my parents. But I wanted to talk to you, because . . . because I think you went to school with my birth parents."

I thought I'd heard everything by then, but clearly I hadn't.

"Didn't you graduate from Beverly in 1974?" Gordon asked.

"Yes, I did."

"Did you know Gary Belstrom?"

I did know Gary Belstrom. We were on the football team together and were good friends. Gary was the guy who hid behind a door and hit me in the chest on Freshman Friday. When I told Gordon this, he asked if I also knew someone named Jessica Ventor. I knew Jessica, too. She'd been part of my core group of friends, a really great, classy girl. Just hearing their names took me straight back to my time at Beverly—to hanging out after games and driving downtown for burgers.

"I think those are my parents," Gordon went on. "They went to the prom together, and I think I was conceived that night."

I guess I wasn't quite prepared for such a discussion. I mean, this wasn't helping a kid learn to run a fly pattern down a football field.

"Coach," Gordon said, "I was wondering if you could call them for me."

"Today?" I asked. "Right now?"

Gordon nodded.

Making this kind of call isn't exactly in the job description. But I could tell this was a profoundly important moment for Gordon. He needed to know who his real parents were. He'd talked it over with his adoptive parents, and they had given him their blessing. Now he wanted me to help him solve the central mystery of his life.

"Okay," I said, "let's call 'em."

I dialed Gary first and reached him in two rings.

"Hey, Gary, I don't know if you remember me or not, but my name is Carter Paysinger and we went to Beverly together."

"Carter?" he said. "Of course I remember you. How are you, buddy?"

We caught up for a bit before I told him why I was calling.

"Gary, I have a question for you."

"What's up?"

"I'm not really sure how to say this, but . . . I have a kid in my office who thinks you might be his father."

There was a long silence. Finally, Gary spoke up.

"Carter, is Gordon there with you?"

"Yes, he is."

"Carter, I've been waiting for this call for eighteen years."

I could hear the raw emotion in Gary's voice. At Beverly I'd always looked up to Gary. He was so big and strong and well conditioned, and he was one of the best players on the football team. I admired his toughness, and I strove to be as tough as him. After college he became a large animal veterinarian, tending to cows and horses. He was a man's man in every way, and here he was, on the other end of the phone, on the verge of blubbering. His voice was cracking, and he was sniffling loudly. I could feel my own eyes begin to water.

"Yes, Gordon is my son," Gary said. "I dated Jessica when we were in high school, but when she got pregnant, her mother moved her away and asked Mrs. Kane to adopt the baby. I was hoping this day would one day come. My whole family knows about Gordon, but we didn't know if he'd ever want to see us. My two young kids have been waiting for the day they can meet their older brother."

Then, after another hesitation, Gary said, "Can I talk to him?"

I handed the phone over to Gordon. Slowly, he raised it to his face. Gordon was struggling to keep his composure, and so was I. I felt a tear roll down my cheek, and I quickly wiped it away. I wiped the next several tears away, too. I didn't want to break down in front of Gordon, but I couldn't stop the emotion from washing over me. This would be Gordon's first conversation with his birth father. I could hardly imagine a more meaningful moment in a young kid's life. As I listened to Gary and Gordon stitch together their separate lives, I noticed tears running down Gordon's cheeks, too. But he was too busy connecting with his father to wipe them away.

After ten minutes, Gordon and Gary exchanged phone numbers, and Gordon hung up the phone. He took a deep breath and looked at me. I knew what was next. I picked up the phone and called Jessica Ventor.

"Carter, of course I remember you," Jessica said. "How are you?"

"Jessica, I have a kid in my office named Gordon, and Gordon thinks you might be his mother."

Another long silence.

"Yes, Carter, Gordon is my son," Jessica finally said in a soft voice. "My friends and I go to lunch every year on his birthday to celebrate him in our hearts. I've been waiting for this moment for eighteen years."

Gordon took the phone and spoke with his birth mother for the first time, and by then both of us were openly crying. I got up, walked around, and tried to pull myself together. Gordon made plans to meet with Gary and Jessica later that week, and their dinner together kicked off a warm and loving relationship that endures to this day.

Normally a coach or teacher doesn't get to witness such a dramatic moment in the development of a student, and I was lucky enough to have gotten that chance. I watched Gordon's life change right in front of my eyes. This is an extreme example of helping a student navigate the complexities of life, but basically this is what we do all day, every day.

And it's exactly why I loved my job so much.

———

IN MY FIRST YEAR AS head football coach at Beverly we had a pretty good season and made it into the play-offs. Unfortunately, we were matched against the top seed in our division—Schurr High School near East Los Angeles. No one gave us much of a chance. Sure enough, with just ten seconds to go in the game, the Normans were down by seven points.

Our quarterback dropped back to pass. He looked to his left, then his right, then fired a pass downfield. Our best receiver ran toward the ball. Without breaking stride he caught it and ran into the end zone.

Touchdown, six points. With just a few seconds left, we were now down by one.

We could have played it safe, kicked an extra point, and tied the game. But in practice we'd drawn up a play to try and get a two-point conversion. If we managed to get the ball in the end zone again, we'd get two points and win the game. From the sidelines I called for the play. The center snapped the ball to the quarterback, and he pitched it backward to our running back, who ran hard to his left. Just ahead of three or four defenders, he dove into the end zone.

A two-point conversion.

David had beaten Goliath.

That was an amazing way to start my tenure as head coach, but our next season was even better. Beverly won the Ocean League Championship and made it all the way to the semifinals of the play-offs. After the season I got a call from someone at the *Los Angeles Times*.

The paper had named me Westside Football Coach of the Year.

Everything was going great. I was proving myself as a head coach, and I was helping kids like Jamie and Gordon. Every morning when I set foot on campus, I had the feeling I was exactly where I belonged. The only problem was, the more successful I became at school, the less time I had to devote to helping Karen with our business. I couldn't stop thinking I was being unfair to my wife.

And so, every once in a while, as I walked along the sidelines of the football field, watching our players go through drills, I'd stop and ask myself, *Carter, are you doing the right thing here?* Don't get me wrong, I loved my students and I loved the school, and that should have been reason enough to stay. Yet there was always a nagging question I couldn't really answer: Was staying at Beverly the right thing? Would I ever know what else was out there for me if I never left?

CHAPTER

10

C OACH, YOU WANTED to see me?"
"Andrew, come on in."

A big, handsome white kid who clocked in at a chiseled six feet and 240 pounds, Andrew folded himself into a chair in my office. He had a big smile on his face, but then, he usually did. On top of being an outstanding athlete, Andrew was one of the friendliest, most popular, most charismatic kids at Beverly. He grew up in Beverly Hills, and his parents were very wealthy. From the outside he seemed to have everything going for him. Sitting there, he could have been the poster boy for Beverly's privileged youth.

In truth, Andrew was the single poorest kid at the school.

"I just wanted to make sure you understand my policy regarding office hours," I told him. "And that is, I don't have office hours. No matter where you are on campus or what's going on, you can always come see me. Come 'round and tell me what's going on."

I gave the same speech to all my students and players, but I wanted to make extra sure Andrew understood it. Not because he

122 Carter Paysinger and Steven Fenton

was one of my best players. But because he was one of the most messed up.

Andrew's parents divorced when he was in the third grade. He lived with his mother for a while before she moved away. Then he lived with his father, but they didn't get along. By the eighth grade Andrew was living on his own, first with friends, then in a tiny apartment in Beverly Hills he rented with his older brother.

When Andrew arrived at Beverly Hills High, I had no idea he was living on his own. I didn't know his parents were essentially ignoring him, sending him some money now and then but never consistently. I just saw a bright, talented kid who showed leadership potential but had some issues and got in lots of trouble. Andrew skipped a lot of classes but always seemed to have a clever excuse. He failed to turn in assignments, then talked his way out of doing them. He got into fights and was suspended more than once.

He also routinely hustled other students, sometimes persuading them to do his homework for him, sometimes luring them into late-night, curfew-busting poker games and winning hundreds of dollars from them—money he desperately needed for rent and books and food.

Andrew always had some scheme working, and he seemed to know just what he could get away with. He was incredibly resourceful because he had to be. Andrew wasn't a bully, but he could be manipulative. People wanted to be his friend, unaware of what he really was—a survivor who would do anything to get by.

Though you might not think it, Andrew experienced some of the same culture shock I did at Beverly. He went to his friends' parties in Beverly Hills and saw elephants, zebras, and major rock bands rented for the night. The next day he would be in his tiny apartment, eating dinner out of a can. He vowed to never let anyone know just how dire his situation was. He refused to have anyone feel sorry for him.

Over time, however, I did learn about Andrew's predicament. The other coaches and I knew we had a special player in Andrew, and he was clearly driven to get even better. He wound up being one of the best offensive guards we ever had. But we also knew he was on a dangerous path. None of his actions, on their own, were that alarming, but taken together they showed a disturbing lack of a moral code. If he was allowed to continue with his scheming, he would likely grow up to be an even bigger schemer, and possibly worse.

Together with my former Beverly coach Chuck Kloes, who was now part of my staff, I took a special interest in Andrew. Our goal was to turn him into more than just a great player—we wanted him to be a true leader. Andrew was so talented and charismatic; all his teammates looked up to him. One morning I showed up at our weight room at 6:30 a.m. for a workout and saw something like forty students waiting to get in. It was the biggest crowd we'd ever had for an early workout—and it was all because Andrew had rallied his teammates and made them want to come.

But being a leader means more than just being charismatic. It means setting a positive example for your troops. It means doing things the right way, not taking short cuts. It means making everyone around you better, not just yourself.

Andrew was nowhere near ready to do that.

What worried me most was Andrew's temper—I'd seen him demolish a chain-link fence once after a bad football loss. I also knew he had a habit of storming out of classes when things didn't go his way. He had a lot of respect for the athletic coaches, because sports meant so much to him, but very little respect for his teachers. He was easily frustrated and often self-destructive. I didn't yet know exactly what Andrew's issues were, but I knew something was wrong.

Eventually, Andrew began dropping by my office—just as Steven Fenton had. And, like Steven, he often stayed for lunch. At first it was just to chat or to let off steam whenever he got too frustrated by something. Over time he started confiding bits and pieces of his personal life. He didn't talk very much about his situation—he was so determined not to let it victimize him—but from the little he did say it was clear he was struggling. At one point Andrew's father remarried, and Andrew allowed himself to hope he might find a place in his father's new family.

But that didn't happen. His mother and father seemed to have little interest in his life.

Andrew never talked about what his parents' neglect did to him inside. Only many years later did he articulate the pain it caused.

"It's like if you take a shiny new hundred-dollar bill and you crumple it up and throw it on the ground and step on it and dirty it up," he explained. "It's still worth a hundred dollars, but it doesn't look or feel right. It looks less valuable. That's what I felt like inside. I had a lot of confidence and self-esteem issues. I was sick of being the poorest kid at Beverly."

My approach to Andrew was to treat him like any other kid. I didn't make any concessions to his situation; if anything, I demanded more from him. Though we didn't talk about it, the fact that I came from South Central and not Beverly Hills made it easy for Andrew to trust me. He knew I hadn't seen myself as a victim just because I had less than my classmates did, and he knew I wouldn't treat him that way either.

Doesn't matter where you come from. Only matters where you stand.

In Andrew's freshman year, the freshman squad had lost every single game heading into our final one against Santa Monica High. I heard through some of my players that Andrew knew the opposing quarterback—a year earlier, the quarterback and some of his friends had beaten Andrew up in a mall. I didn't know what kind of revenge Andrew had in mind, but I knew this could be a great teaching moment. I found Andrew on the field and pulled him aside.

"If you want to get revenge on this guy," I told him, "get it the right way. On the field."

For the rest of the week I used this to motivate Andrew to work even harder. When the game rolled around, Andrew was ready. He went on a tear and devastated Santa Monica's defense, *Offense* getting to the — quarterback for something like six sacks. It was an awesome display of focused power, and in many ways it was Andrew's coming-out party as a football player. Even better, we won the game—Andrew's first ever victory in organized football.

After the game I found Andrew and congratulated him. "You did it," I told him, "and you did it the *right* way."

Years later Andrew told me what that moment meant to him. "I never felt better about myself in my entire life," he said. "I can't even describe the sense of confidence that gave me, to know I could do what I did on that field. To this day that's still one of the top five moments of my life."

————

AS GOOD AS ANDREW WAS getting, he still wasn't a leader.

He might have been the most driven athlete I'd ever worked with, but for the longest time all he cared about was making himself better. He'd get up in the middle of the night and go to the weight room and work out for two hours all alone, just because he didn't think his earlier workout had been hard enough. I understood why he was so sin-gle-minded—he was on his own, and if he didn't take care of himself, no one would. But if he wanted to be a leader, he would have to learn the meaning of teamwork—of making *others* better.

In his senior year, Andrew was the best player on a great team. We coasted through the season before losing a couple of sloppy games heading into our final contest against Culver City. It bothered me that the team played so poorly this close to the end of the season. I was par-ticularly upset with Andrew, who wasn't showing much leadership. The Monday after the second loss, I pulled Andrew out of a class and had him meet me in the gym.

"What's up, Coach?" he asked.

"Sit down, Andrew. Let's talk about the game."

We sat together on the bleachers, and over the next hour I told him stories. I told him about other great players I'd coached, played with, or known. I told him how they got to be great and how they got to be leaders. How they prepared, how they played, how they handled their teammates. What they did before games, during games, and after games. What they said in the locker room, what they screamed out in huddles. Everything they did to get the team a win.

Basically I gave Andrew a blueprint for how to win our last game. And the only way it would work was if he became a true leader. I don't think Andrew said a single word the whole hour. He just listened and soaked it all in.

During practice that week, Andrew was a monster on the field. He took his own game to another level, and he dragged his teammates with him. If any of them let up, Andrew grabbed them by the collar and chewed them out. I'd never seen the team practice with such in-tensity.

But during warm-ups on game night, the team was flat again. Dead flat. I was worried they'd left their best games on the practice field. The pregame locker room was deathly quiet.

That is, until Andrew stood up.

And went nuts.

He told the team they would get their butts kicked unless they woke up and woke up fast. One of our injured players was standing on crutches nearby, and for emphasis Andrew grabbed one of his crutches and smashed it against a locker. He did the same with the other crutch. I felt bad for the kid, but I stood back and let Andrew do his thing. When the wood finally stopped flying, Andrew, huffing and puffing, stared his teammates down.

"You ladies can stay in here and take a nap," he said. "I'm going out there to beat the hell out of those guys."

Then he literally broke down the locker room door and ran out.

There was a stunned silence in his wake for a second—but only a second. Then the rest of the team got up and yelled and screamed and jumped over the broken door and followed Andrew onto the field. The game that night was hardly even fair. Our guys destroyed Culver City.

Andrew, in particular, was unstoppable. He was a blur of energy, pushing his teammates relentlessly, making impossible tackles, keeping the intensity level sky-high. He was so jacked up that, after one play, he ran over a pile of players and sacked the quarterback after the whistle. The referee ejected him from the game.

Andrew came to the sidelines, and I ran over to see him. I'm sure he expected me to chew him out, but by then the game was essentially over. I knew what I had to say.

"Andrew," I said, grabbing him by the arm and spinning him to face me, "in my twenty years of coaching I've never seen anyone take a team on their back like that and lead them to victory."

Then I threw my arms around him.

"You laid out the plan for me," Andrew recently told me. "You reinforced it, and then you let me execute it. You taught me how to get the best not only out of myself but out of my teammates, and that is a gift I still use today. You built me up to a place I didn't think I could be built up to. That was the best moment of my career, even better than when I was drafted by the NFL."

Andrew went on to play professional football with the St. Louis Rams for three years before a series of concussions forced him to retire. He is now the founder and managing director of a highly successful sports investment banking company, Park Lane, headquartered less than a mile from Beverly Hills High. He has built and sold two other companies. He is also happily married with three beautiful young children. We don't talk as often as I'd like to, but when we do, we share a lot of laughs and memories. Our Beverly bond is strong as ever.

"I'm constantly aware that my life could have gone the other way," Andrew says now. "But the beautiful thing about life is that it's a lot like football. There are so many bad breaks and bruises, and you get so banged up along the way, and a lot of the time it's extremely painful.

"But then years down the road you look back on it, and what you remember are the good moments. The happy moments. The people who came into your life. And even though I was the poorest kid in school and I didn't always know where my next meal was coming from, some of the happiest moments of my life were at Beverly."

CHAPTER

11

ARLY IN OUR marriage Karen made it clear she didn't want kids. Well, at least not right away. Waiting was not a problem for me since we were both so young and so busy launching our careers. But all along I was absolutely certain of one thing: I wanted children.

Eventually, Karen and I agreed to try and start a family. Our real estate business was off the ground, and my job at Beverly was going great. The timing was finally right. We were both from big families, and Karen came to like the idea of a bunch of little critters of our own running around. I was more excited than I can describe.

Not long after we decided to start trying, Karen had a routine doctor's visit. During the exam the doctor stopped and eyed Karen with concern.

"What's wrong?" she asked.

"You suffered a miscarriage," he said.

"What? But I didn't even know I was pregnant."

The news was jarring, but we tried our best to put it behind us and move forward. A few months later, Karen got pregnant again. When she took the home test and told me the result, it was one of the happiest moments of my life.

But then, a week or so later, we were getting ready for bed when Karen suddenly doubled over.

"Karen? Are you okay?"

"It's my stomach. Something is wrong."

As I held her, I noticed drops of blood on the carpet.

We rushed to the hospital, and a doctor confirmed our worst fear—another miscarriage.

This one was devastating. It was one of the hardest things we've had to go through as a couple. I'd see Karen crying and feel so angry and so helpless. I wanted to fix things, but I couldn't. I wanted to say just the right words to take her pain away, but there are no words for that. I wanted to feel strong so I could be strong enough for the two of us, but that strength just wasn't there. At the same time Karen was feeling like she had somehow let me down. It was all I could do to convince her that wasn't true. The saddest part of all of it was that we were both so hurt by what happened that it was easier not to talk to each other about it. And because of that we both wound up suffering in silence. For me, the knowledge that we'd certainly try again, in time, gave me some small measure of comfort.

Karen, however, wasn't sure she wanted to try again.

"If it happens, it happens," she said. "But I don't want to plan it."

Within a few months Karen was pregnant again. This time I wasn't excited at all; I was scared. We began tiptoeing around the house, careful not to do anything that might upset Karen's health. It felt like we were balancing a fragile piece of china on a stick.

One night when I was in the kitchen, I heard a cry from the living room. I ran out and found Karen slumped on the sofa, holding her stomach. Fear, confusion, and despair hit me all at once. I drove her to the hospital and held Karen while we waited. Neither of us said a word.

This was our third miscarriage. For the next few weeks we went about our lives with a kind of stunned, quiet anguish. After the first miscarriage we got a lot of sympathy and support from friends who knew we were trying to have a baby. But with the second and third pregnancies we didn't tell anyone; that's how afraid we were of something going wrong. Maybe we should have been more open about it, but honestly, the thought of everyone asking us how it was going, and possibly having to break bad news to them, was too much for us to handle. Instead we chose to make it just our burden to bear.

What I didn't realize until many years later was that, for Karen, the burden was even more solitary. She was going through feelings and emotions I wasn't aware of, mostly because she didn't want to upset me further. She put on a brave face and got on with whatever business was at hand, outwardly seeming strong and resilient. But inside she was in more pain than I ever realized. The hurt of losing those babies made it very hard for her to even be around pregnant women. When her sister-in-law was pregnant, Karen was as happy and supportive as anyone else, and genuinely so, even though seeing someone else have a healthy baby only deepened the hollow ache in her heart. For a while it was even tough for her to be around large, happy families. She didn't show any of this on the outside, of course. Like me, she was stoic and brave. But the pain was there. The pain was always there.

After the third miscarriage, without saying so, we both knew we couldn't go through something like that again.

Eventually we went to see a specialist, who explained Karen had fibroids—uterine tumors that can interfere with pregnancy. We talked about causes, treatments, and probabilities. The more we talked, the clearer things got. When we left the doctor's sleek office,

we both understood a sad, terrible truth: there was a strong likeli-
hood Karen wouldn't be able to have kids.

It was all such a cruel twist of fate. Here Karen had finally decided
to have a child—partly because she knew how badly I wanted one—
and now she was getting knocked down over and over again. Those
were some of the darkest times of our lives. We were heading into our
forties, and we knew we had a window of time that would eventually
slam shut. But could we keep subjecting ourselves to such emotional
turmoil?

All I knew was that I didn't ever want to see Karen so hurt and so
devastated again.

———

I WAS IN THE WEIGHT ROOM one summer afternoon when I heard a
voice behind me.

"Excuse me, sir?"

I looked up and saw a big, tall black kid who was clearly a college
student visiting Beverly to train or meet friends or something.

"My name is Adam," he said, "and I was hoping to talk to you
about coming here and playing football for you."

I stood up, shook his hand, and tried to hide my surprise that he
was still in high school.

"Pleased to meet you, Adam," I said. "So, what's your story?"

Adam explained that he lived in Watts and was a rising senior at a
high school there. I knew about the school, and I knew it wasn't great.
I'd later learn that while Adam was there, robberies, lockdowns, and
shootings were common. Adam had witnessed shootings in the classrooms, hallways, and even the school bus; one day he saw police
swarm the school because a bank robber had fled there and was hiding

in a classroom. Pretty much all of his friends were in a gang, either the Bloods or the Crips. There were only two white kids in the whole school, twin brothers who were *both* in the Crips.

"Sir, I'd like to know how I might be able to attend Beverly High School," Adam said.

"Well, we have this permit for incoming students, which is how I got in," I explained. "But that's only for first-year kids, so you wouldn't be eligible for that."

"Is there anything else I could do?"

"Only one other thing, Adam. Move to Beverly Hills."

I realized the absurdity of my words as soon as I said them. Just move out of one of the worst areas in the country and move into one of the best, that's all. I wished I had a better answer for him, but I didn't. And what made it worse was that I knew he wasn't just looking for a new high school or a new football team.

He was looking for a lifeline.

Adam seemed to slump a little, and for a while he didn't say anything. Then he stood up and stuck his hand out.

"Okay then, sir," he said. "See you in the fall."

"See me in the fall?"

"Yes, sir," Adam said. "I guess I'm just going to have to find a way to move to Beverly Hills."

I thought, *Now here's a kid with some character, some gumption.* Then I thought, *I'll probably never see him again.*

A few weeks later, on the first day of varsity football practice, I noticed a big kid in workout gear jogging on the field.

I made my way toward him, and when he saw me, he smiled the biggest smile.

"Adam, what are you doing here?"

"I'm here to practice, Coach."

"I don't get it."

"This is my new school," Adam said. "And you're my new coach."

———————

WHEN ADAM WAS IN THE third grade, both his mother and his father were sent to jail for drug possession.

His father had abandoned the family once he got out of jail. His mother didn't use drugs, but he believed that she had sold them. After she was released, she went on welfare to support her family. Adam, his older brother, and his younger sister basically grew up with nothing. Plus, Adam had a speech impediment, and he was dyslexic. And he was living in a community plagued by drugs, gangs, and violence.

Any way you looked at it, Adam's future was bleak. His chances of going to jail were significantly higher than his chances of going to college. Adam, it seemed, was one of the doomed. In the sixth grade his teacher, Miss Rivers, asked him what he wanted to do when he grew up.

"I want to be a successful businessman," he said.

Miss Rivers laughed.

"Why are you laughing?" Adam asked.

"Because with your attitude you will either be dead or in jail by the time you're eighteen," she said. "Your only opportunity in life is to work harder than everyone else, and I don't see you working that hard."

Adam thought about what Miss Rivers had said. In her classroom there was a big banner that read, "An Educated Black Man is an Endangered Species." For the first time, Adam understood what that meant. He put two and two together, and he decided he was going to change his ways. He was going to refuse to be extinct.

Which is exactly what Miss Rivers had in mind when she laughed.

Adam became one of the best players on the high school football team, and it was one of his trainers who brought him to Beverly to work out with some students there. On the drive over Adam prepared himself for the kind of wealth and extravagance he expected to see in Beverly Hills. But the homes he saw were even bigger and more opulent than he'd ever imagined. He couldn't even fathom such wealth, luxury, and privilege. They were concepts that didn't exist in his world.

The next surprise was Beverly, which at first Adam thought was a college campus. No high school could be that beautiful. The biggest shock, though, was when he knocked on my door. The last thing he expected to find was that the head football coach in a place like this would be a black man, like him.

After seeing the school and meeting me, Adam was determined to find a way to get into Beverly. His trainer, Mr. Jackson, saw how important it was to Adam and contacted a friend who owned rental properties in Beverly Hills. Adam made a strong enough impression on the friend that he allowed him and his sister and mother to move into a one-bedroom apartment for the same low rent they paid in Watts.

When his high school friends got wind of his plan, they were merciless. "Get lost! You don't care about us; we don't want you around," they told him, only in much stronger terms. In Watts, trying to better your station in life was equivalent to betraying your friends. That was something I could well understand.

Not long after our talk in my office I called around and found out what I could about Adam. I learned he was not only a great football player but also a smart, purposeful kid. Still, I didn't expect he would find a way to move to Beverly Hills and enroll in the school. So when I saw him on the field, I broke into a big smile, too. I never intentionally decided to take Adam under my wing, but that's just what happened. Because of the similarities in our lives, we gravitated toward each other.

Adam had an even harder time adjusting to Beverly than I had had. He came in with even more rigid preconceptions of what white kids in Beverly Hills were like. In turn, many white students at Beverly believed that, because Adam was from Watts, he was a gangster. This was something I certainly understood.

Adam was walking on campus one day when a white student came up to him.

"Where's your rag at?" the student asked.

"What?"

"Your rag. Where's your rag at? Are you a Blood or a Crip?"

At the time there were several mainstream movies depicting the gang culture in South Los Angeles, and in those movies gangbangers wore colored rags signifying their gang affiliation.

"I've seen it in the movies; everyone's got a rag," the student said. "So where's your rag?"

"Not everyone in Watts is a gangbanger," Adam said. "Not all of us have rags."

Then Adam said, "Hey, can I borrow a hundred dollars?"

"What?" the student said. "I don't have a hundred dollars."

"You don't? 'Cause I thought all white kids in Beverly Hills were rich. So where's your money?"

The student smiled. "I get it," he said. Then they went their separate ways.

––––––––

RIGHT FROM THE START ADAM began hanging around my office, same as Steven Fenton and Andrew Kline had. In our talks I shared stories of my childhood and of my time at Beverly. I told him about my parents, and we talked about the lessons my mother and father had taught me. I told Adam that when I first enrolled at Beverly I had a lot of the same preconceptions about kids there as he had.

"But Adam, what I learned is you have to take people as who they are, not as who you *think* they are," I said. "It's like all the kids who think you're a gangster. That's because they don't know you. They're going on what you look like and where you're from. So you want to show them you're more than that—you want them to judge you by what's inside, by what you achieve. Turn around, and do the same for them. Don't think you know them, because you don't. Find out who they are. You can't fight ignorance with ignorance."

Adam and I had talks like that several times a week. At the end of one of our talks, Adam got up to go back to practice.

"Thanks, Pops," he called, before running out.

It took me a few seconds for what he said to register. Up until then he'd always called me Coach. Suddenly, I was Pops.

A grin broke out across my face.

———————

ONE DAY I GOT A call from the principal, who said the mother of one of my white players was accusing Adam of slashing her son's tires. I left my office to look for him and found him on the field.

"I need to ask you a question," I said.

"What's up?"

"Where were you this weekend?"

Adam said he'd been back in the Watts area with some friends.

"So you weren't in Beverly Hills at all?"

"No, sir. What's going on?"

I told Adam about the parent's accusation, and I watched his reaction. As best I could tell, he was crestfallen.

"I wouldn't do that," he said. "Why would I do that? I barely even know that guy."

"I'm not accusing you, Adam."

"I didn't slash his tires. What would that do for me? Why does she even think it was me?"

"Adam, I . . ."

"Coach, I didn't do it. *I'm not that kid!*"

I put my hand on Adam's shoulder.

"I believe you," I said. "I just needed to ask the question."

"I understand, Coach," Adam said. "You were doing what you had to do. Don't worry, I got your back."

We eventually found out someone else had slashed the tires. But from that moment on, Adam trusted me completely, and I him.

Some nights I gave him a ride home after practice. I'm pretty sure we met and talked at least once a day. Eventually Adam met Karen. They got along great. This was around the time Karen suffered her miscarriages. I don't think it's surprising that for both of us, Adam began to feel like family. He began to feel like a son.

On the football field, Adam was amazing. He played his heart out, and no one worked harder. But I noticed that, several times a game, he would stop and look into the stands, as if he were searching for someone. When I asked him about it, he said it was an instinct—that sometimes he didn't even know he was doing it. But he knew *why* he was doing it.

He was scanning the stands for his mother, who, sadly, never showed up.

He was also looking for his father, whom he hadn't seen in years.

The very first game we won with Adam on the team was memorable. I don't remember how he played; I just remember what he did afterward. When the final gun sounded and the players hugged and celebrated on the field, Adam made a beeline straight to me on the sidelines. Then he found me and wrapped me up in a big hug. That took me by surprise, but I hugged him right back. It's not easy hugging a big guy in bulky shoulder pads.

A hug became our ritual, right before games and right afterward. Many years later, Adam reflected on the significance of those hugs. "The thing is, Coach Carter was *there*," he said. "Coach was always there. He was the guy I knew I could count on. So at the end of games I would start looking at the clock, and I would gravitate to where Coach was. And when the game ended, I would rush right over and give him a hug. Those hugs were so important to me. Emotionally, it was the feeling a child gets from a parent when he accomplishes something, or even after a defeat. A hug is how you know someone cares for you. Coach Carter was my go-to person for hugs."

ADAM WAS ONLY AT BEVERLY for one year, but he played so well that several major colleges wanted to sign him up. He asked me to go with him on all his recruiting trips, something a parent usually does. Adam eventually accepted a scholarship to the University of Oregon and played well until a broken bone in his left foot ended his college career and his hopes of making it to the NFL. But by then, he already had a plan B.

Adam became a guidance counselor and a high school football coach.

"I am doing for these kids what Carter did for me," he says now. "And every day there comes a moment when I think, *What would Carter do in this situation? How would he handle this?* And if I can't figure it out, I call him."

Adam is married and has four young kids of his own. He lives in Oregon, but a couple of times a year we'll get together somehow and catch up. And he does call me a lot, just to talk or get advice.

Those calls always start with Adam saying, "Hi, Pops."

———

THE SAME YEAR ADAM GRADUATED, I was offered the job of athletic director of Beverly. I would still be head football coach, but I'd also be in charge of a program that included nearly nine hundred students, some fifty-six teams, and fifty-seven different head coaches.

I accepted the job.

CHAPTER

12

"CARTER, WE HAVE a problem."

A security guard was in my office with three Beverly students. One of them was Calvin, the star of the baseball team. I went off to the side with the guard and asked what had happened; he filled me in.

The guard was on routine patrol of one of the parking lots when he noticed a student quickly tossing away a cigarette. He went over, picked it up, and saw it was a joint. Our policy in matters like that is to search the backpack, locker, and car of the student in question.

"Calvin," I said, "before we search your car, is there anything in it we should know about?"

"No, Coach," he said.

I motioned for the guard to go ahead and conduct the search, but before he could even leave my office, Calvin stopped him.

"Wait a minute."

"What is it, Calvin?"

"Coach, I do have something in my car."

"What do you have?"

"A pipe," he said softly, "and some other stuff."

"What other stuff?"

"Pot."

The guard searched Calvin's car and came back with a decent amount of marijuana. As soon as I saw it, I was pretty sure Calvin would have to be suspended for the rest of the baseball season. Calvin was a senior, and he had several colleges interested in giving him a scholarship. Suspending him because of drugs would pretty much end his chances.

I wrote up the incident, and the school conducted an investigation. At the end of it the decision was made to suspend Calvin for the season. I wasn't at all surprised when Calvin's father—who had gone to Beverly with me and graduated the same year—called me at my office.

"Carter," he said, "isn't there anything we can do to make this go away?"

"I'm sorry," I said. "There isn't."

"You're costing him a scholarship. You're ruining his future."

"You know the drug policy. He did it to himself."

Calvin's father was angry now. He was no longer trying to trade on our friendship.

"Carter, I hate to go this route, but I'm not sure you guys handled this matter properly," he said.

"What do you mean?"

"You searched my kid's car against his will."

That wasn't true—Calvin told us the drugs were there and gave us the keys. But his father didn't want to hear it. He called me again several times over the next four days.

On the fifth day I got a call from Calvin's attorney.

As soon as a lawyer got involved, I was forced to turn the whole thing over to our legal department. Their investigation revealed Calvin had not only been using marijuana, he'd been selling heroin on campus, too. He'd also enlisted other Beverly students to run drugs for him. Before we could do anything with this new information, Calvin's parents pulled him out of school. I never saw him or his father again.

For every kid I was able to help at Beverly, there were probably a dozen others who needed my help that I couldn't reach. Calvin, for instance, had a serious problem. But his father seemed more concerned with his son's baseball career than with his health or his character. Sometimes I just couldn't get past a student's parents. Sometimes, it seemed to me, parents sabotaged their own kids.

I was coming up on my fifteenth year on staff at Beverly, and the longer I was there, the harder I took the failures. I know it was unreasonable to think I could help every kid in need, but still it was tough to see any student fall through the cracks. Some things just aren't in our power to fix or control.

"HEY, CARTER, DO YOU KNOW why the multicultural permit is on the school board agenda?"

Wanda Greene, an old friend and Beverly alum, was on the phone. Wanda was the sister of my pal Michael Greene—the kid who called me over to his table my very first day in Beverly's cafeteria. Wanda volunteered on several district committees, and we'd run into each other on campus every now and then. We'd been friends for going on thirty years.

"What are you talking about?" I said. "Where'd you hear that?"

"The permit program is on the agenda for the next board meeting. Do you think they're trying to get rid of it?"

I immediately went to see Principal Bushman. He confirmed the board was planning to vote on whether or not to scrap the multicultural permit. I was stunned. This was the very permit that had gotten me in the door—the permit that changed the lives of all four Paysinger boys and countless other kids. To me it was an integral part of the history of the school and a perfect illustration of Beverly's values. It's true the school had been struggling lately, but I always believed we'd pull through the problems and emerge stronger. I had faith Beverly would hold onto the things that mattered most and not let them be lost in the strife and contention. The multicultural permit was one of the clearest demonstrations of what we were made of. How was it possible someone wanted to shut it down?

I asked around and found out there was a board member, a former schoolmate of mine named Barry Brucker, who believed the permit had outlived its usefulness. Apparently, he believed Beverly was already diverse enough and didn't need the permit anymore. That didn't make much sense to me or to Wanda. She organized a huge group of people to show up at a public hearing to protest the plan.

Some of the people who came to the hearing were people who'd received a permit themselves, like me. Others were parents of kids who got in on permits. Several white students who hadn't needed the permits but felt they were benefiting from the diversity it guaranteed showed up, too. So many people came to the hearing that it had to be moved from a conference room to an auditorium.

The moment from the hearing that's stayed with me all these years involves one of my former players, Craig Karlan. Craig, who is white, had been a wide receiver and one of the smartest kids I'd ever coached. Now he was a well-respected judge for the city of Beverly Hills.

Craig got up and spoke from the heart with passion and power. He talked about how Beverly prepared him academically for his career in law and how, just as importantly, Beverly exposed him to so many people from so many different backgrounds. It was his relationships with kids who got in on permits, he said, that taught him how to understand people and helped him become a successful judge.

Forget for a moment the black kids who get in on permits, he was essentially saying. Focus on how important the permit is for *white* kids.

"Before you vote, I would ask that you please weigh all the benefits that this program has afforded the students who live in Beverly Hills," Craig said. "My experience at Beverly was absolutely necessary for me to succeed in life."

When Craig finished, the crowd cheered as if he'd just scored a touchdown.

The speeches in favor of the permit were so persuasive and Wanda Greene's efforts so tireless, Barry eventually caved in. The board renamed it the Diversity Permit, but the important thing is they kept it.

Even though the good guys won this battle, however, there was something unsettling about the permit vote. I couldn't really put my finger on it, but neither could I escape the feeling that more such battles were looming. And as it turned out, I was right.

In the early 2000s things began to change at Beverly and in the whole school district. Newer and younger people were being voted onto the five-member board of education, including some old friends and teammates from my own years as a student. This could have been good. After all, some of these were people who knew and loved Beverly like I did, or so I thought. But then the accepted way of doing things at Beverly began to face questioning. That didn't strike me as a bad thing, at least not at first. Change is difficult but often necessary, and I was open to new ideas. I think most people at Beverly were.

At the same time I was very protective of the school's values and traditions. I didn't believe we had to throw everything out in order to

make Beverly better. After all, you can't know where you're going unless you know where you've been. But as time passed, I began seeing
that the values I'd revered since I'd first arrived at Beverly were suddenly up for grabs, and I wondered how people I had thought of as
being on the same page as I was suddenly weren't. Were we losing
sight of Beverly's identity? I'm sure there is some level of politics in
every school district in America, but in Beverly Hills the decision process was becoming _highly_ politicized. The battle to save the multicultural permit was just the tip of the iceberg.

For instance, it had long been a tradition at Beverly to hire from
within. Years of experience at the school counted for something. The
same was true of all the other schools in Beverly Hills and of its many
administrators. But over time the school board began hiring more and
more people from outside the district—people who had no real investment in Beverly or the city. Things would eventually get so bad
that the local paper, the _Beverly Hills Weekly_, criticized the board for
"knowingly skipping over more qualified internal administrative applicants in order to bring in outside applicants who tell them what they
want to hear."

Over the next several years more traditions and policies also came
under fire. It didn't matter that these policies had made Beverly one of
the most successful schools in California for decades. The new wave of
city and school officials seemed bent on change for change's sake.
"These are radical and unnecessary departures from the way the Beverly Hills United School District has been run for the last seventy
years," the _Beverly Hills Weekly_ said. "We do not support these
changes."

Look, I understood this was the way bureaucracies often worked.
The field of education is comprised of endless committees, meetings, boards, and administrators, and the decision-making process

can become hopelessly convoluted. There's always a danger newer school officials will unnecessarily try to reinvent the wheel. And once a school gets caught up in the gears of a bureaucratic battle like that, it is very, very hard to pull it free.

That, it seemed to me, was what was happening at my school. It was agonizing to watch. We were once a lighthouse district, but now it felt like we were going the wrong direction on a one-way street. There was a battle on for the soul of Beverly.

Not long after the permit fight, there was another unsettling incident that involved me personally.

ONCE THE RENAMED DIVERSITY PERMIT program kicked off, one of the first beneficiaries was my brother Donald's son, Justin Paysinger. Justin filled out his application and waited to hear back from the admissions officer, though his acceptance was basically a formality because of my family's ties to the school. When I got in, it pretty much opened the doors for my brothers and now their children.

Sure enough, Justin was accepted.

Not much later, though, I got a visit from Chuck Kloes, now an administrator at the school. As soon as he walked into my office I could tell Chuck was upset.

"What's wrong?"

"I just got kicked off the Diversity Permit committee," he said.

Chuck sat down and explained what had happened. One of the stipulations of the permit program is that a candidate's application must be "complete." It turns out Justin's application had been missing one page—the sheet that verified his address and personal information. It was probably the most standard part of the application and not something anyone would ever leave out on purpose. But for whatever reason, that page was missing from Justin's application.

When Chuck noticed it wasn't there, he called Justin's mother and asked her about it. By then Chuck was like a member of our family, and he didn't think twice about helping my nephew sort out the situation. Justin's mother swore she remembered putting the sheet in, but in any case she ran a copy over to Beverly that afternoon.

The next day, an official from the Beverly Hills district called Chuck into his office. He scolded him for even considering Justin's application since technically it wasn't complete.

"We don't even know who lost the sheet," Chuck argued. "It might have been someone in our office."

But the official wasn't having it and kicked Chuck off the committee.

"He told me I have no integrity, and I'm a low-character guy," Chuck said. "He said he didn't want me in his district at all."

I was horrified. I couldn't believe my friend and mentor was having his integrity questioned over an issue that involved my nephew—and a seemingly inconsequential issue at that. Should Justin's application really have been tossed because one page was missing? Should a kid's future really hinge on a little slipup that might not have even been his slipup?

I could see the pain and weariness on Chuck's face as he sat slumped in my office. His reputation at Beverly was spotless, or at least it had been. Now he'd been saddled with a humiliating disciplinary action.

That very spring, Chuck announced his resignation.

———

I DON'T THINK CHUCK EVER got over having his integrity questioned like that. He accepted a job at UCLA supervising their teaching training program, and just like that Beverly lost one of its best people. Chuck had been such an important part of my own career; he'd coached me as a kid, taught me in history class, and shown me the ropes when I came back as a coach.

Most importantly, Chuck was my friend.

Losing Chuck hit me hard. How could the district allow someone as popular as Chuck Kloes to be subjected to such harsh criticism after all he'd done for the school? Was this how they planned to run the old guard out? We'd gone through three superintendents in three years, and that is never a good sign for any school. Still, there wasn't very much I could do about it.

I still had faith that somehow Beverly would straighten itself out. But then, more defections followed. A teacher who'd been at Beverly for thirty years. An assistant principal who was an alum. Coaches I had known forever. One after another. These moves might have made sense if we were talking about young staffers eager to see if the grass was greener elsewhere, but the people who were leaving were part of the fabric of Beverly, people who should have wanted to retire there.

Instead, they were bailing like it was a sinking ship.

At night I'd go home and talk about the turmoil at Beverly with Karen. "I love the school and I love what it stands for. That's why I've stayed there all this time. We're working our butts off because our work is important. But what if Beverly isn't the same school anymore? What if it's turning into something else altogether?"

Karen didn't have an answer, and neither did I.

CHAPTER

13

K AREN AND I sat in her doctor's office, hoping for the best, bracing for the worst.

After Karen's third miscarriage we weren't sure we should even try again. But as time passed, we both realized we weren't ready to give up. Karen had to have two surgeries to remove the fibroids, but when she recovered, we found a fertility specialist and began the process of in vitro fertilization. Months passed with no results, and months turned into years.

We were almost ready to give up again when a home pregnancy test came up positive.

A week later, Karen miscarried again.

We drove in silence to the office of Dr. Surrey, our fertility specialist. Dr. Surrey was one of the leading experts in the field, so we knew we were in great hands. But by then we were both starting to think that maybe it wasn't God's plan for us to have kids.

"I know you both want to have a child very badly, and I can see how hard you're trying," Dr. Surrey said, "but unfortunately this is a cycle that's just going to keep repeating."

I glanced at Karen and squeezed her hand. I wanted to say something, but I didn't know what to say. Karen turned to Dr. Surrey and, in a low, sad voice, asked the question neither of us wanted to ask.

"Is this it?" she said. "Is it over for us?"

Dr. Surrey slowly nodded. "My suggestion would be for you to have a hysterectomy."

His words cut to my very core. We'd spent so many years and a small fortune trying to have a child, but the result was only heartbreak and disappointment. We still had options—surrogacy, adoption, even taking in a foster child. Yet even when we decided to keep trying— and find a surrogate mother—we were reluctantly starting to resign ourselves to the idea of never having a child of our own.

My sister-in-law was gracious enough to agree to be our surrogate. We harvested some of Karen's eggs, and for a while our hopes were raised. But sadly that procedure failed, too. Next we went to an agency that found us another surrogate. We interviewed a woman who lived in Los Angeles and took to her immediately; she was smart, lovely, and, as far as we could tell, dependable. After careful deliberation, we decided to try again with her. We signed a contract and set a date for the procedure, and we allowed ourselves the luxury of thinking maybe fate wasn't against us after all.

One evening at home, the phone rang. Karen picked it up.

It was our would-be surrogate.

"I changed my mind," she told Karen. "I'm not going to do it."

We were blindsided. We'd had no hint anything was wrong. You'd think by then we'd have been used to last-minute disappointments, but human beings don't work that way. We *always* find a reason to have hope. But it was like being run over by a truck . . . over and over again.

Just when we'd put all the broken pieces of our hearts back together into some kind of working shape, we'd get pummeled anew and our hearts would shatter all over again. After our surrogate bailed, the flicker of hope dwindled even more, and we spent more time resigning ourselves to not having children than plotting a next move.

"We have so many wonderful nieces and nephews," Karen would say. "You work with all these wonderful students. Maybe all these children *are* our kids."

Karen was right. We were already greatly blessed in our lives. If this was God's plan for us, then so be it.

It didn't help, however, that as we got older, more and more people came up to Karen and me and asked, point-blank, "How come you two don't have kids?"

We'd always find a polite way to explain it away. We still want to travel, we'd say, or we're not ready, or there's still plenty of time. But the questions kept coming, year after year.

"You're so good with kids. How come you don't have your own?"

"What are you waiting for? You'll make great parents."

"I don't get it. How come you two haven't had a child already?"

None of them meant any harm, I'm sure, but it got to where I truly hated these questions. One afternoon, I realized Karen felt the same way. An acquaintance approached us on the street and asked the fateful question.

"So how come you two don't have kids?"

Before I could say anything Karen jumped in.

"Because I can't have children of my own," she said forcefully. Our acquaintance mumbled an apology and hurried off.

None of what we were going through was pleasant. In my quieter moments it was difficult to shrug off that feeling of bitter disappointment. And I know it was even harder for Karen than it was for me.

AS IF ALL OF THAT weren't hard enough, Karen and I were suddenly having serious financial problems, too.

We'd invested a great deal of money in our real estate business in a market that was, for much of the early 2000s, robust and healthy. But in the mid-2000s, that began to change. The real estate market got soft, then collapsed. Like a lot of people, we got stuck with unsellable properties. All of a sudden we were staring at the very real possibility that everything we'd invested in our dream, all the money and all the hard work, might be completely lost. Every day became a kind of battle to keep going, to endure. We had to scale back our business, and Karen, who had a degree in sociology, had to go to work as a teacher for the Los Angeles Unified School District to help make ends meet.

Not in a million years had I imagined this was where I would be at this point in my life—fighting every day just to get by. Not after all of my mother's lessons, and all our hard work, and all our big dreams. I wasn't raised to feel sorry for myself, and I didn't. But part of me just couldn't believe this was the path my life was taking.

AT BEVERLY, THINGS WEREN'T MUCH better.

As athletic director I worked hard to make sure sports at Beverly went hand in hand with academics. When I was AD, the grade point average for all students who were on a sports team was 3.0 or higher—a statistic I'm extremely proud of. Plus, our record of sending teams to the play-offs improved; one year, we sent every single one of our teams into the postseason, something that had never happened before.

In the late 1990s I earned my second *Los Angeles Times* Westside Football Coach of the Year award, and in 2002 I won an Apple Award, which honors the teacher of the year for each school in the district. I can't tell you how proud I am of those awards, and in particular the Apple Award. It was important for me to be recognized not just as a coach but also as a teacher.

Yet the slow, steady decline of Beverly continued. The state of California evaluates student test scores and creates an Academic Performance Index (API). A school's API number can be anywhere from 200 to 1000, though the state's target for every school is 800—a score lower than that and your school is really in trouble. The best schools have an API in the 900s. From 1999 to 2008 Beverly averaged an API of only 817, and sometimes barely cracked 800. We went from the twenty-third best high school in the state in 1999 to only the forty-third best in 2004. "Something is going wrong," an editorial in the *Beverly Underground* student newspaper concluded. "Test scores are either constant or declining. It seems we have everything it takes to be one of the best public schools in the nation . . . yet something is faltering. We aren't even one of the top high schools in the *county*."

How could we hope to reverse this trend? "More teacher incentive to perform," the *Underground* declared. "More teacher involvement in curriculum decisions."

Yet more and more teachers and administrators were leaving. By this point we were on our sixth superintendent in six years. The new hires in the school district office were paying less attention to the details that had once made Beverly great: the feeling of family among its staff, the close bond between teachers and students, the devotion of alumni intent on sending their own kids there, even the condition of the once pristine campus. Now the lawns and flowers were drying out and dying from lack of care, and the buildings were falling into shabby disrepair. The deteriorating physical state of the campus reflected the problems slowly eating away at the school from within. Beverly was slipping, and everyone knew it.

Our biggest saving grace was my former coach and mentor Ben Bushman. One of Beverly's best principals, he kept a close watch on the state of affairs at Beverly, and in particular the sports department. He could always be counted on to cut through bureaucratic red tape and do what was best for the school. A lot of sports-related issues and problems never even made it to my desk because Ben—who understood sports at Beverly about as well as anyone—handled them quickly and decisively.

Then, in the spring of 2003, Ben came to see me in my office. Sadly, I already knew why he was there.

In a sad reversal of the day I'd given him my resignation, now he was coming to tell me he was walking away from Beverly and the school district altogether. We were losing one of our pillars, one of our biggest champions—and the man who had taken every step of my Beverly journey with me. Ben was irreplaceable; it was like watching your star quarterback go down with a busted knee.

Of course I tried to talk him out of leaving, but I recognized a weary resignation on Ben's face. Seeing him so defeated was tough to take.

"Carter, I would rather leave now while I still have a good feeling about this place," he said. "I'm not ready to retire, but this is something I have to do."

Ben's words were ominous. His resignation forced me to think hard about what was happening. I couldn't just hunker down, blindly believing things were eventually going to get better if I just soldiered on. The year Ben resigned marked my thirteenth year as head football coach. It marked my twenty-third year as an assistant coach or coach. And it marked thirty-two years since the day I'd sat across from Mr. Hoag in his office.

Why was I still there? What was keeping me at Beverly?

My mother and father raised me to work hard and persevere, and I like to think I worked as hard as anyone—on top of being the athletic director, I was still the head football coach. But after Ben left, I started to really feel the strain. Maybe Beverly really wouldn't ever be the same again. Maybe there were just too many factors going against it. What's more, some of the people causing the downward spiral were the very people I had gone to Beverly with. That was an especially difficult pill to swallow. And if Ben Bushman couldn't fight through it any longer, what chance did I have?

As hard as things were at Beverly, they were even harder at home. Karen and I were struggling to cope with the emotional devastation of trying to have a child and failing time and time again, while at the same time teetering on the verge of financial ruin. We had both worked so hard for so long, yet here we were facing crises in every single area of our lives. The pressure this put on us was tremendous.

It all came to a head one Friday evening.

THE FOOTBALL TEAM WAS PLAYING our old rival Torrance High School. Unfortunately the Normans weren't a very good team that year, and we'd yet to win a home game. But then, late in the game, we were ahead by five points. We had a real chance to win our first home game and give Beverly the big morale boost it sorely needed.

With less than a minute to play, Torrance had the football on their own ten yard line, which meant they had to go ninety yards in a very short period of time. On the sidelines, I was feeling pretty good about our chances. On the first play, the Torrance quarterback threw a pass that fell incomplete. The crowd went crazy. The band was playing, and the cheerleaders were in a frenzy. It was like every single fan in the stands was willing us to victory.

On the second play, the Torrance quarterback faked a running play, then threw a pass to a receiver dashing across the field. Even if the receiver caught it, I figured he'd be tackled right away for very little gain. We were creeping closer and closer to a win.

From the sidelines I watched as the Torrance wide receiver caught the ball and took off downfield. I watched as one of our defenders was fooled by the fake running play and charged hard toward the scrimmage line, away from the actual play. I watched as another defender read the play correctly and made his move to tackle the receiver.

Then I watched as he tripped and fell.

The Torrance receiver was now wide open. He galloped ninety yards for a Torrance touchdown, and we lost the game.

On the sidelines, I was stunned. The band abruptly stopped playing, the fans stopped cheering, and everyone filed out in shocked silence. Our players trudged off the field, heads down. I know it was just a football game, but where I work, football matters. Football means something. We try to keep things in perspective, but sometimes that's hard to do. Sometimes a loss is absolutely crushing.

Instead of following my players I hurried past them to the coach's locker room. I couldn't be around anybody. I was exhausted and dejected and completely at the end of myself, and not just because we'd lost the game. I sat in a chair in front of my locker, my head in my hands. I had the terrible feeling my life was falling apart, and there wasn't anything I could do about it.

After a few minutes Beverly's principal and assistant principal walked in.

"That was a tough one," the principal, Dan Stepenosky, said. "Are you all right, Carter?"

"Yeah, I'll be all right," I answered, not looking up and trying hard not to let my desperation show.

Dan heard the heaviness in my voice. "Carter, is there anything we can do to help?"

For whatever reason, that was my breaking point. I couldn't hold back my frustration any longer.

"I don't know if I can keep doing this," I said, my voice haggard and halting. "The student complaints, the parent complaints, buses, officials, vendors, hiring coaches, evaluating coaches, calls, emails, forms, student eligibility—I have to do it all. And I'm the only full-time football coach, so all the off-season stuff falls on me, too. Honestly, I just don't know..."

I trailed off, choking back tears. Dan and his assistant didn't say anything. They just stood there. It wasn't a full-blown breakdown; I didn't toss a chair or kick a Gatorade bucket or anything like that. But it was as close to a breakdown as I'd ever come. Reciting a litany of grievances wasn't like me at all, and neither was showing my emotions. I'd always done my job at Beverly without incident or complaint. But now I felt up against the wall.

And yet my heavy workload wasn't the main problem—that's just what came spilling out of me at that moment. My real problems ran much deeper. I didn't pose it as a question to Principal Stepenosky, but basically that's what it was—a question.

What am I still doing here?

After my outburst I stood up and composed myself. As head coach I was supposed to be in the players' locker room addressing my team, and that's where I went. Since I was late, one of our other coaches was addressing the players. I stood by quietly and let him finish. When he was done, I took over.

"Tonight, we suffered a tough loss," I told my team. "But I want all of you to know that we are going to come back from this. We are going to come back stronger because of this. This loss will make us a better, hungrier team. Just don't stop believing in yourselves."

It may not have been my best speech, but I've never spoken words that came more directly from my heart. Because the truth is, I was addressing myself. I was challenging myself. Would I be able to overcome all the setbacks and heartbreaks and seemingly insurmountable obstacles in my life to regain my fighting spirit? I hoped that I would. But honestly, I wasn't so sure.

After the speech I showered and changed and took a walk by myself out to the football field. By then it was empty and quiet. More than three decades earlier I'd gazed down at this field from the top of a hill, and I'd thought it was the most beautiful thing I'd ever seen. But the field felt different now. As I walked up and down the sidelines, I said a prayer to God, and I asked him to give me strength.

"Please, Lord, help me do the right thing."

But there was no thunderbolt that night, no flash of inspiration. There was only darkness and questions. How could I hope to be a mentor to kids if I couldn't straighten out my own life? How could I teach them about courage and perseverance if all I felt was utter despair?

I stood on that football field, and I felt like I'd given so much and simply had nothing left to give.

For the first time ever in my life, I felt completely defeated.

THE THUNDERBOLT, IT TURNED OUT, came later.

A few weeks after that crushing loss I was coaching our team in a home game. At halftime the players jogged into the athletic building toward the locker room. I ran in behind them. Once we were through the door and into the tunnel, my players veered right to the locker room. I kept going straight, to my office.

But before I could take two steps, I looked up and saw a man standing at the other end of the tunnel.

The man had blond hair and a crooked half smile. When I saw him, I stopped in my tracks, and so did he. We stood there like that, not moving, saying nothing, for what seemed like a lifetime. It was like we were in some kind of trance.

I realized I hadn't seen this man in almost twenty years.

Finally, I walked toward him, and he walked toward me. In the middle of the tunnel I put my arms out, and we hugged. If I had to time it, I'd say that hug lasted a good ten seconds.

"Hey, Coach," Steven Fenton finally said to me.

"Hello, Stevie," I said to my old friend.

CHAPTER

14

I N THAT TEN-SECOND hug, nearly twenty years melted away.

Steven hadn't changed all that much. He'd always been very youthful, and at thirty-six he still was. It wasn't hard for me to summon an image of that eager little kid who ran up and shook my hand at freshman baseball tryouts. We'd promised to keep in touch after he graduated, but we'd both broken that promise, something I regretted. Early on I'd heard Steven was working in Hollywood, but after a while I lost track of him completely. No visits, no phone calls, nothing. Most of my former players either called or came back to see me, and I guess I figured Steven would have, too. But for whatever reason, he didn't.

And yet, in that tunnel, it was like no time had passed at all.

"It's really good to see you, Coach," Steven said.

"Well, it's really good to see you, too. How are you?"

"Good," he said. "I'm good."

But I could tell he wasn't good at all.

When Steven asked how I was, I gave the same answer: "Good." I'm pretty sure my expression and demeanor gave nothing away; I was great at keeping things under wraps. Even so, Steven eventually told me he knew I was lying, too.

He could tell by how hard I'd hugged him.

It was only halftime of the football game, so as much as I wanted to sit down and catch up with Steven, I couldn't. We made plans to see each other that week for—appropriately enough—lunch. Steven gave a little wave and walked away. I looked after him for a moment, feeling the tug of nostalgia, as well as disappointment in myself for not trying harder to keep in touch. Then I turned and headed to the locker room to get back to coaching.

A COUPLE OF DAYS LATER I met Steven for lunch at a little local place near Beverly. We talked for the next four hours.

Steven opened up about everything that had happened to him in the years we were apart. It wasn't a happy story. Of all the kids I ever coached, I would have bet on Steven as the most likely to find success and happiness. He was just so driven, so relentless, so focused. I couldn't imagine him ever struggling to find his way in life. And yet that's just what happened.

Like me, Steven had a dream to play professional baseball. After attending Pitzer College in Claremont, California, where he was a four-time All-Conference player and a two-time regional All-American, he was invited to try out for three pro baseball teams—the San Diego Padres, the Kansas City Royals, and the Cleveland Indians. When the Major League Baseball draft rolled around the summer after he graduated college, Steven waited anxiously to hear his name called.

But it wasn't.

Yet Steven, also like me, had a plan B. When he was little, he used to cut the Nielsen TV ratings out of the paper every Wednesday and tape them in a big red scrapbook. He was fascinated with Hollywood, and after college he landed the most sought-after starting job in show business: working in the mailroom of the William Morris Agency.

His time in the mailroom was a rude awakening. The idea was to put your time in, move up in the ranks, and eventually become a talent agent. But that process usually took years. Steven, though, was in such a hurry to prove himself and make something happen with his life that, after less than a year, he walked away from William Morris and started his own talent management company.

Maybe a bold move, but not a financially rewarding one. In his first year he made all of $8,000.

After that, Steven came up with a new plan: he got a job as a junior manager at a small management company in Hollywood that represented an eclectic mix of people. He was hired at $250 a week with a $50 a week expense account. His first week on the job he got kissed on the cheek by two of his bosses' clients: former porn star Traci Lords and the actor Harvey Fierstein.

"Come here, dimples," Harvey would say, before wrapping Steven in a hug.

During Steven's first year as a junior manager a publicist friend asked him to take a meeting with his client, an actress named Gail O'Grady. At the time, Gail was starring in one of the hottest shows on TV, NYPD Blue. Steven set up the meeting and met Gail in his office. They hit it off immediately, and Steven signed his first prime-time star.

Just a year or so later, Steven and Gail fell for each other and were married.

Here he was, twenty-four and on top of the world. Great job, great wife, great future. But sadly the joy he felt was short-lived. By his own telling, Steven was emotionally unprepared for marriage.

"Gail wasn't very good at being married, but I was worse," he told me. "I was in completely over my head. I didn't have the life skills I needed. I got jealous easily, and I was very judgmental. Gail stopped feeling safe with me. I was at my worst in that marriage."

A day after Gail filed for divorce, Steven drove to LAX to hop on a plane to Chicago and get away from everything. At the airport he picked up a copy of *People* magazine and, in a daze, leafed through it. He glossed over the stories until he saw his own face smiling back at him. A photo of him and Gail was right there next to a heart that was broken into two pieces.

"O'Grady and Fenton: Divorcing in LA," the headline read.

Steven hadn't even had a chance to tell his parents about the breakup yet, and now he didn't have to: *People* magazine had done it for him. Right there in the airport, Steven broke down and cried for a good fifteen minutes, something I'd never known him to do. It must have been humiliating and just plain painful to have his personal failure splashed all over the media.

"I felt like my life was over," he told me. "You know, I always thought it would be great if I made it into *People* one day. I just never imagined it would be for my marriage falling apart."

I hated hearing the ache in his voice, but there was more. After the divorce Steven's mother begged him to move back to Beverly Hills and start over. But Steven just couldn't bring himself to do it.

"I didn't want to come back as a failure," he explained. "I didn't want to be the first of the guys in my class to have crashed and burned. It was such an embarrassing situation for me and also, I thought, for my family. I barely recognized the face staring back at me in the mirror, and I couldn't stomach the idea of running into any of my old Beverly friends or coaches who believed in me and having to explain how far I had gotten from who I wanted to be." His mother had always told him not to embarrass the family. The thought that he might have done just that was enough to drive Steven away.

And so, fleeing from his old life, Steven skipped the Coldwater Canyon exit on the 101 freeway—the exit for Beverly Hills—and headed instead for the Laurel Canyon exit, which took him into Hollywood Hills and a small apartment that was off the beaten path, a place he could hide. He'd lost his wife, his biggest client, and his confidence. Now he'd exiled himself from his hometown, from his community.

During that time Steven *did* occasionally wander back into his old neighborhood, but only late at night when the chances of running into anyone he knew were slim. He would drive west on Santa Monica Boulevard and park on a street as familiar to him as the back of his hand. Then he'd walk across a darkened high school campus on his way to a place that had been his best and safest place.

Late at night, Steven would walk onto Beverly's baseball field.

"I'd lie down in the grass in the infield," he told me. "Right between first and second base, right in the spot where I used to play. I'd stare up at the sky and look for some kind of sign."

I guess I hadn't been the only one to wander an empty field in search of answers.

———

STEVEN EVENTUALLY PICKED HIMSELF OFF the ground and moved into a bachelor pad at the top of Mulholland Drive with a friend who was one of the hottest young agents in Hollywood. Then he got back into the talent management business. It was there Steven finally got to indulge in something he'd deprived himself of in college: the swinging, carefree bachelor life. He drove around Hollywood in a restored 1967 Mustang convertible he bought from one of his better-known clients, the actor Charlie Sheen. No longer needing to discipline himself for sports, he made up for lost time and jumped in the fast lane of parties, movie premieres, and women. For Steven, finding girls to date was not a problem. He was handsome, charming, and outgoing. The problem was what happened once he found them. Basically, Steven hopped from woman to woman, as reckless with their feelings as he was with his own. At one point his conquests included beauty pageant winners from three Midwest states, and for good measure another from the Northeast.

All this was surprising to me. The Steven I remembered was a very different kid. He'd had only one girlfriend all through high school, and he was a very committed and loyal person. I didn't know if this complete turnaround was due to the brokenness of his first marriage, or a fear of getting close to someone again, or something else. What I did know was that he wasn't proud of this time in his life. When we talked, he was hesitant and a bit guarded, as if he was afraid of disappointing me. I just listened and didn't say much. Just like in the old days I tried to create a safe, supportive place for Steven to get it all out.

He took me through the rest of his story, showing me how, bad choice by bad choice, his life continued unraveling. When Steven was in his late twenties, he served as a groomsman in a friend's wedding at the Hillcrest Country Club, one of the most prestigious clubs right outside Beverly Hills. He drank too much and hooked up with an ex-girlfriend on the eighteenth green of the golf course, not far from the rest of the guests. Some other groomsmen eventually found him doubled over and throwing up on the green.

The Hillcrest wedding should have been the wake-up call Steven needed. But it wasn't.

Steven was showing up late to his parents' house for the Cowboy games he'd always religiously watched with his dad, and after being out most of the night, he routinely dozed off by halftime. Those games had been a sacred father-son time, but even that was starting to fray.

For one of his birthdays, Steven had a blowout party, and Steven and some friends invited fellow agents, producers, studio executives, actors, and actresses—some of the heaviest hitters in Hollywood. They put a security guard at the door so no lesser lights could get in.

Steven also invited the woman he had just started dating, Sara.

For most of the party Steven ignored Sara while he flirted with other women. Then, fueled by arrogance and confident he could get away with it, he snuck off to his bedroom with a few female executives he knew.

When Steven finally emerged again, disheveled and unsteady, Sara confronted him by the pool.

"Where have you been?" she asked.

"I fell asleep," Steven said.

The look on Sara's face said it all. Steven knew he'd broken her heart. Without a word Sara left the party and disappeared from his life.

As his birthday party raged around him—as some of the hottest stars and executives in Hollywood drank and danced to pounding music around his shimmering swimming pool—Steven stood in the spot where Sara had left him. Eyes bloodshot, head down, he stood there motionless, absent from the party, absent from his life.

"I didn't move for a long, long time," Steven told me. "I just stood there and thought, *What am I doing? What have I become?*"

———

AROUND THAT TIME STEVEN GOT bad news: his grandmother Rose was dying. To Steven, Rose was the ultimate survivor, a fighter and a warrior. She'd survived war-torn Berlin, and she'd survived hours adrift in the freezing Atlantic. She was beloved and revered by the entire family. Steven got one last chance to say good-bye in her nursing room before she passed away.

Not much later, Steven lost another towering figure from his youth, his beloved Little League coach Big Al Silvera. Big Al had been the first mentor to have a profound impact on Steven. "Anything is possible if you're focused and determined," Al taught his players. "You will your own luck and success." To many of us who knew him, Al was living proof of that—he'd even willed himself to beat brain cancer. Originally given three months to live, he ended up living for more than twenty years after the diagnosis. There was something mythic and indestructible about him.

But now he was gone.

At the funeral Steven sat next to his old teammates from his Little League glory days and listened as a stream of people eulogized Al.

"Al may have lost some games in life," Joe Sutton, another of Steven's old coaches, said in his speech, "and he endured a disease that would have defeated a lesser human being. But to me, Al is a champion. A champion is someone who never quits nor asks for mercy, no matter the terms or conditions of his battle."

A champion is someone who never quits.

Steven heard those words and broke into tears. He sat a few rows from Al's casket and wept uncontrollably. He was mourning his old mentor, but he was also mourning the slow slipping-away of the life he'd expected to have—of the person he'd expected to be. Perhaps he thought back to when he was a confident little kid spraying base hits all over the field. Or maybe he thought of all the promise that lay ahead of him then. His life had seemed to have only one path—the path leading straight to success and happiness.

And yet it hadn't led him there at all.

Searching for some kind of meaning, Steven reconnected with an old friend—a girl who had been homecoming queen when Steven was at Beverly. They fell in love, and Steven bought a condo so that she and her daughter could move in with him in Beverly Hills—just a few hundred feet from the campus of Beverly Hills High School. Steven was getting his life back in order, and at last he seemed ready to come back to the fold.

Steven had a plan. First he would buy an engagement ring and propose to his girlfriend. Once he was engaged and had his life on track he would gather up his courage and walk across the street from the condo to reconnect with his old coach—me.

But then he got blindsided when his girlfriend suddenly broke up with him, feeling the relationship was going too fast. His chance to be both a husband and stepfather disappeared. Just one week after closing on the condo, Steven, humiliated once again, turned around and sold it. Then, rather than walk that few hundred feet to my office, he went the other direction. He quickly fell back into old habits, dating four or five women at once.

He was more lost than ever.

"At Beverly there was a way you were expected to act," Steven told me. "But in Hollywood, nothing is off-limits. Nothing is forbidden. Nobody talks about integrity and character—those things aren't rewarded. There is no code of conduct I had to adhere to. So I didn't."

One night in 2006, in one of his darkest moments, Steven got in his car and drove around aimlessly. He was angry and confused and couldn't seem to get out of his own way. He didn't know who he was or what he stood for anymore.

Rolling down the windows, he tried to clear his head. Just a few minutes into the drive he was in tears. He kept driving, kept searching, for something, for anything.

Absently, he drove up to Charleville Boulevard and Lasky Drive and, almost out of habit, signaled for a left and turned down Lasky. In the distance, he saw a light.

It was the light tower on the Beverly football field.

Normally, Steven never wandered onto the Beverly campus when anyone was there. He was too ashamed and afraid to run into someone he knew. And since the field light was on, that meant something was happening at Beverly. A game, or an event, or something. Normally Steven would have just driven away.

But that night, without thinking about it, Steven parked his car and started walking.

He headed toward the field, but at the last minute veered toward the athletic building, which connected the field to the locker rooms. In a numb, trancelike state, he walked through a set of double doors and into a drab white cinderblock tunnel. His head was down, but he heard a familiar sound: the clatter of cleats hitting a concrete floor. Steven looked up.

Down the hall, several high school football players in full uniform were coming in from the field, just like Steven had done a million times. Steven watched them turn right and go into the locker room.

As they disappeared, another figure came into view. He'd been there all along, but the players were so big he had been hidden behind them. When they turned into the locker room, Steven could see plain as day who was there behind them.

It was someone he recognized.

Someone he hadn't seen in a long, long time.

CHAPTER

15

I T WAS HARD to learn how far Steven had fallen, but at the same time it was great to be able to sit across a table from him again. Steven was someone from Beverly's glory days—heck, from *my* glory days. He'd represented so much of what was good and special about Beverly—passion, commitment, a desire to win, a desire to better oneself, all rolled into one dynamic kid. In our four years together at Beverly we had indeed accomplished something special. And it felt good to be reminded of that. Seeing Steven was good for my soul.

I could tell it was good for Steven, too. He seemed so relieved to be opening up about his life that he barely touched his food.

At first I didn't share any of the details of my own personal struggles. That just wasn't my way. I did fill Steven in on some of the things that had befallen Beverly, but again I didn't tell him the whole story. Though Steven pressed me for more details, I didn't want to launch into a long sermon—not yet, anyway.

"This place is not the same anymore" is basically what I told him. "It's not the same school you and I attended."

Over the next few weeks Steven and I talked a lot, and we began confiding more and more in each other. I told Steven all about the revolving door of principals, teachers, and staffers in the district.

"Steven, we have leadership that believes in doing away with the old completely and starting over," I told him. "The problem is, they're turning their backs on history. I could understand it if we had been failing as a school, but we were once one of the best. And they're just throwing that all away."

Steven began coming by my house in Ladera Heights, about a half hour from Beverly. He was genuinely interested in what was happening. I agreed to take him on a tour of the campus, and one day we walked it from end to end.

I could tell Steven was shocked by how run-down the facilities had become. He'd wandered onto the field many times over the last few years but always at night, so he had no idea how the rest of the campus looked. For one thing, not a single building or facility had been restored for a long time, and the whole place felt dilapidated. The outdoor basketball rims had no nets, and the backboards were rusted; the locker rooms were grungy, and the blackboards in disrepair. Nothing had been painted or fixed for years. Maybe I hadn't realized quite how bad it was myself because seeing it through Steven's eyes broke my heart all over again.

"Carter, I'm going to look into this," Steven said after our tour. "I promise you, I'm going to look into this."

Over the next few weeks Steven spoke to several people in the community to get a handle on how things could have gone so wrong. What surprised him the most was the exodus of talented teachers and administrators. He simply couldn't wrap his head around the idea that people no longer wanted to be at Beverly. He was astonished to learn that, for the first time in the eighty-year history of the school district, both Beverly's principal and the district's superintendent had resigned within a few weeks of each other. Nothing close to that had *ever* happened when Steven was a student. Back then, principals and superintendents were like columns holding up a roof—they never budged.

Even worse, in his swings through the community Steven found a level of apathy about what was happening. People simply didn't care all that much that the school wasn't what it used to be. Parents just sent their kids to private schools, and administrators focused on other problems. Essentially, everyone was writing off Beverly as a lost cause. To them, the school had become a joke.

It was clear to me that figuring out how to fix Beverly was becoming something of an obsession for Steven. I wondered if, in the midst of his own problems—and frustrated that he couldn't get his own life on track—he was gravitating toward something he felt he could fix. Maybe he had to connect to his old self before he could put the pieces of his life back together. Maybe in order to move forward, he had to revisit where he came from.

Whatever the reason, Steven's interest in the school wasn't a passing thing. On the contrary, he latched onto it like it was a lifeline. We talked all the time about what was happening and what we could possibly do to turn things around.

But here's the thing about Steven: he's not just a talker; he's a doer. So he didn't just discuss the situation; he did something about it.

For starters, Steven turned to the one group of people he knew wouldn't be apathetic about what was happening: former Beverly athletes like himself.

Steven suggested we form something called the Beverly Hills Athletic Alumni Association—the BHAAA. The idea was for Steven to create a board made up of sixty or so ex-jocks who would help raise money for Beverly's athletic department. Two of the first guys he contacted were his old teammates Mike Sutton and Albert "Bubba" Silvera—Big Al's son. Not surprisingly, they both quickly agreed to help. Just like that, Steven had reunited the Three Musketeers.

Steven made hundreds of other calls and assembled an impressive team of alumni. Still, no one gave him much of a shot to make a real dent in Beverly's problems.

But in its first year the BHAAA raised a million dollars from generous alumni. That money went straight to the athletic department at Beverly and helped revitalize the program that had touched so many lives.

Then Steven had another idea—he wanted to create an annual fund-raiser centered around Beverly's Athletic Alumni Hall of Fame. The problem was that, while Beverly did have a Hall of Fame, it didn't have an actual *hall*. There was no special place on campus where inductees were commemorated. Steven petitioned the district to give him actual space at Beverly for the hall—a special room, or even just a wall.

Out by the football field, behind the goalposts, there was a big blank wall that was part of the athletic building. Steven set his sights on that. He went to the five-member board of education for their approval.

Now, the board members already knew Steven was raising serious money from alumni, so there wasn't much reason for them to turn him down. It should have been an open-and-shut vote. But it wasn't. Steven was persuasive, and in the end he got his wall by a vote of 3 to 2. It was the first board of education vote in four years that was not unanimous. As best we could figure there was likely some resentment toward Steven, possibly because he was seen as a prodigal son who was suddenly making a lot of noise back home.

LEFT: Carter's parents, Lessie and Carter Sr., in Muskegon, Michigan, before their move to Los Angeles in 1957.

ABOVE: The Paysinger brothers— (clockwise from top) Carter, Carlton, Donald, and Vonzie—with Santa.

LEFT: Carter and his younger brothers in front of the family's Mercury Montclair.

RIGHT: Carter and his brothers at a neighborhood Tom Thumb party (a mock wedding for children) in South Central.

LEFT: Carter (left) playing baseball at Beverly Hills High in his senior year.

RIGHT: Carter and his mother, Lessie, outside their home on the day of his graduation from Beverly in 1974.

ABOVE: Carter getting ready for a baseball game at California State University, Los Angeles.

RIGHT: The Paysinger brothers all grown up: (from left) Donald, Carter, Carlton, and Vonzie.

LEFT: Carter and his fiancée, Karen, are toasted by her father, Joe, at their wedding rehearsal dinner.

ABOVE: The newlyweds Carter and Karen cut their wedding cake at the reception in San Fernando Valley in 1981.

ABOVE: Jamie Marks, one of the first students Carter helped, in Beverly Hills.

RIGHT: Adam, one of the many kids at Beverly whom Carter mentored. Adam is like a son to Carter and Karen and calls him "Pops" whenever they talk.

RIGHT: Steven's grandparents Rose and Karl Freudenthal brought the family to Los Angeles after fleeing Nazi Germany.

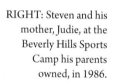

LEFT: Budding star: a young Steven playing T-ball at Hawthorne School in 1978.

RIGHT: Steven and his mother, Judie, at the Beverly Hills Sports Camp his parents owned, in 1986.

LEFT: Steven with his sister, Jenny, and brother Gary, at the legendary Trader Vic's in Beverly Hills.

RIGHT: Steven, Carter, and Frank Fenton on the day of Steven's graduation from Beverly in 1988.

LEFT: After losing touch for nearly two decades, Carter and Steven pose with Steven's father, Frank, in 2006—their first photo together since 1988.

RIGHT: Steven and some fellow Hollywood talent representatives: Brad Slater (left), a partner at William Morris Endeavor, and Jason Barrett (right), a Beverly friend and also Steven's roommate in the Hollywood Hills.

LEFT: Carter and Steven at Steven's fortieth birthday party, reuniting with some old friends, Damon Marshall and Josh Reims, who played baseball for Carter along with Steven all four years at Beverly.

LEFT: Carter with his mother, Lessie, in Palm Springs, California, before she fell ill.

B.H.E.F. Apple Ball
05.05.2009

ABOVE: Carter and Karen at the 2009 Apple Ball, an awards dinner for the top teachers in Beverly Hills.

LEFT: *Beverly Hills Weekly* endorsed Steven when he ran for a seat on the board of education in 2007 (that's Carter in the background). (Courtesy of *Beverly Hills Weekly*)

RIGHT: Steven hugging his dad just after swearing him in as mayor of Beverly Hills in February 2009.

ABOVE: Steven, Leeza, and Carter at the Beverly Hills High School Alumni Hall of Fame.

ABOVE: After he reconnected with Carter, Steven's life took on new meaning, and luckily for him, Leeza Gibbons came on the scene. Here they are at an American Red Cross event honoring Will and Jada Pinkett Smith. (Photograph by Steve Granitz)

ABOVE: Chandler Paysinger at two and a half. "The first time I held him felt like a miracle," says his mother, Karen.

ABOVE: Carter, Karen, and their son, Chandler, with Carter's nephew Spencer (Donald's son), a linebacker for the New York Giants, after an NFL game in 2012.

LEFT: Steven and Leeza's wedding day (April 20, 2011); his stepchildren, from left, are Troy, Lexi, and Nathan. (Photograph by Christian Scott)

RIGHT: Proud parents Carter and Karen pose with their son, Chandler, after he was named student of the month in his preschool class.

ABOVE: Steven and Carter with their beautiful wives, Karen and Leeza.

RIGHT: A family tradition: Lawrence Tolliver, owner of Tolliver's Barber Shop in Los Angeles, has been giving haircuts to Paysinger men for more than four decades.

"Maybe they're thinking, *Who does this guy think he is? Why does he even care?*" Steven reasoned. "*He disappears for twenty years, and all of a sudden he knows what's best for Beverly?*"

None of that mattered to Steven—all that mattered was that he got his wall.

———————

"CHEVY, WE'RE GOING TO DO everything in our power to help you get back on track."

Erik Kritzer, Steven's old friend from his William Morris mailroom days and his partner in the management company Fenton Kritzer Entertainment, was doing the talking. Somehow Steven had managed to put the pieces of his management career back together, and he and Erik had landed some pretty major clients, including Burt Reynolds, Arsenio Hall, Chuck Norris, and Anne Archer.

Now they were talking to the actor Chevy Chase about revitalizing his career.

Steven had been in hundreds of meetings like this one, and ordinarily he would have jumped at the chance to help a star like Chevy Chase. He'd have made it his personal crusade to make his client's dreams come true. But sitting in that meeting, Steven felt nothing. He felt no energy, no desire.

"That's when I knew I was nearing the end of my career," he told me. "The more I was helping my school, the more Hollywood felt empty to me."

When I ran into Steven in that tunnel, he wasn't quite the Steven I remembered. I can't recall ever seeing him glum and unhappy about anything back in the Beverly days, but in that tunnel he seemed dejected. He was missing the fire and energy that had defined him as an athlete. But now that he was back in my life and back at Beverly, I could see the old flame returning. Suddenly he was more animated, more energetic.

Beverly was bringing out the best in him again.

But there was something else besides Beverly that was also reinvigorating Steven. When he came back to town, he persuaded his father, Frank, not to run for reelection as Beverly Hills treasurer but to run for the city council instead. Steven, naturally, would manage Frank's campaign together with his mom.

"Why would I want to give up being treasurer and run for city council?" Frank asked him. "So I can listen to people complain about streetlights all day long?"

"First," Steven argued, "because the city needs you. And second, because this is the one thing in the city you haven't done yet."

This was true. Frank had served on the board of education and as city treasurer, and if he was elected to the city council, he'd be the only person to ever win a seat in all three elective offices in Beverly Hills. Steven, ever the competitor, was motivated by that challenge. But Frank didn't seem to care. Still, with both Steven and his wife Judie pushing him to do it, Frank gave in.

The campaign lasted ninety days, and Steven took a leave of absence from his company so he could go door-to-door with his dad. This gave Steven the chance not only to reconnect with Beverly Hills but also to team up with his father—his hero.

But to Steven's surprise, Frank showed barely any interest in campaigning. "That wasn't like him—shaking hands and meeting people was his strength," Steven said. "Suddenly he was depressed and withdrawn. He looked like he was just going through the motions."

Steven figured his father had already given a lot to the community and perhaps didn't want the stress of campaigning, so he took the responsibility on himself. On election night, he was at city hall gathering voting results from the city clerk and calling his parents, who were at a friend's home, with the numbers. There were ten precincts in Beverly Hills, and after each precinct was announced, Steven called his folks.

"You won another precinct!" he'd excitedly report, only to be met with silence.

When all the votes finally came in, Frank had won a seat on the council. Frank Fenton had made history.

Between the excitement of his father's campaign and the impact he was having at Beverly, Steven was finding a new direction and purpose in his life. It was around that time that he came to my office to announce he'd made a pivotal decision that would affect both of us.

"Carter," he said, a familiar twinkle in his eyes, "I'm going to run for public office."

Steven had long thought of following in the footsteps of his hero. Despite the pressure it had put on him when he was younger, he now envisioned himself assuming the mantle from his civic-minded father and furthering the legacy Frank Fenton had built over three decades of service. It was way back in the eighth grade when Steven first tried emulating his dad by running for student council president. That was the election he quit at the last minute rather than risk the embarrassment of losing.

It may have taken him a few years longer than planned, but Steven was finally ready to redeem himself. And this time, he was running to win.

THE IDEA OF HAVING A guy like Steven anywhere in city government was exciting. He'd be not only an ally but also a defender of everything that had once made our old school great. I'd always be able to call him when something else fell apart at Beverly.

That is, if I still had a job at Beverly myself.

Around the time Steven decided to run for office, I attended a meeting of the executive committee of the California Interscholastic Federation Southern Section. CIF was the governing body of athletics for the entire state of California, and for years I'd served on the Football Advisory Committee. One year, the foundation named me the Character of Champions Coach of the Year, and the next year they named me State Coach of the Year, two enormous honors. I had a great working relationship with everyone at CIF, and I was proud to be a new member of the executive committee.

After the meeting one of the commissioners pulled me aside in the hallway.

"Carter, there's going to be an opening for an assistant commissioner position at CIF," he said. "I think you should consider applying for the job."

I was flattered and intrigued. I'd always wondered what I'd do if a great opportunity came along, and now I was about to find out.

I went home that night and talked it all over with Karen. I was surprised to find the idea of leaving Beverly not quite as unthinkable as it once had been. For one thing the prospect of starting a new career in sports administration was exciting, and the extra salary sure wouldn't hurt, considering how things were going at home. I still loved Beverly, and I believed Steven could eventually have a positive impact on the school. But did I really want to wait around for something that might or might not happen several years down the road?

For the next couple of days I thought about the suggestion constantly. I realized I was on the verge of a life-changing decision, one that involved walking away from the place that had been my home for more than thirty years. It would be a monumental move, but even so, I felt like I already had one foot out the door.

I knew it was time to get some advice. I needed to talk to someone who understood my dilemma—who loved Beverly as much as I did, but who also recognized the reality of what was happening there. Someone who had both my interests *and* Beverly's interests at heart. More than anything, I needed to talk to a friend.

I needed to talk to Steven.

Just a few months after he sought me out because he needed me, I found that suddenly it was me who needed him.

I dialed his cell number, and he picked up in his office.

"Steven," I said, "I may have another job opportunity, and I'm seriously considering it. I can't stay at Beverly and watch what's happening there anymore. I just love this school too much to do that."

"Carter, I want to talk in person," Steven said. "Can I come over?"

Steven drove to my home, and we sat with a couple of beers in my backyard. We spent the next couple of hours talking about our old school. To some, seeing their alma mater slip from greatness to mediocrity might not have been that big a deal. But to us it was a *very* big deal.

We both knew what Beverly had done for us, but more importantly we knew what it had done for hundreds of students like us. Now there were countless Stevens and Adams and Andrews and Jamies coming through the pipeline who needed Beverly just as much as we had. Who would look out for them? Who would fight for their futures?

I'd been taught never to quit, never to concede a fight. At the same time there comes a point in any fight when you have to ask yourself if it's still *your* fight. I had all but reached that point.

"Steven, I don't know if I can do it anymore. I don't know if it's worth it."

As we spoke, I could practically see the gears turning in Steven's head. Slowly but surely he'd been coming out of his funk, fired up by his efforts to fix Beverly. But a Band-Aid here and there wasn't going to save the school, and Steven and I both knew that. A much more concerted effort—a much more daring play—was needed, or else the clock was simply going to run out on Beverly . . . and on me.

All of a sudden Steven jumped out of his chair and looked me square in the eyes.

"Carter," he said, "I'm not going to run for my father's seat anymore."

"You're not?"

"No, I'm not," he said. "I'm going to run for the Beverly Hills Board of Education."

I sat in silence and let his declaration soak in. If Steven got on the board of education, he'd be one of five people in charge of making *all* decisions regarding Beverly. He would be in a position of real power, and possibly enough power to change the course of events currently taking place.

This was a daring play indeed.

But Steven wasn't finished.

"Look, it's killing me to know the teachers and coaches I grew up with are disillusioned and frustrated enough to leave," he said. "It's killing me to see that even you are thinking of leaving. Carter, if I can get on the board of education, I think I can make a real difference. I think I can turn things around."

"I think you can, too, Steven," I said. "I think you should do it."

"I *am* going to do it, Carter. But I have two conditions."

Conditions?

"Number one, you have to promise not to leave yet. You have to give me a chance to see what I can do."

As excited as I'd been by the CIF job opportunity, the idea that someone had just jumped alongside me and joined in the fight changed everything. I wasn't alone anymore. I had an ally, and not just any ally—I had one of *my guys* with me. If Steven was serious about running for the board, I believed it was worth sticking around long enough to see how it all turned out.

"Steven, you got it," I said. "I'll do whatever I can to help."

"Great," he said, "because here's the other condition."

Steven leaned in, eyes blazing in the late afternoon sun.

"Carter," he said, "you have to agree to become principal of Beverly Hills High."

CHAPTER

16

I T'S NOT LIKE I hadn't thought of running for principal of Beverly. In recent years I'd thought about it more and more. I looked around and didn't see anyone who was more qualified, more passionate about the school, than I was. I had a bachelor's degree in social science and had since earned a master's in education as well, but even more important I'd been at Beverly for more than three decades. I knew the teachers, the students, the parents, the way things worked. To me, at least, the idea that I could be principal made a lot of sense.

Yet at the same time I was also thinking about leaving Beverly. I was being pulled in both directions—stay and fight to make the school better, or leave and find out what else was out there for me. When I learned about the opportunity with CIF, I had to sit down and finally answer the questions that had been nagging at me: What was keeping me at Beverly when so few seemed to care anymore? Did I want to stay and fight? Was it my destiny to be at Beverly, or had that season come to a close?

I'm not sure I would have ever been able to answer these questions on my own. Luckily, I didn't have to. Luckily, a whole bunch of people answered them for me.

PEOPLE LIKE LUKE ZIMMERMAN.

At a football practice several years back, a couple of my players, Eric and Chris, came running up to me.

"Hey, Coach, there's this really cool kid named Luke we think you ought to meet," Eric said. "He really loves football."

"Yeah, we're hoping you might consider letting him be on the team," said Chris.

A day later I ran into Luke near the practice field and invited him to my office. Luke was friendly and cheerful and funny and just an all-around great kid, and boy, did he love football. He knew most of the players on the team, and he came out to all the games. He was so passionate about the team he'd cry after a loss and feel bad for several days. And when the team won, Luke was over the moon. Honestly, I'd met very few people who were as passionate about anything as this kid was about football.

Luke Zimmerman was born with Down syndrome. Doctors believe people with Down syndrome never progress mentally past the age of eight. As Luke neared the end of elementary school, most people figured he'd stay in a special education program all through high school. But Luke and his parents had other ideas.

Luke enrolled at Beverly Hills High as just another student.

In my office we talked football for a while, and he impressed me with how much he knew about the game.

"Hey, Luke," I said, "I have a question for you. Do you want to be on the football team?"

"Yes, Coach," he said quickly, "I want to be on the team."

We didn't have any free roster spots, so Luke became our nonplaying manager. But we gave him a jersey and a set of shoulder pads, and we let him practice with the team. Luke was only about five foot four and 130 pounds, but he was a bundle of energy. He came to every practice, even the two-a-days, and he ran special solo drills we devised for him.

The next season a roster spot opened up, and we listed Luke as a wide receiver. We issued him his own jersey and helmet, and gave him number 51. After a while it didn't seem to any of us like we were doing Luke a favor by having him on the team; he just became part of the squad, like any other player. He spoke to the team in the locker room before and after games, and if any of the guys were too wrapped up in plays and strategy and Xs and Os, they weren't anymore after hearing Luke talk. His speeches were pure inspiration.

During games Luke mostly stayed on the sidelines, cheering his teammates as they came off the field. Luke worked hard at whatever he did, and that rubbed off on the guys. How could they not be as upbeat and positive as Luke? If he never gave up, how could they?

Luke was the emotional heart of our team.

The Beverly football team won only two games the year before Luke came aboard. The year he was manager we improved to six wins and five losses. The year he played, we had eight wins and only one loss. Coincidence? I can't say for sure. But honestly, I don't think so.

Luke played in a handful of games at Beverly. He was also a member of the swim team, the orchestra, the chorus, the photography club, and the piano club. He became the first person with Down syndrome to graduate from Beverly Hills High. On top of all that, the kid is a pretty good actor. After high school he earned a major role on the ABC Family show *The Secret Life of the American Teenager*. He is, in every way, a phenomenal person. His heart is as big as a mountain.

What I remember most about Luke, though, is how much the players loved him—and one small moment in particular that captured that love.

In Luke's very first game against Morningside I noticed our star running back, Aaron Kogan, following Luke on the field on his first play. I was confused; Aaron wasn't supposed to be in the game. But before I could say anything, Aaron dashed back to the sidelines, and we ran the play. After the game I asked Aaron why he'd followed Luke like that.

Aaron, a three-time All-League running back, a straight-A student, and a hugely popular kid, started to laugh.

"Coach, Luke's pants were falling down," he said. "I just went out and pulled them up for him."

It was just a tiny gesture, lost to most and possibly even to Luke, but to me it meant so much. It showed me I was among people who truly cared for one another. It reminded me what a special place Beverly was.

It was where I belonged.

Luke. Aaron. Steven. Jamie. Gordon. Andrew. Adam. Hundreds of other kids like them.

I had to stay and fight, if anything, for them.

———

WHEN I HAD PHONED STEVEN and told him about the CIF job opportunity, I think I knew deep down I wanted to stay. It wasn't just my calling to be a coach and teacher—it was also my destiny. It was what I was *meant* to do. But the situation at Beverly had changed so much I guess I just needed a little assurance that staying was the right thing to do. I needed someone to agree with me that Beverly was a place worth fighting for.

And Steven came through for me, just like he had so many times before when he was my second baseman. He not only wanted me to stay; he wanted to help me become principal, too.

Even so, I wasn't sure he'd thought it all through.

"You're the best leader we have," Steven went on in my backyard, "and it's time for you to start leading more than just kids. It's time for you to lead every student, every faculty member, every member of this community. It's time for us to take Beverly back."

"Steven," I interrupted, "I have no doubt I'd do a heck of a job running Beverly. But I'm not sure you know what you'd be getting yourself into. This could be a tougher battle than you think."

"I know it'll be tough, but that's okay, because—"

"Steven, I'm talking about people who won't want to see me as principal. People who won't be happy with a principal who is *black*."

Steven flinched, as if my words stung. Then he was quiet for a while. I don't know if he'd even considered race to be an issue, or if he thought so highly of Beverly Hills as a community that he couldn't believe people there would block me because of my color.

But Steven couldn't see Beverly Hills through my eyes.

He didn't know, for instance, that when I went for a morning jog through the streets of Beverly Hills, I'd see white women clutch their purses tighter as I ran by. He didn't know that I would jog clear across Santa Monica Boulevard rather than run up behind a white person who would see me as a threat—even though I might have been coaching their kids at Beverly High. Steven had never experienced the way some white teachers and parents measured their words when they spoke to me, or tensed up when I joined a conversation, or otherwise acted like they had to be careful around me. These were small and subtle things that someone like Steven wouldn't notice—but I could sense them, and I sensed them all the time.

"Boy, just keep living," my father had once told me. "There's gonna be a lot of things you're not gonna believe."

I felt I had to let Steven know what I believed might lie ahead if we pursued this idea.

But that didn't mean I wasn't up for the fight.

Not once in my life had I ever shied away from a challenge. In fact, the longer the odds against me, the more I wanted to win. That drive was one of my mother's many gifts to me, and I always tried my best to honor it. And I knew Steven was made of the same stuff. That's why he was there in my backyard, eyes on fire.

"So," I finally said, "you really want to do this, Stevie?"

Steven looked at me and grinned.

"Carter, I really want to do this."

I stood up and stuck out my hand. Steven reached out and shook it.

"Well, then," I said, "let's do it."

PART
3

CHAPTER

17

WHEN I WAS nine years old, on one of my family's trips to Louisiana, I saw a group of men wearing white sheets and white hoods.

It was a summer Saturday afternoon, and my father had taken my brothers and me and some of our cousins to spend time in Bossier City, which wasn't too far from his hometown, Plain Dealing. He parked on a street in downtown Bossier, and we all jumped out, eager for whatever adventure lay ahead.

As soon as I got out of the car, I spied a group of ten or twelve men standing across the street from where we parked. They were wearing white sheets and hoods. I could tell they were watching us from across the street, and suddenly I felt afraid.

"Daddy," I asked, "is that the Ku Klux Klan?"

I don't know how I knew about the KKK at such a young age; I just did.

"Yes, son," my father said, putting his hand on my shoulder. "They meet down here a couple of times a month."

I couldn't believe what was happening. The dreaded KKK was right across the street, yet my father was acting like it was nothing.

"You mean it's okay for them to just walk around like that?" I asked, my voice full of astonishment.

"One thing about the South," my father said, "is that they don't bother us, and we don't bother them."

That was the last we spoke of it that day. And my father was right: we didn't bother anyone, and no one bothered us.

It was only on the long drive back to South Central that I asked my father about what I'd seen in Bossier City. I didn't understand how black people and people who hated black people could coexist that way.

"It's just a part of life," my father explained. "You can't always control it. You boys just do what you do, and be who you are. Don't let anyone else define you."

My father went on to explain two different kinds of racism—the overt kind and the hidden kind.

"The difference between racism in the South and racism in California is that in the South you know where you stand. In the South, they don't pull any punches. They don't like you and you don't like them, and you both know where you stand.

"But in California some people will smile at you and pretend they like you, and all along they have a white sheet in their closet."

I had no frame of reference for this at the time, so my father's words didn't mean that much to me right then. But over time, they would.

———

THE FIRST PART OF OUR crazy plan was getting Steven elected to the board of education, and he set the plan in motion in July 2007 by filing papers to run in the upcoming November election.

By then Steven had already started calling old friends, classmates, and neighbors, asking for their support. He went door-to-door and shook a thousand hands, same as his father had done for years. But what Steven didn't do was tell anyone his ultimate goal: getting me into the principal's office.

Instead, Steven campaigned as a youthful reformer with roots in Beverly Hills. For the first time in memory both local papers, the *Beverly Hills Courier* and the *Beverly Hills Weekly*, endorsed one and only one candidate for election that year: Steven Fenton.

The *Beverly Hills Weekly* went so far as to anoint Steven as something of a savior for the community. They called him "The Man with a Plan." Unlike recent board hires from outside Beverly Hills who tended to stay for only a year or two because "they don't feel invested in the community in the first place," the *Weekly* said, Steven "understands what makes Beverly Hills great and what could make our schools great, too. We not only believe him, we can't wait to see him get started. Fenton gets it."

For me, the best thing about Steven's campaign was seeing how it made him come to life. He was reconnecting with old friends and classmates and getting them excited about Beverly's future, and this invigorated him like nothing else, not even high-wire Hollywood deal-making. He put up more than a thousand campaign lawn signs—some kind of Beverly Hills record—and every day he grew more confident.

He was brushing away the cobwebs of a long, wayward stretch.

There would be setbacks, though. Before Steven had officially filed to run, Steven's mother arranged for him to have lunch with Barry Brucker's wife, as Barry had become a big community leader and was a family friend. Even though Barry had opposed the multicultural permit in the past, Steven still expected to win his and his wife's support for his campaign, but it didn't go quite that way.

"Let's face it," she told Steven, "your parents are getting older, and so are their friends. There's a new generation of people coming up, and I think you need to wait your turn." She hadn't even bothered to listen to Steven's thoughts and ideas about how to turn the district around. Those things didn't seem to matter. But Steven, scrappy fighter that he was, just turned around and campaigned even harder.

On the night of the election Steven invited Karen and me to Xi'an, a Chinese restaurant on North Canon Drive, for the election party. I watched nervously as someone fed Steven results over his computer. Steven was confident and excited—I could tell he believed with every bone in his body he would win. I believed it, too, but still I was nervous. Steven had campaigned on the idea of hitting the reset button on the entire district. Obviously, the people currently in power weren't exactly crazy about that idea. But in the end the establishment underestimated its opponent. After all, these people had never seen Steven play second base, and they had no idea how driven, aggressive, and focused he was.

A couple of hours into the voting, the numbers looked good. All Steven had to do was be one of the top three vote-getters, and he'd win a seat on the board. As the evening wore on, it looked more and more likely that Steven would win a seat. He was on the verge of making Beverly Hills history as part of the first father-son team to both hold elected office at the same time. At some point Steven left Xi'an with his father and headed to the local news station for a live interview.

But something was wrong with Frank Fenton.

Throughout the campaign Steven had made sure not to ask his father to do too much. He knew his father was burned out, and he didn't want to burden him with more obligations. He did bring him along to the coffee meetings with voters, partly to emphasize the proud Fenton tradition, partly to try and bring his father out of his funk. Most of the time, though, Frank seemed to be in his own world. He clearly wasn't the same old Frank people knew.

On election night, things weren't much better. The excitement of the evening, the hustle and bustle and constant well-wishes, seemed to be overwhelming Frank. He wasn't responding to comments or picking up threads of discussions. He seemed like he was somewhere far away.

In the end, Steven got more votes than any other candidate and won by the widest margin in board history. But even so, he was not in a mood to celebrate. He was distracted. A terrible thought was forming in his brain.

My father is sick.

Just then, Frank pulled his son aside. Suddenly, Steven noticed an old, familiar spark in his father's eyes. Frank hugged Steven tight and told him something he will never forget.

"I am proud of you, son."

For Steven, hearing that was the sweetest victory of all.

AROUND THE TIME OF THE election an assistant principal position at Beverly opened up.

A lot of people sought me out and told me I should apply. It felt like the right time, not least because of the plan Steven and I had hatched. I went through the formal process of applying, and the interviews went smoothly. Soon, I heard through the grapevine that I was the leading candidate.

In the spring of my thirty-third year on the campus of Beverly, I was offered the job of assistant principal.

But there was a hitch.

I was offered the job right before the start of football season. I was still Beverly's head football coach, and we were busily preparing for our first game. I was happy to move up to assistant principal as long as I could continue as head coach for the upcoming season. I felt it would be grossly unfair to my players to abandon them right before the season. Plus, there was precedent. A few years earlier my friend Chuck Kloes had been both an assistant principal and the football coach, and he did both things quite successfully. I figured there'd be no problem with me doing the same.

Unfortunately, there was.

Beverly's principal and the district superintendent both told me I'd have to stop coaching, and they gave me only a few weeks to detach myself from the program.

Their decision didn't seem fair, to me or to my players. Why had Chuck Kloes been allowed to work both jobs and not me? I went in and strongly pleaded my case. I explained I'd be doing double duty for only three months, and I was certain I could handle both sets of responsibilities for that short period of time. I emphasized how wrong it would be to abandon my players and my coaches right before a new season and how that would unnecessarily damage the team.

But they didn't budge. Their answer was still no.

The truth is, I felt slighted. I took their stance personally. It put me in an unnecessarily difficult position—I could advance my own career, but only at the expense of my players. Or I could stay with my team and say no to the new job. It was either one or the other.

This was the first confirmation of what I'd suspected: that my path to the principal's office would not be straight or easy.

After talking it over with Karen, I called the principal and told him I was passing on the job.

The fallout was immediate. Several school officials came looking for me on the football field to tell me I was making a big mistake. Even the district superintendent came out and advised me to reconsider. I asked again if I could continue as head coach for the upcoming season. Once again, she said no. I told her that left me no choice. I wasn't taking the job.

"What are you going to tell people when they ask you why you didn't take the promotion?" she asked.

"I'm going to tell them the truth."

Understandably Steven was upset with my decision, too. I'm sure he saw it as a setback to our plan, and I guess it was. But that's the thing about taking a stand—it's always hard, and it always comes with a price. I guess I could have compromised my values and quit the team and convinced myself it was for the greater good. Instead I took a stand and passed on the job. The price was setting back both my career and our plan, and that was a pretty steep price.

But every time I stepped on the field and saw my players busting their butts to learn plays and gain yards and get better, I knew I'd made the right decision. The kids were the end goal. Whatever the price, I would just have to pay it.

So there we were: Steven on the board but outnumbered and essentially powerless, and me having just let the assistant principal's job slip through my fingers.

Our plan to save Beverly was off to a great start.

TWO YEARS PASSED, AND THOUGH we never discussed it I'm sure there were times both Steven and I doubted our dream would ever come true.

Then, two things changed.

First, a new round of elections gave Steven the chance to get another ally on the board. If he could get just one more person on his side, he'd be in the majority and have the power to execute our plan.

At the same time, another assistant principal position opened up at Beverly. For me, the timing was perfect—I could go after the job and still give the football program plenty of time to replace me. And so, once again, I applied to become an assistant principal.

It was during the application process, though, right when it looked like things might go our way, that I suffered the worst setback of my life.

It was something so cruel and so painful I had to stop the application process in its tracks.

CHAPTER

18

WHEN I WAS nine or ten, my mother dropped me and my brothers off at Trinity Baptist Church in South Central so we could practice the Easter program with our Sunday school class.

After the practice, which ended early, we waited in the church for our mom to pick us up. I'm not sure how long we waited, but at some point we got the bright idea to save her the trouble and just walk home. We lived five miles away, but that didn't strike us as an obstacle. So without telling anyone, the four of us left the church and began walking.

About five blocks into our journey we saw our mother drive right by us in the opposite direction. When she saw us, she did a quick U-turn. In my young mind I was sure our mother would be proud of us for trying to walk home alone. Boy, was I wrong.

"Where in the world are you all going?" my mother demanded.

"We were walking home," I explained.

"Do the ladies at the church know you left?"

I looked at my brothers, who looked at me. "I don't think so," I said.

"They just let you go?"

I could see my mother's fury start to boil. She hustled us into the car, did another U-turn, and drove straight to Trinity Church. There, she stormed over to the Sunday school ladies and let them have it.

"You let my babies leave this church on their own?!"

"We're sorry, Mrs. Paysinger. We had no idea they left."

"They were walking down the street five miles from home! Anything could have happened to them!"

"We truly apologize. We should have kept a better eye on them."

"Just know that if I drop my babies off at the church, either me or their father will be here to pick them up," my mother said, her wrath subsiding. "*Always.*"

I was mortified to see these poor church ladies get dressed down by my mother. It didn't seem to be their fault, and I felt bad they got yelled at and we didn't. I should have known our turn was coming.

On the car ride home our mother let us have it, too . . . good.

When I think of that day now, it shows me how ferociously my mother stood up for her family. It is not an exaggeration to say that she lived for her children. There was nothing she wouldn't do for us, no detail too small for her to approve or disapprove.

But having her as our champion came with a price, too.

It meant we had to hold up the high standard she was setting for us. If we didn't, our advocate became our critic. She was as hard on us as she was on anyone that she felt did us wrong. That is how my mother taught us the importance of doing things the right way. *Don't take shortcuts. Don't cut corners. Being a Paysinger means striving to be better than everyone else.*

My mother never stopped drilling those lessons into me. Not even when I was head football coach at Beverly.

Because all four of their children went to Beverly, over the years my mother and father probably attended as many athletic events there as any other parents. In a very real way, they became a part of the Beverly family, too. One day, after watching a football game I was coaching, my mother asked me why the concession stand at games wasn't better.

"Why is it so pathetic?" is what she actually said.

"We can't get anyone to commit to running it the way it should be run," I explained. "As it is, the other coaches and I have to set it up and take it down."

"Nonsense," my mother said. "From now on you guys concentrate on winning football games, and your daddy and I will run the stand."

I looked over at my father when she said this, and he gave her a withering look. But he was smart enough not to challenge her. The next weekend both my parents worked the concession stand.

After the game my mother asked me, "How much do you usually make at the stand each week?"

"I don't know, between two and three hundred dollars."

"Well," my mother said, "your football program just made $1,500 tonight."

After that, hundreds of other parents and volunteers went on to work at our concession stand and turned it into an enduring success.

You see, "good" was never good enough for my mother.

AROUND THE TIME STEVEN AND I reconnected, my mother started complaining of back pains.

She'd always been active, but now, in her late sixties, her back was slowing her down. My father took her to the doctor, who said she was having muscle spasms and prescribed relaxants. Then she had a hip replacement, which sidelined her for a while, but afterward she was back to being her normal active self.

Then the back pain returned.

By then my parents were living in the same neighborhood as me. I saw them all the time, and we had dinner together at least once or twice every week. I'd listen to my mother complain about her back, but I knew my father was taking her to see doctors, so I figured eventually they'd figure it out and her pain would go away.

Then, one morning, my mother awoke with such excruciating pain she couldn't stand up. My dad rushed her to the hospital, where doctors ran a battery of tests before sending her to another hospital, which ran even more tests. I was with my parents as they sat across from a doctor in his office when the test results came in.

The look on the doctor's face terrified me.

"I have never seen anything like this," he said, holding up an X-ray, "and I don't know if there is anything we can do about it."

My mother was diagnosed with myeloma, a serious cancer that affects the bones. The cancer, apparently, had spread to her spine.

I was stunned. I reached over and held my mother's hands and tried not to cry. Momma had always seemed immortal to me, larger than life and tough as they come. I never even considered the possibility of her not being there. The diagnosis was absolutely shattering for all of us.

We told the doctor we wanted to get a second opinion, but the next physician just confirmed my mother's myeloma could not be cured, only treated with chemotherapy to reduce the pain. She was prescribed heavy painkillers and sent home. Despite the diagnosis, none of us were ready to give up on her, and we convinced ourselves that if anyone could beat this disease, it was Lessie B.

At first the chemo and painkillers did seem to work; my mother had less pain and more energy. But after a few months we noticed she was losing weight. She was also less active because the painkillers made her lethargic. My father and I went with her on several doctor visits, and they'd show us where the chemo was working . . . and where it wasn't. Any gains she made were tiny and incremental, while physically she was just growing weaker. Those months were such a struggle for her, and for us all. Still, we believed somehow she'd pull through.

None of us ever spoke about the alternative.

It was around then that I applied for the assistant principal position at Beverly for a second time. One night I went into my mother's bedroom, where she was resting, to tell her I'd soon be interviewing for the job.

Now, my mother was always a little nervous when any of her sons talked about leaving one job and taking another. I suppose that's a sentiment many parents share.

But at the same time, I could see she was extremely proud of me. She understood what an important position this was and how much influence I'd have over generations of children passing through Beverly. And, in a way, becoming assistant principal meant coming full circle in a journey that had started more than three decades earlier, when she took me to the well-appointed office of Mr. Hoag.

In essence, I would now be sitting on the other side of that big mahogany desk.

Carter, this is your moment, she'd told me back then with nothing but a squint of her eyes. *Carter, you can do this.*

And now, in her bedroom, weakened by the chemo, Momma told me pretty much the same thing.

"Go for it," she whispered in a soft, trailing voice. "You can do it."

I was right in the middle of the interview process at Beverly when, one February night, I got a call from my father.

"Your mother can't breathe," he told me. "We're at the hospital. Come now."

Momma had been feeling better of late. The doctors even told us there was a chance they could get her cancer under control. Then one night she couldn't catch her breath. I raced to the hospital and found my father in the waiting room, hunched over and staring at the floor. He was a mess. Eventually all the children arrived, and we sat in that waiting room for nearly two hours without any word. We weren't allowed to go in and see our mother. All we could do was wait.

Finally, I asked a nurse what was happening. The nurse's face went white. She called the doctor, who took us all into another room.

"I'm so sorry. She didn't make it."

That is how I found out Momma, my heart, my rock, was gone.

––––––––

THEY HANDED US A BOX of tissues and told us we could see my mother in her small, dark hospital room. We all went in, except for my father, who refused to go.

Her body looked impossibly small in the bed, nothing at all like the larger-than-life mama bear of my memories. We stayed with her for more than an hour, each of us having a private moment, thanking her, expressing our love, touching her hands, touching her face.

Saying good-bye.

It turned out the morphine my mother was taking had slowed down her heart, which led to the heart attack that killed her in the hospital.

In the end, the cancer didn't get her after all.

My first reaction was anger—I couldn't help but think how much time had been wasted believing her pain was only muscle spasms.

What if the doctors had diagnosed her correctly from the start? I was consumed by rage and a deep feeling of injustice. This was not the way it was supposed to end for someone as strong and towering as my mother. I wanted to lash out at someone for the unfairness of it all.

But I didn't. That wasn't the Paysinger way.

Later that night we all gathered at my father's house. I heard the doorbell and looked up and saw Steven Fenton. He was carrying two big bags filled with pizza and pasta. Putting the food down, he came over and gave me a hug. Then we sat by ourselves at the dining room table to talk.

Except I couldn't talk. I couldn't say anything. I hadn't really cried yet, but as I sat there with Steven, it all came out. A waterfall of tears. Sheer, raw grief. I'm pretty sure it was the first time Steven ever saw me cry.

Steven didn't say anything as I wept. He just put his hand on my shoulder and let me cry.

A FEW DAYS LATER WE held the funeral at Trinity Baptist Church— the very same church where Momma had scolded the teachers for letting us walk home by ourselves.

The service was beautiful, or so people tell me. It's hard for me to think of it in those terms. The church was packed with relatives from Louisiana and Michigan, old and new neighbors, friends from South Central, coworkers, churchgoers. My mother had touched so many people in her lifetime, and that day it seemed like they were all there, pouring out their respect, affection, and love.

I got up and said a few words, though the truth is I was too emotional to keep it together for long. I do remember my cousin Earl getting up and giving a beautiful speech. He explained that my mother had many professions—architect, doctor, soldier, lawyer—all unlicensed, all unpaid.

"She wasn't schooled at Harvard or Yale and didn't even earn a law degree," Earl said. "But she was a fierce defender of a client called family. And she never lost a case. Woe unto the one who would test the resolve of her argument. The proof she presented was her own family. And the jury that voted unanimously in favor of her life's work is more than just twelve people. It is legions. It is all of us."

After the service we drove to the cemetery in Inglewood, and we laid my mother to rest.

What I remember most about the funeral, though, was how many people from Beverly Hills were there.

Dozens of teachers and staffers from Beverly Hills High School. Board members and district officials and cafeteria workers. The parents of people who had been my classmates, and countless current students who knew her from football games. Every time I'd ever been at Trinity Baptist I'd looked over the congregation and seen a sea of black faces. But not this day. This day, I saw white faces interspersed with the black ones, side by side, everywhere, pew after pew. What I saw was a sea of *people*, all mourning the same loss.

So many folks from Beverly came to honor my mother they basically had to shut the school down for the day.

When I was in school, I had been so careful not to bring South Central to Beverly Hills.

But now my mother had brought Beverly Hills to South Central.

AFTER HER FUNERAL I SPENT many dark weeks praying for my mother's soul and crawling through a life that suddenly seemed emptier. Losing her knocked me to my knees.

Her illness and death made it impossible for me to focus on the assistant principal job, so I told the interview panel I was withdrawing my application, at least temporarily. I didn't know if withdrawing meant losing any chance of getting the job, and part of me didn't care. Without my mother around, what was the point? Without my rock to hold onto, how could I be sure I wouldn't fail?

In those dark times I talked to my mother every day. It took me a while to realize I was talking more to my mother after her death than I ever had when she was alive. But I guess that makes sense because suddenly I needed her a lot more.

And what I came to realize was simply miraculous.

When I needed my mother the most—after her death—is when she was most with me.

Everything she had ever told me—all the lessons, scoldings, urgings, and praise—all of that was still with me, and it would never go away. My mother could still talk to me through the very same words she'd used while she was here. In my darkest moments I could practically hear her saying those things to me, as if we were standing side by side in the kitchen, like in the old days. *You can do this, Carter. You are strong. Do the right thing. Be better than everyone else. This is your moment.*

My mother may have left me, but she did not leave me unprepared. She left me with a heart filled by her wisdom and love, an endless reservoir of strength and courage and hope.

All my life, everything she ever did—from the Tom Thumb wedding to chewing us out for leaving the church to insisting I go to Beverly to a million other things—had all been designed to prepare me for the complexities of life. To shape me into a strong, resilient man.

It was only in the weeks after her death that I truly realized how well her plan had worked.

I missed my mother painfully in those first few months, and as I said, part of me lost interest in the goings-on at Beverly. But deep down I knew full well that's not what Momma would have wanted for me. She would never have allowed me to back down from any challenge, however great or small. After all, one of the last things she ever said to me was, "Go for it."

And when my mother makes a decision, it's final.

Three months after my mother's death, I told the officials at Beverly I wanted to continue the application process to become an assistant principal. They were kind enough to allow me to pick up where I'd left off. I was no longer the top candidate, as I'd been the first time around, so the interview process was even more important.

But in July of 2009, four months after my mother passed, I was once again offered the job of assistant principal at Beverly Hills High.

This time, I took it.

And when I did—when I became the first African-American assistant principal in the history of Beverly—I could hear my mother's sweet voice say, *Carter, I'm so proud of you. I knew you could do it.*

CHAPTER

19

WHEN I WAS a student at Beverly back in the 1970s, there was a groundskeeper and custodial worker there named Sylvester Harris.

Everyone loved Mr. Harris. He was kind, friendly, and funny, and he was always happy to talk to freshmen and help them feel a little less nervous, a little more at home. He would show up at games and cheer the team on, and for hundreds of students over the years Mr. Harris became a kind of Beverly institution.

Nearly forty years later, Sylvester Harris was still there.

But then, toward the end of Steven's first two years in office, I learned district officials were trying to get rid of him.

They didn't fire him outright, but it looked to me like they were trying to make his life miserable so he would quit. They demoted him and put him on a rotation with other schools. This would save the district a few thousand dollars, but it meant Sylvester would have to travel a lot more and work many nights. The problem was, Sylvester was living with and taking care of his ailing ninety-year-old mother, and everyone knew that. Disrupting his life that way struck me as downright cruel.

When I found out, I called Steven and told him what was happening. Steven rushed the matter onto his agenda, and he managed to arrange a board vote to save Sylvester's job at Beverly.

Steven and his ally, Brian Goldberg, voted to save it.

But the other three members voted against it.

After the vote, Steven drove to Beverly to see Sylvester in person.

"I'm sorry for what is happening," he told him. "We fought hard to save your job."

"I appreciate that," Sylvester said.

"But listen, I want to tell you something," Steven said. "Don't leave. Do not leave. Tough it out for as long as you can. There's an election coming up. We are going to bring you back."

It wasn't all that different from what Steven had told me in my backyard. And just like me, Sylvester looked into Steven's eyes and believed what he was saying.

He didn't quit his job. Instead, he toughed it out.

"MOM, I THINK DAD IS sick."

For the longest time Steven and his mother had written off Frank's sluggishness as burnout or depression or some other ailment that came with getting old. But Frank's lack of excitement about his son's campaign convinced Steven something was seriously wrong. He spoke with his mother about it, and they finally took Frank to see a doctor.

Frank was diagnosed with the onset of Parkinson's disease, a degenerative disorder of the central nervous system that can cause depression, dementia, and paralysis. There is no cure, only medicine that can possibly slow its progression. Frank was not in the full throes of Parkinson's—he didn't have tremors, and his mind was still reasonably intact. But he was often depressed and distracted, and he was having trouble swallowing and smiling. The disease was starting to affect the nerve endings in his mouth.

As things worsened, the elements of his sickness started looking more and more like Lewy body disease, a form of dementia. Sadly, Frank was forced into retirement shortly after being installed as mayor of Beverly Hills.

Steven took the news about his father's illness just as badly as I had taken the news about my mother's cancer. Frank was Steven's hero, the one he went to for advice and encouragement—the guy he'd watched Cowboy football games with every Sunday for decades. Like me, he hadn't even considered a future without his hero in it. And now, watching Frank lose a bit more sharpness every day—and understanding he might be reduced to a shell of himself—tore Steven apart.

One of the worst aspects of it all was that, after Steven got elected to the board, he needed his father's advice and counsel more than ever. He was still in the board minority, and the establishment seemed to take pride in outvoting him at every turn. It wasn't a position Steven was used to being in, and I could feel his frustration every time I talked to him. The one person who could have given him the advice he needed—*be patient, Steven; don't act recklessly; don't lose your cool; win and lose with class*—wasn't able to give it to him.

Then we caught a break.

Around this time our eighth superintendent in eight years came aboard. His name was Jerry Gross, and he was an ex-football player who was older, distinguished, and well respected in the community. Hollywood couldn't have cast a more elegant elder statesman.

Steven and Jerry hit it off right away, and in some ways, Jerry became Steven's guiding force on the board. When Steven got angry about being outvoted again, it was Jerry who told him he had to stay calm.

"You need to start acting more like your dad," Jerry told him.

Turns out that was all Steven needed to hear.

Steven began sharing our plan with Jerry Gross. Jerry recognized right away that it was a risky plan, and that most of the board members would strongly oppose it. But he took the time to get to know me and my family anyway, and in the end he joined our side. It was fate that brought him to us, and I'm grateful he had the courage to go out on a limb and become a fierce advocate for me in the days to come. With Steven newly invigorated and Jerry on our team we could finally sense the tide starting to turn.

———

AROUND THAT TIME THE MAYOR of Beverly Hills pulled Steven aside at a meeting.

"You need to run for your father's seat on the city council," he told Steven. "It's your legacy; it's your time. I will back you, and you'll get elected. Why take all this abuse on the school board?"

It's true; Steven was being marginalized on the board. He was in the minority, and it was hard, if not impossible, for him to make any real headway. Plus, running for a seat held by his father—assuming the mantle directly from him—had long been Steven's actual dream. Here, finally, was his chance. He went home and slept on it, and the next day he drove out to Beverly and came to my office.

"Carter, we need to talk."

Steven explained the mayor's offer to me. I sat and listened quietly as he spoke in his usual animated way about what an opportunity it could be.

I didn't know what to say, so I said nothing.

When Steven finished speaking, we both sat in silence for a while. I was waiting for the shoe to drop, and I presumed Steven was waiting to drop it. Without Steven on the board of education, there was con-siderably less chance, and maybe no chance, of us executing our plan. The existing board members clearly didn't support his agenda in any way, so even with Steven on the board our plan was a long shot. But without him?

It could be the end—the end of our efforts to save Beverly.

Steven leaned forward in his chair. He always had a way of focus-ing on you as if your conversation was the only thing that mattered in the world at that moment. That's how I felt as he leaned toward me—like something important was about to happen.

"Carter," Steven said, his voice low and serious, "you and me, we're in this thing together, right? You are with me, aren't you?"

Now it was my time to lean forward.

"Steven," I said, "I am with you one hundred percent."

"Okay then," Steven said. "I'm not running for my dad's seat. I'm staying right here with you."

And that was that.

IN NOVEMBER 2009 TWO SEATS on the board of education were back up for grabs. If Steven could find a way to get one more ally elected, he'd go from the minority to the majority. He'd finally have the power to get things done.

Steven and his friend on the board, Brian Goldberg, handpicked two people to run for the vacant seats—Jake Manaster and Lisa Kor-batov. Steven and his mother oversaw Jake's campaign, while Brian helped run Lisa's. Steven, a natural campaigner, pulled out every stop to get his two picks elected. In no small way his future, and mine, de-pended on them winning.

That November, both Jake and Lisa won their elections.

Steven was now part of a four-vote majority, lined up against the fifth member of the board—a woman named Myra.

Myra was smart and tough, as well as an old family friend of Steven and his parents. She had been on the board of education when Steven was first elected two years earlier, and on the face of it they should have been allies. Both were considered heirs to the old Beverly Hills establishment, and both were, in their own way, in the shadow of one of the city's greatest power brokers, Frank Fenton. But they never got along. Myra led the three-vote majority that made it so hard for Steven to make any progress on the board. They wound up fighting about nearly every issue, and during one particularly heated meeting a board member's spouse confronted Steven, telling him he was "through in this town." A security guard had to escort him out of the building.

I believe Myra and the rest of the board came to see Steven as something of a flamethrower—an impatient guy with radical ideas. It's true Steven was aggressive; I knew that about as well as anyone. Steven was always the kid with the dirtiest uniform, and now, as a grown-up, he still wasn't afraid to mix things up. He may have even enjoyed it a bit. Most of all, I knew Steven wasn't interested in playing it safe and following the majority opinion—if he had been, he would never have backed me for principal. Steven was interested in doing whatever was necessary to fix what was broken. Steven was the runner barreling into home plate; Myra was the catcher, trying to block his way.

It wasn't lost on me, or on Steven, that by lining up against Myra, Steven was in effect lining up against his parents. Granted, his parents couldn't have foreseen the conflicts that lay ahead when they helped Myra get elected, but still it couldn't have been an easy thing for Steven to square off against her. But I think back to the story of Steven quitting his first election in the eighth grade rather than risk embarrassment by losing. I think about him not wanting to return to Beverly Hills out of fear he'd brought shame on his family by failing. At some point Steven had to take a stand and fight his own battle, regardless of the risk of failure and what it might mean to his parents. He had to step out of their shadow and do what he thought was right, regardless of the consequences. That would be his path to redemption, if he was brave enough to take it.

And he was.

The tradition on the Beverly Hills Board of Education is to rotate the presidency of the board among its members, with the most senior member assuming the title whenever there was a changeover. That meant Myra, then the board vice president, was in line to be president. There would still be a vote to confirm her, but ordinarily it would be a formality.

Except that it wasn't.

Steven invited me to the school district office on the day of the board vote to name a president. I took a seat in the auditorium and held my breath. If Steven could somehow get himself named president, our plan would pick up all the steam it had lost, and then some. Several hundred people filled the auditorium, and I looked around and saw a lot of familiar faces, including Judie and Frank Fenton. The tension was palpable. A lot was riding on what happened next.

The district superintendent banged a gavel to start the proceedings.

"Does anyone want to nominate someone for president?" he queried.

"I do," said Brian Goldberg. "I want to nominate Steven Fenton."

"Will anyone second that nomination?"

"I will," said one of the two new members of the board, Jake Manaster.

The matter was now clear to be voted on. One by one, the superintendent asked all five board members to say either yes or no to Steven's nomination. The final vote was five to zero.

"Congratulations," he said to Steven, "you are the new board president."

Even Myra, apparently seeing the handwriting on the wall, had voted for Steven.

The crowd broke out in applause. But not everyone was pleased. Abruptly, in the middle of the auditorium, Barry Brucker, current city council member, and his wife got to their feet and walked out the door. Murmuring and sideways glances rippled through the crowd, but Steven wasn't at all rattled.

He took the podium to give his acceptance speech. He was thirty-nine years old and the youngest board president in Beverly Hills history.

I wasn't surprised that one of the first things Steven did in his speech was bring up Sylvester Harris.

"I watched last year as our superintendent—the eighth one we've had in ten years—recommended that after thirty-eight years on the job, Sylvester should take a pay cut of a few thousand dollars and have his duties in the athletic department severed," Steven said. "I am here to tell everyone that I will be putting on the agenda for our meeting in January an action item to restore his position and salary retroactively. Sylvester, I am sorry for everything that happened. We will make this right."

Cheers rang through the auditorium.

Then Steven spoke of Beverly's illustrious past and why it was so crucial to honor it going forward. "Our future," he said, "lies within the sanctity of our past."

Finally, Steven drew his line in the sand.

"I am here to send another message to all five hundred employees of our district," he said, pausing dramatically before going on.

"If you don't bleed Beverly, please leave now."

The auditorium erupted. Cheers, whoops, applause. Just like in the old days, whenever Stevie would get a big base hit.

Three days after being installed as board president Steven called a special meeting. The very first order of business was doing right by Sylvester Harris.

Steven put the matter to a vote. Only Myra voted no. By a count of four to one, Sylvester had his job back.

The battle for Beverly was on.

———

AS BOARD PRESIDENT, STEVEN'S PLAN was to replace four school principals in the district with four people he knew and trusted—people he believed could turn things around.

I would be the fourth.

He wasted no time getting started.

"My father always told me, strike while the iron is hot," Steven said to me one day. "If you've got a hot hand, play it and run the table. Momentum is everything."

Still, such a sweeping changeover of principals had never happened before. It was sure to be messy and controversial, and there was a good chance it wouldn't work. People could conclude Steven was overreaching. Yet if he tried to get me in as principal right away—before the other three prospective principals—people might say he was just doing his old coach a favor. Either move was risky, but Steven was determined to overhaul the culture of mediocrity that had taken over.

The thing is, Steven didn't just randomly draw up a plan of action. He was not a casual analyst of talent—in fact, it was his profession. As a talent manager, he made his living by putting people in the best position to succeed, and he did it at a very high level. He also had a deep understanding of how things worked in Beverly Hills.

Steven was probably better suited to overhaul our school system than anyone else.

Over the next several months Steven removed the principals of three of Beverly's schools, transitioning some into administrative positions in the district and replacing them with people who had deep roots in the community. One of them had been a sports hero at Beverly and a teacher at Horace Mann for thirty-five years. Yet he'd never held an administrative position, which meant he wasn't on track to becoming principal; in fact, no one had ever made the jump straight from the classroom to the principal's office. But Steven picked him anyway, and he got the job.

In fact, all three of Steven's new hires were people who had been part of the Beverly Hills school system back in its glory days. He wasn't just picking people off the street. He was bringing back some of the top-notch talent that had slipped away.

Then it was my turn.

There had been no formal announcement about me running to be principal, but people were starting to figure it out. It was time to go public. My first step was to discreetly and informally meet with two board members to gauge their reactions to my running. While I thought I was ready for anything, their reactions surprised me.

"Why would you want to be principal?" one board member asked me. "I thought you were leaving to go work for CIF or something?"

"I want to be at Beverly. I believe in Beverly," I told her. "I have no doubts I can do a great job and move us in the right direction."

She looked at me like I was suggesting a trip to the moon.

"What do you know about algebra?" she asked abruptly. "Do you know anything about algebra?"

I was taken aback. There wasn't a principal in the country who had an intimate knowledge of every subject taught at his or her school. Some of them had math backgrounds, some liberal arts, some administrative. I had a degree in social science and a master's in education. The idea that I had to subject myself to an algebra pop quiz to prove I was capable of being principal was absurd—and insulting.

"I know our algebra support classes aren't working, but we'll work on that," I responded. Then I ended our meeting before I could say anything I'd regret.

Never mind that I'd taught classes at Beverly and served as an athletic director and assistant principal. Never mind that Beverly had other principals and assistant principals who were former sports stars and coaches and that, as far as I could tell, had always been considered something of a plus.

Now, with me, it was suddenly different. My background in athletics was something people could use against me, to show I was unqualified. I'd bet my bottom dollar no other candidate for principal would ever be asked what they knew about algebra.

The second board member I met with wasn't any more welcoming. When I told her I wanted to apply, she said some people might have a problem with me being principal. Then she told me the story of how, back in the 1970s, Beverly Hills High went on a nationwide search to find a new principal. "The man they picked was an older, distinguished Jewish gentleman," she explained. "He fit the profile of what a principal should look like. And to some people, fitting that profile is very, very important."

After a brief pause, she added, "But I don't feel that way."

The insinuation was that I didn't fit the profile. Never mind my background, or my qualifications, or anything else—the biggest problem was my appearance. Not surprisingly, the board member didn't elaborate on why I didn't fit the profile. Was it because I wasn't older and distinguished enough? Or because I was black? Was she saying

Beverly couldn't have a black principal because it had never *had* a black principal? Was she suggesting I was being presumptuous to think I could change that?

I'd long since come to the realization that in Beverly Hills, where only 2 percent of residents are black, there would be times I'd be judged by my appearance and not the content of my character. Sometimes it would be subtle and relatively easy to forget—like hearing the click of a car door locking as I walked by—and sometimes it would be more difficult to just shrug off. This was one of the more difficult times. I'd warned Steven the color of my skin might be a problem for us, but even so I was startled to hear the board member talk about my "profile." I couldn't shake the thought that it was just a polite way of saying I couldn't be principal because I was black.

Those meetings with the two board members did have one positive effect, though—they wiped away any hesitation I might have had about becoming principal.

Back when I was a growing up in South Central, my friend Tony asked if I wanted to play in a game of basketball against him and his friends. I said sure. Then he told me the biggest, best player in the neighborhood was on his side. He was trying to intimidate me, but his words had the opposite effect. Now I wanted to beat him twice as badly.

"Doesn't matter who you have on your team," I said. "I'm gonna whip you anyway." And I did.

After the meetings with the board members I was not only convinced I should pursue the job; I was determined to get it no matter what. If I didn't fit their "profile," they were just going to have to come up with a new one.

In the spring of 2010 I filed papers to formally apply for the job of principal of Beverly Hills High. Our secret plan was secret no more.

CHAPTER

20

W HAT ABOUT ADOPTION?"
Karen and I had asked each other that question many times over the years. Early on the two of us—and me more than Karen—wanted to exhaust all other possibilities before we went that route. Now we had. After many discussions and a lot of back and forth we contacted an attorney in Century City, and the adoption process began.

Nothing about it was easy or cheap. The retainer for the attorney was thousands of dollars, and it was several thousand more to advertise ourselves as parents looking to adopt. But whatever it cost, Karen and I were determined to do it. We'd gone through too much to give up now.

The attorney found a woman named Tameka, a single mother of five who was eight months pregnant. Tameka didn't think she'd be able to raise a sixth child, so she wanted to place the baby in a good home. Karen had already had preliminary conversations with several other possible candidates, but her talk with Tameka was the best one yet.

We arranged to meet with her, and she struck us as a lovely woman in a very tough spot. She had no real family, and her living arrangements were not ideal for five children, let alone six. We knew it had to be extremely hard for her to give up a child, and we tried to be as sensitive as we could throughout the whole process. But in private, we were starting to feel some excitement. We were allowing ourselves to have a tiny bit of hope.

Our conversations with Tameka went so well we all agreed to move forward. We met in the attorney's office and signed the papers. Everything was falling into place.

A few days later we were scheduled to meet Tameka for dinner at 6:30 at a P.F. Chang's in El Segundo. By 7:00, Tameka still wasn't there. We called her a few times, and she finally answered at 7:30. She told us she'd overslept. That seemed plausible. She was eight months pregnant, and she had to be exhausted.

A couple of weeks later Tameka missed another appointment with us. Some doubts began to creep in, but still it was reasonable to believe that, given the circumstances, Tameka was just impossibly stressed.

Days before Tameka was set to give birth we worked out a plan to have her call or text us when she went into labor. We wanted to rush to the hospital and be there for the birth. Seeing the child being born was very important to both of us. A few nights later, Karen and I were out for dinner with her sister Deborah when I heard the text message alert on Karen's phone. It was from Tameka.

"What's it say?" Deborah asked.

"She said she had the baby. She's beautiful, and they're both fine. And she will call me later."

Deborah was excited—"You're going to be a daddy!" she screamed at me—but Karen and I were subdued.

"She was supposed to contact us before she had the baby," Karen said. "I'm calling the attorney to see if we should call her."

The attorney told us to take a deep breath and let him look into things. He called the hospital to find out when the baby was born, but there was no record of Tameka being there. We started thinking the baby might have been born one or two days earlier, and Tameka hadn't told us about it. By now, we were starting to panic. The attorney eventually located Tameka and called us after he spoke with her.

"Let's give her some space," he said. "Let's not pressure her. Let's see what happens."

Finally, Karen got Tameka on the phone. She told Karen she just wanted to spend a few days with her baby, and then she would hand her over to us. That hardly made us feel better. The attorney warned us some mothers change their minds at the last second and, pressured by their families, decide to keep their babies. Still, we wanted to be positive and hopeful because we wanted this child so badly. We tried to ignore the growing pits in our stomachs and stay optimistic.

The day before we were supposed to pick up the baby, Karen called Tameka to arrange the meeting. And then Tameka went off.

"Don't call me anymore; I will call you!" she said. "I told you I just want to spend time with my baby. Don't call me again!"

Monday came and went without a call. So did Tuesday and Wednesday and the rest of the week.

We would not hear from Tameka for another six weeks.

Long after we'd come to the sad conclusion we weren't getting the baby, Karen opened an email from Tameka. In it, Tameka explained why she did what she did. She felt worse about giving up her daughter than she'd anticipated, and she felt she was getting the short end of the stick in our arrangement. She apologized for what she put us through.

Then she told us what had happened to her baby.

She hadn't been able to care for her daughter after all, so Child Protective Services came and took the baby away. A child that might have been ours was now lost to the system.

The news floored us. "It's just not our fate to have children," Karen said, and hearing her say it broke my heart. She was being dragged through a terrible, emotional process full of pain and sadness. And there was nothing I could say or do to make things better. I could tell by her reaction she was setting up a defense mechanism, to spare us both. She was convincing herself that everything would be fine even if we never had a child. She was getting very close to giving up the fight and resigning herself to never being a mother, and she was "okay with it," as she often told me. I knew that she wasn't, but I also couldn't expect her to keep trying forever.

The truth is, I was ready to throw in the towel myself.

It wasn't long before we heard from our attorney again: this time, he had a candidate in Washington, DC. She was homeless and giving birth in a week or two. If we wanted the child, we had to act fast. We hired a separate lawyer to work through some interstate commerce issues, and we booked a last-minute flight and hotel room. All told, we spent several thousand dollars. But as we packed our suitcases the night before the flight we were buoyed by a sense of hope, however unfounded it might have been. This time, we felt certain, it would be different.

I was folding one of my shirts when the telephone rang. Karen picked it up. I could tell from her side of the conversation she was talking with the homeless woman in DC. After a few minutes Karen hung up and filled me in on their conversation.

"Don't come to my hospital room until I call you," the woman told Karen. "I want to spend a day or two with my baby before I hand him over."

I called our attorney, who advised us not to get on the plane.

"Don't go until she is ready to give the baby up," he said.

We skipped the flight, lost the money we'd paid for the hotel, and waited at home for the woman to call. Two days passed without a word. We called the woman, but she never picked up or answered our messages. Finally, on the fourth day, our attorney called.

"It's not happening" was all he said.

By then our skins should have been hardened to last-second disappointments, but they weren't. If anything, we were more vulnerable this time. After I hung up with our attorney, Karen slumped in a chair in our living room, and I knelt beside her. Neither of us said a word. Including Tameka and the woman in DC, we'd seen a total of five potential adoptions fail to materialize for us. No matter how hard our prayers and how strong our faith, the result had always been the same—a surge of hope, then crushing disappointment. Finally, after a long while, Karen spoke.

"It's my fault," she said. "I'm the reason we don't have a child. You wanted one when we were younger, and I didn't. And now we'll never have one."

Karen's eyes were swollen and red. I tried to say something, but a huge lump in my throat stopped me. The thought of Karen blaming herself—and possibly believing I'd always be secretly resentful toward her—filled me with sorrow and dread. I put my arms around Karen and held her as she let out a deep, sad sigh.

"I'm done," she said. "I'm done. I can't do this anymore."

I cannot express the immense disappointment we both felt at that moment. It was truly one of the most harrowing times in our lives.

Several weeks later, one quiet night at home, I got a call from our adoption attorney. He'd found a seventeen-year-old woman in South

Carolina who was pregnant and needed a good family to raise her baby.

"I'm sorry, we've given up," I told him. "We just can't survive another failed adoption."

"Look, just give me this one last shot before you give up, okay?" the attorney said. "Don't give up just yet."

I told him I'd get back to him. Then I went to find Karen in the living room. I wasn't sure I was even going to tell her about the call. How could I ask her to go through this again? The failed adoptions were knocking her down over and over again, yet she kept bravely getting back up. But for how long? Another year? Three or four more years?

At moments like that, there aren't any rulebooks to help you make a decision. There is only what's in your heart to guide you.

The last two years for us had been emotionally exhausting. First, Karen's father had died, and then my mother passed. We were still recovering from the crash of the real estate market, and I was just entering what was sure to be a contentious fight to become the principal of Beverly. On top of all that, we were both drained after four miscarriages, three attempts at surrogacies that didn't work out, and five failed adoptions. Could we really get up off the ground and go through it again? Did we really want to?

I sat with Karen in our living room, and I told her about the seventeen-year-old girl in South Carolina.

"So," I said, "what do you think we should do?"

———

AT BEVERLY, A THIRTEEN-MEMBER SELECTION committee made up of teachers, staffers, and district officials vetted ten or fifteen different candidates for principal and narrowed it down to four.

I was called in for a series of interviews with district officials. I'd been through two rounds of interviews to be assistant principal, so I knew what to expect. The questions were fairly standard: Why did I think I'd make a good principal? What were my plans for the school? What had I learned in all my years at Beverly? I had no problem answering any of them. Then came the final question.

"What does Beverly Hills High School mean to you?"

I was surprised to feel my eyes begin to water.

Like I said, I almost never show emotion in public. But sitting there, I couldn't help it. I thought about my first ever interview at Beverly with Mr. Hoag. I thought about my mother driving me to Beverly that day in her cafeteria dress. I thought about all the sacrifices my parents had made to get my brothers and me into this school.

And it struck me, then and there, that it was because of my mother and father that I believed I understood Beverly better than anyone else.

"This school isn't a place for the elite or the privileged," I said. "It's a place for everyone. Because to me, Beverly isn't just about its students—it's about its teachers, its coaches, its administrators, its alumni, even its custodians and cafeteria workers. Beverly is like a big family, and I am living proof that everyone in that family can thrive if given the chance. Now, some of that unity of purpose has been lost over the last twenty years, and I want to see it restored. I want Beverly to be a family again."

I pulled myself together and left the interview feeling pretty good. I even heard whispers I was the leading candidate.

Sadly, those weren't the only whispers I heard.

As we got closer to the board vote, the opposition got louder. Some of it I expected. Some of it I didn't.

I would soon learn that a full year before I even applied, several people in the community, sensing what Steven was up to, began gearing up to block me from getting the job. One afternoon, Steven met a family friend for lunch at the Peninsula Hotel in Beverly Hills.

"I know what you're trying to do, and you're never going to pull it off," she told Steven. "There will never be a black principal at Beverly Hills High. Never."

Steven hid his shock and answered with only two words:

"You're wrong."

A few months later, Steven phoned me at home to say his mother, Judie, had just received a call from one of my old friends who I had known for a long time. He was a successful executive from a prominent family. He was an influential power broker in Beverly Hills. He wasn't the type to throw his weight around, but just a few words from him could affect the balance of power in the city.

"What did he have to say?" I asked.

Steven paused for a moment.

"He said, 'Carter's not the guy.' "

I was stunned. Several years earlier we'd had a misunderstanding about some school issue. We didn't become enemies, but our friendship was now strained. We'd still say hello when we ran into each other and we'd even shoot the breeze, but we just weren't as close as we'd once been. Even so, I'd fully expected him to stand behind me when I ran for principal. He'd been one of Steven's biggest advocates before my candidacy had come up. I didn't expect a big, formal public pronouncement, but I knew he could support me quietly. He could tell the right people, "Carter is my guy."

Instead he said the opposite.

What bothered me most was *how* he said it—I wasn't the man for the job. What did that even mean? He didn't articulate a solid reason why I shouldn't be principal. No one did. All of the criticism, it seemed, was veiled and purposely general. I didn't fit the profile. I wasn't the right guy. I possibly didn't know algebra. What were these people really trying to say?

In the weeks before the board vote several other people I knew and admired approached me and told me I should drop out of the race.

"Why are you doing this?" they asked. "You really shouldn't do this." No specifics, just a general argument that I wasn't the right man.

Basically, it was Steven and me against the world.

We were the sports team at an away game, looking uselessly up into the stands for support . . . except we had thought we were playing a home game.

My candidacy became a big story in the community. It was written up in the papers, and it became a hot-button issue. Supporting me became a very divisive thing to do. One evening my wife and I attended an awards dinner for top teachers in our district. On the way into the ballroom a man I didn't know stopped me. He had a drink in his hand, and it probably wasn't his first.

"Carter Paysinger!" he said loudly. "The most controversial man in Beverly Hills!"

Could that be true? How deep did the opposition to my candidacy run?

Deeper, it turned out, than I ever imagined. I later learned when word of Steven's plan to make me principal had first gotten out, someone had called the Los Angeles district attorney's office and filed an anonymous tip that Steven had been living outside the city limits when he ran for the school board and was thus ineligible to be on the board of education. It was a blatant lie and easily disprovable, but the DA had to investigate it anyway. It struck us both as an attempt to discredit Steven and derail our plan.

Later on, a friend of mine told me someone had even started a Facebook page opposing me as principal. Then, one afternoon when one of my wife's friends was driving through Beverly Hills, a woman came up to her at a stop sign. The woman was holding a clipboard, and she asked if my wife's friend would sign a petition.

"A petition for what?"

"It's a petition that says we don't want Carter Paysinger to be the principal of Beverly Hills High."

When my wife told me about the petition, I shrugged it off and told her not to worry about it. But inside I was surprised by all of this and more than a little hurt. I had come so far and grown so close to this community, and suddenly I felt just like I did that first year I showed up at Beverly—alone and unsure and . . . *different*. Was I that undesirable a candidate? When had all the people who I loved and I thought loved me decided to turn their backs on me?

What was going on?

Then one of my best friends and colleagues pulled me aside and offered words of encouragement.

"Hang in there, Pace," he said. "Don't listen to what they're saying about you."

My first thought was, *What* are *they saying?*

My second thought was, *Do I really want to know?*

For me, one of the great ironies about all the opposition to me being principal was that, just two years before I decided to run, the country had elected the first black president in its history, Barack Obama. My wife and brothers and parents and I all sat around the TV and watched his inauguration in 2008, and like millions of other Americans we felt a special sense of pride. But while the United States had proved ready for a black president, some of the people in Beverly Hills, a community that prided itself on being forward-thinking, didn't seem ready for a black principal. Believe me, I thought long and hard about why so many people opposed me so vehemently without even knowing my plans for the school, and I tried to find some reason that didn't have to do with my race. I was more than ready to answer any legitimate charges about my qualifications. But it's pretty hard to defend yourself against the argument that, for unstated reasons, you're just not right for the job.

Not that any of the comments and petitions and Facebook pages mattered. All that mattered was who the selection committee picked and whether or not the board of education voted to approve that pick.

In the spring of 2010 I learned the committee had recommended me.

Then, on May 11, the five members of the school board gathered for a closed-door meeting in a conference room at the district office and voted on whether I should be the next principal of Beverly Hills High School.

CHAPTER

21

THE SCHOOL BOARD asked that I make myself available the day of the closed-door vote, in case anyone had more questions for me. It was Myra's idea. I found it strange anyone could still have questions they needed answered. After all, I'd been at Beverly for nearly four decades. Everyone knew who I was and what I stood for.

Still, I went to the district office the day of the vote and sat in the reception area, waiting for someone to call me in.

Two hours passed, and no one ever came to get me.

I couldn't know for sure what was being said, what arguments were being put forth against me.

Was there still a question of my academic capability, despite my graduate degree and the fact that previously Ben Bushman, my former mentor and coach who'd never taught an academic class before, had gone on to be a successful principal at the school? Or was there some objection to the selection committee that had recommended me, even if it was exactly the same committee and process that the district used for *every new hire*?

I didn't know. I could only guess as I sat on that bench outside the district office. All I knew was that Steven was in there, fighting for me.

After a couple of hours Steven came out the front door. He saw me in the reception area.

"Carter, your mother would be so proud of you," he said. "You're going to be the next principal of Beverly."

———————

BUT THERE WAS MORE. THERE was a catch. I thought I was ready for anything, but I wasn't ready for what came next.

"Your title will be <u>interim principal</u>," Steven told me.

"Interim?" I said. "I'm *interim* principal?"

"Yes."

I felt like a linebacker had tackled me from behind.

As far as I knew, no other principal had ever been designated an "interim" principal. Even candidates who were brought in from outside the community were not called "interim." They were given the job outright. Had the board been voting on an outsider—and not someone who had been at Beverly for nearly forty years—they would not have used the "interim" disclaimer. But for some reason, they used it for me.

It seemed as if the opposition to me being principal was so intense the board came up with a compromise solution—they would vote for me, but only as interim principal. That meant that I could be quickly fired if I was deemed in any way unworthy.

Steven, seeing my disappointment, tried to give me a pep talk.

"Carter, every principal who comes in is essentially an interim principal. Every principal is on a one-year contract," he said. "They all have to go through performance reviews and prove themselves."

"But Steven, this is different," I said. "You know this is different."

"Carter, if you took the job, you wouldn't act like an interim principal, would you? You wouldn't do the job halfway?"

"Heck no," I said. "I'd do it like I do everything else—full-out."

"Carter, remember what you used to tell me when I was playing baseball? You said, 'It doesn't matter if we win ten to nothing or three to two. A win is a win.' We got the win, Carter. *You are principal.*"

My own words echoed out of the past and traveled through a generation so they could land on my ears again. I understood what Steven was getting at, and part of me knew he was right. I could turn down the job and leave Beverly with an awful taste in my mouth. Or I could take the job and prove everyone wrong.

Still, there was that lingering feeling that I had been singled out. It was like they were allowing me into the principal's office but only through a separate door.

District protocol called for me to accept or decline the offer on the spot so it could be reported at an open board meeting set to start any minute. I told Steven I needed to call my family first. The first person I called was my father. I was almost too embarrassed to tell him what had happened because I knew he was expecting something a bit more triumphant. And to me this wasn't that.

"Tell them you'll take the job, and you can always back out of it tomorrow," my father said. "Just come home."

I found Steven and told him I would take the job.

That night I sat with my family, trying to sort through all that had happened up to this point, the surprising antagonism from people I thought I knew, the painful realization that I was still on the outside looking in, the frustrating outcome of this whole battle. Karen took my hands in hers, gazing steadily into my eyes, and said what she always said: "I believe in you."

The voices of my family chimed in.

"Carter, you are stronger than they are."

"Just hold your ground. Keep going."

"Don't let them win," added my father.

Then I heard another voice, distant but firm, from a place deep inside my heart.

Carter, it's not enough for you to be as good as everyone else. You have to be better than them.

My parents lived in a time when black people had to be better and work harder than white people in order to get the same chance to succeed. It was a lesson they drilled into us, though one I guess I had never fully understood—until that day. If I wanted to be principal, I would have to work harder than anyone else to prove myself.

I thought of Steven. We'd devised our plan in my backyard, and against all odds, here we were at the finish line. I'd seen how all this had pulled Steven out of his long rut and made him come alive again. And I knew how it had invigorated me and kept me from leaving. I believed Steven walked back into my life after nearly twenty years for a reason.

And that reason was that he needed me, and I needed him.

Now, all I had to do was swallow my pride and accept the interim title, and I would be principal. We would have a win. Our plan would have worked, maybe not exactly how we drew it up, but it would have worked nonetheless.

I decided I would keep the job. I would be interim principal.

I went to sleep believing the worst was behind me.

I was wrong.

A FEW DAYS LATER I was on the baseball field when Trish Garcia, the associate student body auditor and one of my best friends on the Beverly staff, came running up to me.

"Did you hear about the board meeting?" she asked.

I had no idea what she was talking about.

"A second meeting," she said. "They're going to have another meeting."

"Another meeting to do what?"

"Another meeting to vote on you being principal."

I was startled and confused. I thought I *was* principal. Why would there be another vote? What was happening?

"No one has said a word about this to me," I said. "Are you sure?"

"Carter, they called for another meeting. For next week."

I called our superintendent, and he confirmed there was another board meeting the next week and that the matter at hand was my candidacy.

"But I'm not a candidate!" I said. "They already voted me in. I'm the principal!"

He could only tell me what he knew—a meeting was scheduled for the following week.

Finally, I called Steven.

"What is going on?"

Steven was silent. That's when I knew I was in trouble.

"They found a loophole," he explained. "They found a way to vote on whether or not to approve your contract. Usually it's just a formality at this point, but . . ."

In baseball there is something called a brushback pitch—when a pitcher throws a fastball up high near your head to intimidate you and make you take bad swings.

Then there is the knockdown pitch, when he actually hits you in the head and you go down in a heap.

This was a knockdown pitch. This was my lowest moment.

It's the moment I realized an awful truth:

They might never stop trying to get rid of you.

CHAPTER

22

MY MOTHER RAISED me never to back down from a fight. But in the end you have to know what you're fighting for. You can't believe in something if you don't know what it is. And what, exactly, was I fighting for? For Beverly Hills High? For the place I thought of as home? Yes, I told myself, that's what I was fighting for. For my home.

But what if Beverly wasn't really my home? Could a place be called home when the people in it didn't want you there?

This latest tactic involved something called a consent calendar. That is when the board groups together around fifty to a hundred different items—from employee contracts to ordering supplies—and votes to approve them. Almost always, they vote on all the contracts at once since there is nothing to debate—the hiring itself had already been voted on and approved. Essentially, consent calendars were perfunctory votes.

Except this time it wasn't.

Those opposing me announced they wanted to pull my contract

from the calendar and put it up for fresh debate as a stand-alone issue. They had fought as hard as they could to make sure I wasn't principal before simply running out of time. Now they had found a way to put more time on the clock. Now they had time to sway just one more board member against me.

When I found out about the second vote, I didn't even tell Karen about it right away. I couldn't. I was even more embarrassed than the first time around, and I just couldn't face my family. There was no way I could tell my father; it would upset him too much. Besides, how do you explain that you've already been voted in as principal, except now you might get voted out before you even started?

How do you explain that?

I needed to be by myself and think.

Why were people so against me becoming principal? Was it just a couple of people on the board, or was it most of the community? Was it the whole city? How badly did people not want me to get the job? To what lengths would they eventually go?

And if they would stop at nothing, what did that say about what I thought was my family?

I had to face the fact that, in spite of everything I held dear, in spite of the fact that I bled Beverly, this place that meant so much to me might never fully accept me as one of its own.

And if that was true, then I was fighting the wrong fight.

I could stop the whole charade and just turn down the job. At least that would put an end to the turmoil I was subjecting my family to. I could leave Beverly and start fresh somewhere else. Steven would understand. Even if my contract was approved, my opponents would probably look for some other way to get me out. After all, I was only an *interim* principal. I could be fired at any time—all that was needed was another meeting, another loophole. You cannot win a battle that never ends. You can only endure it. And what was the point of that?

So much hurt and anger flooded my mind as I wrestled with myself, and I seriously considered stepping aside, even though that meant letting Steven down and letting Myra win.

But I only considered it for a moment.

Because something else ran through my mind that night—Martin Luther King Jr. and the civil rights movement.

Please understand, I am not in any way comparing what I went through at Beverly to the life-and-death battles fought by the brave civil rights pioneers. Those courageous men and women took a stand against unthinkable opposition, and many of them paid with their lives. A bureaucratic nightmare at Beverly Hills High School doesn't hold a candle to what they endured.

I'm talking about what I *learned* from their heroic struggle.

People like Martin Luther King Jr. and other civil rights advocates weren't so much fighting against the police, specific politicians, or people opposed to equal rights.

No, they were fighting *for* an issue, *for* a cause. They were taking a stand because they believed in something much bigger than themselves *and* their opponents.

They believed in what was right.

And they fought and died to give black people the chance to succeed on a fairer playing field. To give someone like me the chance to be a high school principal in Beverly Hills.

That night I decided that I wasn't going to make it easy for my opponents. If they wanted me out, they were going to have to say so—in public, to my face.

On May 27, I went to a conference room in Beverly Hills for the consent calendar meeting. The room had brown paneled walls, an

American flag on a standing pole, and an AV projector screen on one wall. Tables were pushed together to seat the five members of the school board. Steven Fenton gaveled the meeting to order.

THE MEETING WAS SCHEDULED DURING school hours on a weekday morning. That meant teachers and students and staffers at Beverly wouldn't be able to attend. Still, three dozen people or so crowded into the conference room. I sat by myself toward the back. Steven explained each board member would have a chance to state their position and that any speakers present would have two minutes to argue their case. Letters from people who couldn't make the meeting would also be read.

A middle-aged woman who'd sat on the school board years ago and taught in the district for a long time was one of the speakers.

"You have failed us by not doing due diligence," she scolded the board members. "The appropriate action would be to delay this vote until you, the board, have the opportunity to examine all the applicants for principal." Then she turned to the audience.

"What I am saying is not about Carter," she explained. "He sounds like a charming person to spend time with."

"This, for me, is not about Carter," echoed another speaker. "Carter is a wonderful, wonderful man. This is about process."

"I object to the process of selecting this new principal," another long-ago board member said. "Nothing in this statement is intended to question the ability and qualifications of Carter Paysinger. It is about the process."

Several other speakers criticized the "process" of selecting me. But the process was *exactly* the same as the one that had been used to select every principal for years. Procedurally, nothing had changed. The only difference this time around was me.

It wasn't easy for me to sit there and listen. I'd spent nearly forty years building relationships in this community and investing in the family I thought I was a part of, and in the past three months that had all been challenged and tossed in the trash. But it was even harder to sit there and hear people wax on about how nice or charming I was when the message under the surface was that, in the end, they didn't want me.

"Mr. Paysinger, I don't know you, but if you're single, I would love to date you. You're sort of cute," one woman who got up to speak jokingly said. "Meet you at the Peninsula, five o'clock."

Then she argued that by picking me the superintendent had shown "contempt and derision for the community."

There was no way I could know what was in that woman's heart when she said that. But from where I was sitting, and with everything I'd seen in my life, it was hard for me not to think my race had something to do with her comment. My father had talked about how racism can be subtle and hidden, always just below the surface and never on any decent person's lips. Was this what my father was talking about? Contempt and derision hidden behind a compliment?

What were these people really trying to say?

———

THEN SOMETHING REMARKABLE HAPPENED.

The board members began reading letters from everyone who couldn't make it to the meeting. I wasn't sure what to expect.

The first letter was from a special education teacher at Beverly.

"I urge you to approve the recommendation of Carter Paysinger as principal," it read. "He drops by my classroom to spend time with my students all the time, and he always stops and listens to me when I have a problem."

Next, another letter from a Beverly counselor:

"Carter knows how to inspire, motivate, and build a team that works together to accomplish its goal—the best education possible for our students. Carter brings out the best in his coworkers and students."

From a twenty-three-year teacher at Beverly:

"Since Mr. Paysinger's selection there has been a marked turn-around in energy and optimism among both staff and students. For the first time, I am looking forward to my classes in the fall."

From Beverly's head counselor:

"One of Carter's strengths is his ability to relate to *all* people. He consistently treats each and every person in an empathetic manner."

From one of my former players, now a teacher at Beverly:

"Why Carter is 'interim,' I'm still trying to figure out. He's spent three quarters of his life at Beverly. I became an educator and a coach because of Carter. You will not find a better person to lead this school."

From a previous school board member:

"I'm not really familiar with all the details of how Carter Paysinger was selected, but sometimes the choice is obvious. The only thing I don't know is why Carter Paysinger wasn't made principal years ago."

From a Beverly teacher:

"People in this district bandy about words like *respect, integrity,* and *leadership*. Carter is a living example of what those words mean."

From another teacher, who I didn't know well:

"I have an academic background, and if I were principal I would know English but not the other subjects. I would have to talk to people who were experts in those subjects. Any principal would have to do the same. We must also realize that Carter Paysinger's many years of experience at Beverly, as a student and in service to the school, is an invaluable resource. No outside candidate could ever hope to match it."

And from a sophomore student:

"I've only been at the school for two years, but I already look up to Carter Paysinger as a role model. He knows the school, the parents, and the students, and he is extremely honest and straightforward. Everyone in life needs a role model. Carter Paysinger is Beverly's role model."

So many times I had wondered if I was truly making a difference at Beverly. So many times I had asked myself if I was wasting my life.

I never expected to get my answer quite this way.

"WE'RE GOING RIGHT TO ITEM A," Steven said after the last letter was read. "Approval of interim principal of Beverly Hills High School. Do I have a motion?"

"Yes."

"Do I have a second?"

"Yes, I will second it."

"Okay, we have a first and second," Steven said. "The board can now discuss Item A."

Lisa was the first to speak.

"This is not to cast aspersions on Carter," she said. "I am very fond of Carter. I take us to task for lack of process." The vote, she said, "is a dog and pony show. We teach ethics in class, and we talk about Carter's integrity, his honesty, his decency, and he has a reservoir of those, a huge amount—but did this process? I cannot support voting for Mr. Paysinger because this is a vote against lack of process and good governance."

Myra was next. She had never been a teacher herself. She didn't go to Beverly, and she didn't spend a great deal of time there as a board member. She knew me through my dealings with the board, and through Steven and his family, but I cannot say she knew me all that well. She was always friendly and complimentary whenever we were together.

"Carter, my husband, my son, and I have known you for a long time," she began, "and we deeply respect you for a number of reasons. There is no question whatsoever that you are a man of tremendous integrity. We know how much you care for these students, how much you've done for this school, and how much history you have at Beverly.

"And that is why this is such a difficult conversation for me."

Myra's first objection had to do with my lack of classroom teaching experience.

"This is no knock on you, Carter, because you have had a tremendous career, but I think we all understand that your career has not been actively teaching in an academic classroom. I personally feel that firsthand experience in academic teaching is a vital requirement for the job of principal."

No one interrupted her to bring up Ben Bushman, who had never taught in a classroom. But Myra seemed to address that issue anyway.

"The old model of yesteryear," she said, "is not appropriate in the current day."

Then Myra spoke about my years of experience at Beverly.

"Carter, you are probably the one person who could galvanize people at Beverly and bring up school morale. But I do not think that is the only factor for us to consider. I reject the commonly held premise that the high school staff won't work with anyone unless that person has been chosen from their ranks, or unless that person 'bleeds Beverly'—which is a term I detest, by the way."

Myra argued that since a new school superintendent was going to be selected shortly it made sense to delay voting on me to give who-ever was hired a say. "That person must have some input, must play a part, in the selection of a principal," she said. "For us to do it this way is dismissive and disrespectful."

In truth, though, the last several superintendents brought in by the board had played no part in choosing Beverly's principal.

Finally, Myra, like so many others, went after the process.

"There were people with all kinds of experience and credentials applying to be principal in our district, and we ended up with three out of three—and I don't mean to be mean-spirited—we ended up with a strange coincidence that all three are personal friends of Steven Fenton. I apologize if this feels like I am being personal, but we have to be very mindful of who we are employing.

"It's human nature to select someone who is your friend, who does not challenge your comfort level," Myra said. "But I just feel very un-settled about this. For those reasons, sadly, I don't think I can support the recommendation of Carter Paysinger."

Well, I thought to myself, *there goes her vote.*

Brian Goldberg was next to speak. The first thing he said was, "I agree with Lisa one hundred percent in terms of the process."

If Brian was flipping his vote and suddenly siding with Lisa and Myra, it was all over.

———

BUT BRIAN HAD MORE TO say about the process.

"Yes, we need to look at a better way of doing things," he said. "But this process has been in place for *years* in this district. Every one of these selection panels has been stacked with employees from the school. And now here we come, and because our board president knows Carter, therefore the process is fixed. I think that's belittling."

Brian said he planned on voting for me.

So did the fourth board member, Jake Manaster.

Now it was Steven's turn.

"Pam," he said to the clerk, "please call the roll."

"What about your comments?" Myra said, surprised to see Steven moving so fast.

"I will save my comments for later."

"Are you kidding me?"

"I think everyone knows how I feel. Pam, please call the roll."

Myra tried to interrupt again, so Steven was more forceful.

"Pam, *call the roll*."

Pam called Brian's name.

"Yes," he said.

She called Lisa's name.

"No."

She called Myra's name.

"No."

She called Jake's name.

"Yes."

Two yes votes, two no votes, with only one vote left to be cast—Steven Fenton's.

Pam called Steven's name.

"Yes," he said. "The motion passes, three to two. Congratulations, Carter."

And that is how I became principal of Beverly Hills High.

CHAPTER

23

STEVEN AND I didn't celebrate that night. We didn't drink champagne or go out to a restaurant or even high-five each other. After he congratulated me in the board meeting, he moved quickly onto the next order of business. Basically we put our heads down and got on with our jobs. This was something we'd both learned when we were younger. Steven's old Little League coach had always told his kids, "We lose with class, and we win with class." Gloating, my mother would surely have said, is not the Paysinger way.

Steven's moment of triumph—the moment that stood out from all the rest—had actually come days earlier, after the closed-door meeting where I was first named interim principal.

As an undersized freshman at Beverly Steven had jumped on the school bus in his jersey and shoulder pads so he could rush home and show his father his new uniform. All he wanted was for his father to be proud of him.

Now, all these years later, after he came back to Beverly, after he found his way again and somehow helped me become principal, all he wanted to do was share that victory with his father.

After that first vote Steven raced to his parents' home in Beverly Hills. It had been two years since his father had been diagnosed with Parkinson's, but he hadn't really been himself for closer to five years. There were long stretches when he was simply absent from the world around him. Sometimes he didn't even seem to know who he was.

In Beverly Hills, however, everyone knows just who Frank Fenton is.

On the northwest corner of South La Cienega and Olympic Boulevard in Beverly Hills, where there used to be an asphalt parking lot, there is now a beautiful green multiuse athletic field. If you drive by it you will see young kids in their too-big uniforms racing around the bases, dreams of playing pro baseball swirling in their heads. Just outside the field sits a sturdy plaque that tells you why the field exists at all.

It tells you the field is called the Frank Fenton Field.

"Mr. Fenton's personal and tireless leadership, along with the support of his family and friends, made this conversion possible," the plaque reads in raised bronze type. "His contributions to the City of Beverly Hills have helped to make it the world renowned city we know today, and a wonderful community in which to live, work, and play."

Sometimes Steven finds himself driving by Frank Fenton Field, even when it's out of his way.

When he got to his parents' home on Wetherly Drive after the first board vote, he found his father sitting on the sofa by himself, watching TV. Frank looked up blankly when Steven walked in, then looked back at the TV. Lately he had seemed more confused, and the damage to the nerves in his mouth was so bad he could barely speak. Steven sat next to him on the sofa and took his father's hand in his.

"Dad, we did it," he said. "Carter is the principal."

Frank turned and looked at his son again. Steven studied his face for any sign of comprehension. He wanted to know his father understood what he'd done. He *needed* to know.

But there was nothing. A blank stare. Frank turned away and went back to his TV show.

Steven clutched his father's hand tighter. He hadn't been able to really get through to his father in months, so he wasn't sure why he expected to get through to him now. He realized he might never be able to connect with his father again.

Just then, Steven noticed something.

He noticed his father's eyes starting to water.

Frank wasn't saying anything—he couldn't say anything. He just sat, unmoving, as his eyes got redder and redder. Then he slowly turned to face his son again. He looked into his son's eyes through his own tears. This time Steven saw something there, in the face of the man he loved and admired so much. He saw a glimpse of comprehension. He saw understanding.

His father knew. He knew I was principal. He knew his son had done it.

Steven squeezed his father's hand, wiped away his own tears, and thought, *He's proud of me.*

I OFFICIALLY STARTED MY JOB as principal of Beverly on July 1, 2010, two weeks after the second vote. But by then I'd already spent months thinking about what I'd do if I won. A couple of days before the students arrived for fall semester, the board of education called a meeting to get a progress report from me. It would be my first official meeting with Myra since she'd twice voted against me.

I showed up with a long legal pad on which I'd written everything we'd already done and everything we wanted to do. I filled every single line of two long pages with items on my agenda—more than sixty in all. At the meeting I rattled them off, one after another, rapid-fire. Steven was there, and I'm sure I detected a faint smile as he listened to me tick items off my list.

When I finished, Myra looked up from her notes and over at me.

"Well, Carter," she said, "you certainly have hit the ground running. This is impressive."

The truth is I didn't need anyone to tell me I could do this job. Nearly forty years earlier I'd told Mr. Hoag I believed I could make the Beverly baseball team, and he'd been taken by my confidence. Well, I felt the same sense of confidence now—and for the same reason.

All along I believed that what Myra and others thought was my biggest liability—a sports mentality—was actually my greatest asset.

In my more than thirty years on the athletics side I'd come to see that students who played sports were generally more respectful, more motivated, and more productive than those who didn't. In team sports, a big part of being successful is learning how to work with and respect your teammates, and that was always the main message my coaches and I drilled into our players.

The skills they learned from their coaches were directly applicable to their studies and indeed their lives. They learned discipline and focus and determination, and all of those things helped them develop into fine young students and people. I always had the impression our players were doing the right things the right way, and now I wanted every other student—and staffer—at Beverly to buy into that way of thinking.

From day one I brought something of a sports mentality to my tenure as principal. Early on I broke from tradition and held a big meeting for the entire staff. Normally, there were separate meetings for certificated workers—the teachers and administrators—and classified workers—custodians, cafeteria workers, and other support staff. I wanted to do away with that distinction.

We gathered in the Salter Theater on campus, and I gave my first big speech as principal. Honestly, it didn't feel all that different from one of my locker room speeches to my players.

"Look, no one comes into a season saying, 'I want to be a .500 team this year,'" I said. "No one starts by saying, 'We want to be mediocre.' You start by saying, 'We want to be the best.' So that's what I want all of you to be thinking, and that's what I want all of you to say—'We want to be the best school we can be, and one of the top public schools in the country.' We've been there before; we know we can do it.

"So let's go out and do it.

"I want us to think of ourselves as a team. Every one of you is as important as anyone else. If a teacher is lazy, the kids can't learn. If the cafeteria is filthy, that gets in the way of a kid's education. We all have important jobs to do, and the only way we can pull this off is if we all work together, as a team, toward the same goal—making Beverly Hills High School great."

And yet a speech is just a speech—by itself it can't win you any games. The high school had one principal, three assistant principals, eight counselors, and just under two thousand students. I didn't kid myself into thinking that turning Beverly around would be easy.

HARD WORK. PERSEVERANCE. COURAGE. FAITH. If you attack a problem with all of those things, there are few obstacles you can't overcome.

But sometimes, all the hard work in the world isn't enough. All the perseverance and courage and faith aren't enough. Sometimes, a situation is out of your control. No amount of wishing and hoping and praying can change it.

My wife Karen and I, it seemed, were facing just such a situation.

I never told anyone at Beverly about the struggles Karen and I were having starting a family. It was just too personal and painful to share with anyone. And after five failed adoptions we'd both decided we were done. It was time to put the struggle behind us and move on.

That's when our adoption attorney called and said, "Give me one more shot. Don't give up just yet."

I sat down with Karen, and we talked it over and, reluctantly, we agreed to at least get on the phone and speak with the prospective candidate, a seventeen-year-old pregnant black woman living in South Carolina. Neither of us could imagine going through yet another failed adoption, so we went in with no expectations that things would work out. We just agreed to a phone call.

Karen and I were in our car outside my credit union when Karen's phone rang. It was Charlotte, the pregnant young woman. Karen spoke with her for a few minutes before Charlotte passed her on to her mother. Karen spoke with her for a long time; then Charlotte's father took the phone. Before we knew it, Karen had been on the phone for an hour. I stayed parked outside the credit union; I didn't dare pull into traffic for fear we'd lose our cell connection. We clung to the slightest positive sign, and Karen's long conversation was just that.

When she finally hung up, she turned to me and said, "Carter, this is the one. These are the ones."

A week later Karen and I landed in Colombia, South Carolina; drove thirty-five minutes to Orangeburg; and met Charlotte's family in a restaurant off the highway.

The first thing we noticed was that Charlotte didn't look pregnant.

We looked at each other as if to say, "Oh no, not again." Charlotte was tall, around five foot ten, and though she was due to give birth in a month, as far as we could tell there was no baby bump.

But after we shook hands with Charlotte and her parents and went into the restaurant, they assured us Charlotte was indeed pregnant. She'd met a military man at a party, but he'd disappeared before she knew she was pregnant and she had no idea who he was. Because Charlotte's father was a pastor and a board member in his school district, he didn't want neighbors to know his daughter was pregnant. So she hid it under baggy clothing. Not even her brother, who was in college, knew Charlotte was expecting.

It made me kind of sad to know that Charlotte had to hide her pregnancy, but I also understood what their family was going through. Charlotte's parents wanted her to have a happy, fulfilling life, same as my parents had wanted for me. Raising a child at seventeen would certainly make that more difficult. And Charlotte herself had so many dreams for her future; she was a star basketball player and had big plans for college and beyond. She seemed certain about wanting to give up her baby for adoption. Like her parents, she was making a tough but practical decision. But they were adamant about one thing: if they were going to give her baby up, they had to be sure that child would be part of a stable, loving family.

It turned out Karen and I weren't there to interview Charlotte and her parents. They were there to interview us.

Luckily, our lunch went on for more than five hours. Before long we were all laughing and joking like old friends. Karen and I went home feeling more hopeful than we'd ever been.

A few weeks later, Charlotte's due date came and went with no baby. That didn't mean anything, but to us even the slightest hitch was magnified. Just a couple of days after her due date, we got a call from Charlotte's parents—her doctors were going to induce labor. We got on a plane and flew to South Carolina and checked into a hotel near the hospital. The next morning we made our way to the maternity ward.

Karen went into Charlotte's room with her mother, while I stayed with Charlotte's father in a waiting area. I was so conditioned to expect bad news that every time a nurse passed the room I felt my heart jump. I tried my best not to let Charlotte's father see how nervous I was, even though he was pretty anxious himself. We talked about sports and politics—anything but babies.

Suddenly a nurse stopped in the doorway.

"It's a boy," the nurse said. "They're both doing great."

We rushed to Charlotte's room like two little kids. When I walked in, I saw Karen standing by Charlotte's bed as Charlotte held the child. She'd been in the room the whole time; she had breathed out when Charlotte breathed out and pushed when Charlotte pushed and cried when Charlotte cried. When the baby arrived, her eyes got wide and her heart exploded with love. The boy was so small and so bundled I couldn't even tell what he looked like. So many different emotions raced through me in that moment.

I congratulated Charlotte and hugged her mother and father. Before I could make my way over to Karen, I noticed Charlotte holding the baby up in the air.

"Here," she said to Karen. "You hold him."

Karen gently took the boy from Charlotte and held him with both arms. The way she held him seemed so natural and motherly, and the way she stared at his face so loving and real. Seeing him in her arms, his eyes closed, his tiny body tucked safely against her, triggered a wave of emotion. I felt it in my stomach and then in my heart and then in my lips, which were trembling. I felt my composure slip away. The sight of Karen finally cradling a child was more than I could take. I wept in that hospital room, and looking around, I saw everyone else crying, too.

Charlotte and her family let us take the baby the very next day. We'd never gotten this far in the process before, and we were stunned to suddenly have a child in our care. At the very least we had expected the handover to be slow and possibly complicated, but Charlotte's family trusted us so much—and knew how badly we wanted a child—they had no qualms about giving us the baby.

Karen and I marveled at the tiny creature entrusted to our care. He was so beautiful, more beautiful than anything we'd ever seen. But he was also small and fragile, and like a lot of first-time parents we were worried we might somehow break him. Honestly, we didn't know what to do.

What I do know is we fell instantly in love.

Nevertheless, down deep, I know Karen and I were both thinking the same thing. Charlotte could still change her mind. We couldn't be certain this child was ours to keep. That was just a fear we had to live with.

On top of that, the tiny boy was jaundiced, and we had to keep him under a heat lamp. Karen had to continually position him on something called a BiliBed, and when he got fidgety and rolled off, Karen gently moved him back under the light. I remember thinking, *Dear Lord, what have we done?* To make matters worse, I also had to fly back to California that same day and leave Karen alone with the baby in South Carolina. I'd just started my first semester as principal a month earlier, and I had to be there for parent-teacher conferences no matter what. Karen understood, but she was understandably anxious about staying behind with the baby—a baby that wasn't even officially ours yet.

When Karen found herself alone in that hotel room with the baby, the reality of the situation truly hit home. She had no one to help her—it was just her and the boy. One minute she'd been childless, and the next she was a mother. In an instant her whole world changed. Karen had helped take care of our nephew, but she hadn't changed a diaper in years. Her family still kidded her about the time she put a diaper on backward. And yet the first time she had to change the baby's diaper in the hotel room, she did it as if it were the most natural thing in the world to her. "I was nervous," she told me, "but what I felt for the baby was stronger than the nervousness. I felt the mommy bond. I felt it right away."

Adoption officials in South Carolina spent nearly two weeks fussing over the paperwork. Day after day went by with no formal approval of the adoption. In that time I had to fly back and forth from LA two times. Karen spent two weeks in that hotel room cradling and swaddling and carrying that crying little baby, all the while unsure she would get to keep him.

In the South some mothers and grandmothers say a new baby shouldn't ever go outside for the first two or three months because they are so vulnerable to germs. But Karen had no choice. She had to take the baby outside so she could buy diapers and formula and supplies. The first time she took him, she carefully latched him into his baby seat and put a blanket loosely over him to keep away the germs.

"Okay, little man, it's just you and me on this adventure," she said as she started the rental car. "Let's do it."

From the start it was clear to Karen and me that this time was different from all the rest. This time we had the baby in our hands. As badly as we'd been hurt by other failed adoptions, not getting to keep this child would, by far, be the most devastating setback of all. It was such a horrible, unimaginable thought that we never brought it up. We just went about our business and cared for that little baby and waited for the phone to ring.

And in that hotel room something remarkable happened to Karen.

One day the baby was squirming and crying, so Karen took him and laid him down on her chest. Immediately, the baby stopped crying. He just lay there and slept, breathing in and out, as peaceful and perfect as could be. After a while Karen picked him up and put him back on the bed, but as soon as she did he started squirming and whimpering again. Karen put him back on her chest, and the crying stopped. He was letting her know that was where he wanted to be— on her chest, with her. Karen let him stay there as long as he wanted, and she gently stroked his hair and touched his tender skin and marveled at how tiny he was, and as she did those things a powerful feeling swept over her—a feeling she had never before experienced in her life.

"It was the feeling of loving my child," she told me later. "I was surprised by how strong it was. It was a different kind of love from any I ever knew. I felt it everywhere in my body. It just kicked in, and it overwhelmed me. I lay there with that child on my chest and I just cried. I cried and cried and cried."

I cried, too, when Karen told me that. Because I knew that in that hotel room, for better or worse, Karen and the baby had bonded forever.

———

AND THEN IT HAPPENED.

One night when I was home getting ready to fly back to South Carolina, Karen called me from the hotel room.

"They approved it!" she said, her voice cracking. "They approved the adoption!"

That tiny, jaundiced, beautiful baby boy was ours.

Karen flew back to Los Angeles with the baby, and I met them at the airport. I waited by the arrival gate as the first few passengers came through. A businessman, a young couple, a family with two small children. I silently wished they'd walk faster. Then I saw a woman, a beautiful, smiling woman, come through the gate holding a tiny infant in her arms. This was Karen. This was my wife. And she was holding my son.

I raced to Karen and hugged her and the baby. I hugged them tight. Weary travelers brushed by us on their way to their own lives, but we were in no hurry to go. That hug in the terminal was the very first time the three of us were together as an official family.

I held onto that moment as long as I could.

We had experienced so much heartbreak, so much pain, and yet it had all been worth it. God blessed us more than we could ever have imagined.

"God knew what he was doing," Karen told me. "I am a better mother now than I would have ever been in my twenties. That's why I feel so blessed. He has blessed us with love."

Charlotte allowed us to name the baby ourselves. We were so grateful to her and her family that we knew just what we wanted to name him: Chandler, in honor of his biological mother. She was thankful to us for that, but really we were the ones who owed her everything. She'd helped make our dream come true—a dream that, for the longest time, looked like it was unattainable. I thought of that every time I got up in the middle of the night to comfort little Chandler; I thought about how lucky we were.

Chandler is just about three years old now. He's incredibly energetic, and he loves trucks and sports. And you know what? The kid can really throw a ball. I think he's got a future in sports.

LITTLE BABIES GROW UP TO be children, children become teenagers, and teenagers sometimes get into trouble. My son, Chandler, had a
long way to go before he hit his teen years, but my students at Beverly
were right at that vulnerable age. As their principal there were times I
had to be tough on them, to keep them on the right track.

That's why, in my first year as principal, I called the Beverly Hills
Police Department and had them raid the campus.

Fifteen officers and eight drug-sniffing dogs swept through classroom after classroom. One student, high on something, jumped out a
classroom window as soon as he saw the cops and landed on an adja-
cent roof.

"We've got a kid on the roof," the teacher told the officer. The police talked him down and took him to the station.

Why had I called the cops? Why had I sent armed guards and
trained dogs into classrooms?

I did it because drugs have no place at Beverly.

Some people in the community felt the drug sweep was excessive,
and believe me, it wasn't a decision I made lightly. But I firmly believed
we needed to do something dramatic. One of Beverly's biggest issues
when I became principal was one that plagues high school campuses
all over America: drugs on campus. Somehow we had to reverse the
culture that was taking root. And so I called for a raid.

I think we got five or six hits, but that was only part of the point.
What I really wanted to do was send a message to every student on
campus. I'd seen a lot of smart, promising kids get destroyed by drugs
in South Central, and I'd never forgotten the impact of my cousin
Freddy showing me that cocaine in the fridge. In a way I was passing
along what Freddy taught me to my students.

An unlikely lesson handed down through time.

My policy as principal was zero tolerance. One day we found a student with a very small amount of pot on him. We could have given him a warning or sent him home, but instead I called the police. The student was taken to the police station, questioned, and released. Then I suspended him for five days.

Afterward, I got a visit from his mother, who was furious. She couldn't believe I'd called the cops on her son. But I saw this as a great opportunity to teach her child a lasting lesson.

"Look, your son didn't get arrested; he got off with a suspension this time," I told her. "But if he's found with drugs on the street he's not going to get off; he's going to go to jail. This is a great chance for both of us to teach your son a lesson that could save his life."

Not every parent approved of my methods. But over time, more and more of them did.

In my first semester at Beverly the number of students suspended went way up from the previous semester. To some, so many kids missing so much school just didn't seem like a positive thing.

But in my second semester, the number of student suspensions went way down.

The message was getting through.

I made many other changes. Some were minor, like assigning our groundskeeping crew to add Heath Avenue, one of the streets bordering Beverly, to their schedule. The street had long been filthy and unkempt, so we cleaned it up and repainted the curbs red and blue. Heath Avenue, and Beverly, suddenly *looked* better.

Other changes were more significant. Beverly already had a dress code—boys couldn't wear anything gang-related and their pants had to be above the waist, while the girls couldn't wear halter tops or miniskirts. Yet students were routinely breaking these rules, and one of my first orders of business was fixing that.

We emailed all the parents, explaining the dress code and announcing we were going to strictly enforce it. If we saw a female student wearing a halter top on campus, we'd give her a T-shirt to wear the first time, then send her home if it happened again. If I saw a boy wearing droopy jeans, I'd tell him to pull them up. If he couldn't get them above the waist, we'd send him home, too. We actually got a little resistance from one of the school board members, who said, "It's hard for boys to find pants that go above the waist nowadays." Well, I didn't buy that. There are plenty of pants that don't sag, and we couldn't have kids walking around campus with their butts hanging out. So we stuck to the policy, and we sent a lot of kids home.

We did the same thing with Beverly's cheating policy—we didn't make it tougher; we just started enforcing it. Over the years the definition of cheating had changed for many students and even many teachers. For instance, copying another student's homework wasn't regarded as cheating by some. But to me, it was. So we began going after students who, by our definition, were cheating. A first offense, and you'd get an F on the test or assignment. A second offense, and your class grade would be lowered by a letter. A third offense, and you'd probably fail the class.

Another problem was actually proving that a student *was* cheating. A lot of times it was clear to teachers that someone had copied a homework assignment or cheated on a test, but they couldn't prove it. So all a student had to do was deny he or she had cheated. If we punished him anyway, he'd go home and complain to his parents, who would call me and insist, "But my kid swears he didn't cheat."

That's not how it worked when I was growing up. If a teacher told my mother I had cheated, that meant I had cheated. I couldn't go home and plead my case—my folks refused to hear it. I guess my parents understood a kid will *always* say, "I didn't cheat." So I began challenging the parents who automatically took their child's side.

Did some parents get ticked off? You bet. But over time they came to trust our motives, and the policy worked. Incidents of cheating went way down.

But despite all that, in the business of education there is only one real marker of progress, and that is standardized test scores.

Whether I was seen as a successful principal would hinge mainly on the results of the CST—the California Standardized Test given to all high school students at the end of every year. Those were the tests the state used to determine your API score—the ultimate measure of academic achievement.

I could tell kids to pull up their pants all I wanted, but if I didn't help raise our API score my time as Beverly's principal would be short.

———

IN SPORTS, WE TALK ABOUT something called discretionary energy. It refers to the amount of energy a coach is able to get from his players. If you're a good coach, you can get your players to push themselves as hard as they think they can be pushed. But the best coaches find a way to push their players *further*—producing extra bursts of energy they didn't even know they were capable of. This extra energy—an extra gear—is often the difference between being a good player and being a champion. The coach who can motivate his players to produce it is the coach who ends up holding up the trophy.

To me, every teacher at Beverly was a kind of coach. They all had a team of students, and it was up to them to motivate those students to attack their studies with extra discretionary energy. To not just work as hard as they believed they could, but to work even harder. In my time at Beverly I met a lot of exceptional teachers, but I also met some who seemed dejected and tired. They'd allowed fatigue and maybe even despair to turn them into uninspiring teachers who were looking to just get through the day. I believed that if I couldn't change that way of thinking, I would fail as principal.

And so I focused on our teachers and on getting them to rediscover their passion so they in turn could inspire passion in their students. There is no magic bullet that produces higher test scores. I didn't implement any new methods of teaching or test taking. I just spent a lot of time in classrooms, talking to teachers and trying to make them feel more involved and more accountable. I wanted them to form the kinds of bonds with their students that my old coaches and teachers had formed with me. I wanted them to feel *invested* in how their students fared. To believe, as I did, that we were all in this together—teachers, students, parents, custodians, cafeteria workers, everyone. I wanted Beverly to be a team again.

At the end of my first year all the students at Beverly took the CST. The test has four subjects: language arts, science, history, and math. Depending on what year you were in you'd be tested in one of those subjects. The multiple-choice tests were four hours each on four consecutive days. A couple of months later, we would know exactly how Beverly stacked up against every other high school in the state.

For years heading into my tenure as principal, the school's API scores had been in the low 800s. From 1999 to 2010, we averaged a score of 821. This wasn't a terrible score, but it wasn't great. The really elite schools scored somewhere in the 900s. So an average of 821 was just okay. And as my mother told me over and over, "just okay" isn't good enough. I knew I had to get those scores up somehow.

Still, I didn't expect us to make any kind of huge jump right away, and no one else did either. Schools are big, cumbersome beasts that move impossibly slowly, and sometimes change is measured in decades, not years. My fondest hope was that we'd go up a handful of points. My greatest fear was that we'd drop, possibly even below 800.

I tried not to think of the tests at all during the two months it took the state to grade them. I didn't want to drive myself crazy. Finally, one day in August, during the summer after my first year, I got a call from one of my assistant principals. She had just spoken to the district's assistant superintendent, who gave her our CST score.

"Carter," she said, "you're not going to believe this."

"What is it?" I asked, my heart in my throat.

"We went up."

"We did?"

"Yes. We went from 838 to 872."

"What? We scored 872?!"

That was not only the biggest jump from one year to the next in the history of Beverly Hills High, *it was the highest score the school had ever recorded.*

I sat down and let out a deep breath, and I had three thoughts.

The first was, *Thank you, God.*

The second was, *Momma, I hope you're proud of me.*

The third was, *Next year, we're gunning for 900.*

———

STEVEN FENTON STEPPED DOWN AS the board of education president just a few months after I started as principal of Beverly. He'd done what he set out to do, and now it was time for him to move on. On his last day as board president, with the very last item on his agenda, he put the matter of my interim status to a vote.

He had the board clerk call the roll, and the same five board people who had twice voted on my fate voted on my future once again.

The final tally was 5 to 0.

I was no longer interim principal of Beverly Hills High School.

I was just Principal Paysinger.

AFTERWORD

M OST MORNINGS I get up before the sun rises, at 4:30 a.m. I put on shorts and a T-shirt, sometimes three if it's cold, and lace up my old Avia running shoes. I kiss my wife good-bye; then it's straight to my car without stopping in the kitchen—no breakfast for me. A traffic-free, twenty-minute drive takes me where I need to go.

Beverly Hills.

Once I'm there, I park my car, stretch a bit, and start my run. Up South Lasky to where Santa Monica meets Wilshire, west on Whittier all the way up to Sunset. I run on Sunset, past Rodeo Drive, past the Will Rogers Park, heading to Hollywood. After a while on Sunset I circle back to Elm Drive, back to Santa Monica, back to Lasky. The morning sun is just peeking over the mountains now, and I'm on my sixth or seventh mile and sweating pretty good. After all, I'm not a young man anymore.

But you know what—I'm not old, either.

My name is Carter Paysinger, and I'm fifty-five years old. I was raised in South Central, Los Angeles. If you ask me what I do, I will say that I teach. I'm a teacher. One way or another I've been teaching kids for close to forty years. I'm not an athlete, not anymore anyway, but I like to stay in good shape, which is why I take my jogs.

But that's not the only reason I run.

I do it for peace of mind.

I don't listen to music because I like the quiet. Sometimes the only sounds are birds chirping and my own voice, saying prayers. I pray for strength and for guidance, and I pray that I'll always do the right thing. I talk to God, and I thank him for my beautiful family, for our safety, and for helping us get through tough times.

Often I talk to my momma, Lessie B. I tell her I love her and miss her every day. I let her know how things are going in my life.

This is my ritual just about every morning—running through the shiny streets of Beverly Hills. Past the cream-white mansions and the towering hedges and the manicured lawns and the swaying palms. There is something very magical about Beverly Hills, as if it's not only a place but also a feeling, a state of mind. Running through its streets, you can feel for a moment like you're running through paradise.

And when I'm done running, I am back at the spot where I parked my car, in a lot behind the athletic department of Beverly Hills High School. I shower, put on a suit, and start my working day. My head is clear, and my heart is strong.

There are children to teach and lessons to be learned.

————————

DURING MY FIRST MONTHS AS principal no one was more supportive, more encouraging, than my old friend Steven Fenton.

We spoke on the phone a lot, and from time to time he'd come by campus to hang out in my office—same as all those years ago when he'd bring me a hero sandwich for lunch. We didn't talk much about the battle that led to me being principal; basically, we're both for-ward-looking guys. But there was a subtext to our conversations, something only he and I could share—a satisfaction that we had fought the good fight together and won.

It was great to see Steven so alive and full of purpose, in contrast to the way I had found him in the tunnel just a few years before. He had become the Steven I always had expected him to be. What thrilled me the most, however, was seeing how happy he was. And not all of that had to do with our victory at Beverly.

A lot of it had to do with Steven falling in love.

His record in the romance department wasn't great—zero for two in marriages, along with some ill-advised relationships. Still, I believed it was only a matter of time before someone came along and saw the goodness in Steven's heart and turned that record around.

Such a person did come along.

That person was Leeza Gibbons, the beautiful and popular TV host. Steven's relationship with Leeza developed and grew throughout the time Steven and I were trying to turn things around at Beverly. Her calming presence in his life was such a blessing in the chaos, but early on Steven worried the press would drag Leeza into the controversy as a part of the measures taken to derail us. In the end he needn't have worried—Leeza was fearless and unwavering in her support. She had watched her own father—a teacher, a principal, and a superintendent all through her childhood—fight for things that were unconventional, things that mattered. And she stood right with us throughout the course of our battle.

What impressed Leeza the most about Steven was how thoughtful and gently supportive he was of her and her three children. After being responsible for some five thousand children in the Beverly Hills school district, Steven figured he could handle a few more. Lexi, Troy, and Nathan quickly became a fixture in Steven's life, and the love between all of them continued to grow.

"Most men I knew would steal all the oxygen in a room, but Steven isn't that way," Leeza says now. "He jumped in and helped me with my kids and with my charity foundation, but he did it quietly. He wasn't trying to get credit or be the hero. He was just being heroic."

Steven proposed to Leeza on the front lawn of a home they bought together and gave her a platinum band with the initials *L* and *S* on either side of the initials of Leeza's three children. They were married on the roof of the hotel where they first met, in a private ceremony officiated by Leeza's two older children, who were ordained as ministers just for the occasion. They are a beautiful couple, and the greatest gift Leeza gave Steven, I believe, is the gift of allowing him to fail.

Steven was the kind of guy who wanted to save everyone. He never wanted to let anyone down. And so, when he lost his way in life, he fell into a pattern of inauthentic relationships. It's something Steven's friend had coined as "the Fenton Five." Because he didn't want to disappoint anyone, he would overextend himself with ten different obligations, never allowing himself to spend more than five minutes with anyone. He'd pop in, stay five minutes, then run off to the next obligation. He wasn't sharing his true self with anyone.

"Because he's so generous, he offers his energy to everyone, and he can exhaust it," says Leeza. "And I think it was my job to reassure Steven that it was okay to not have an answer for everything. He doesn't have to solve every problem. Steven needed permission to *not* be perfect."

When Steven finally stopped running and focused his energy on something that really mattered—fixing Beverly, for instance—he was once again able to accomplish great things. The fact that I got to play a part in helping him regain his focus and passion fills me with pride.

Being elected principal was great.

But seeing Steven happy was an even better reward.

A LOT OF MY STORY has to do with teaching and learning lessons. Some of the lessons in this book were handed down from my great-grandparents to their children, and then to their children, and eventually all the way down to me.

And one day they will be passed on again, to my son, Chandler.

There is a word for this passage of lessons: "tradition."

I want Chandler to understand where he came from. I want him to feel the same big boulders of support beneath him that I feel every day. I want him to know he is part of a bigger story—part of a rich, enduring history. I know it is up to me to make sure he understands all this.

When Chandler was just one year old, I took him with me to a familiar place—Tolliver's Barber Shop on the corner of Western and Florence in South Central.

I was eight years old when Lawrence Tolliver first cut my hair there nearly half a century ago. Since then, my dear friend Lawrence is the *only* man who has ever cut my hair.

Now I was back with my own son in tow. In my day haircuts were $2.50. Now they were up to $12.50—still a bargain. Lawrence, older now but just as spry, put a booster seat in the barber's chair, and I slid my boy into it. My father came with us and held onto Chandler, or else he might have slid right out. Chandler looked at himself in the mirror with his big round eyes as Lawrence cut his hair. When he was finished, I scooped up my son and ran my hand over his smooth head.

Just a couple of weeks ago I brought Chandler, who's three now, to

Tolliver's for his usual haircut. And for the first time we didn't have to hold him in the chair.

"Come on, Chandler, it's your turn. Hop on up," Lawrence told him, and before I could react, Chandler climbed into the chair on his own. Lawrence draped an apron around him and gave him his first big boy's cut. Around him, men talked sports and argued politics and laughed at bad jokes and tried to fix the world.

The music of Tolliver's has never, ever changed.

"TRADITION," "LEGACY," "CONTINUITY"—THESE WORDS MEAN something. These words matter.

Much will happen in your life to knock you off course. Things may happen to make you question your basic beliefs and values. It was painful for me that so few people I knew and trusted—people I considered friends—spoke publicly on my behalf when I ran for principal. I asked some of them to speak out, but in the end they didn't. They quietly rooted for Steven and me but felt they weren't in a position to do so beyond closed doors. There was a price to pay for supporting me, and they weren't willing to pay it.

But then, just when your faith is most tested, something comes to steady your heart again. Not long ago I went to see a few of my former Beverly athletes play in a college football game at San Diego State. One of them came up and sat next to me in the stands. He was a white kid, the former student body president at Beverly, and an all-around great young man.

"Coach, what was the deal with the board vote?" he asked me.

"What do you mean?"

"Well, when we heard you were running for principal, we all thought it was a no-brainer. We thought you would sail right in."

"Well, it got a little more complicated than that," I said.

"Is it true some people had a problem with your race?" he asked.

"Yeah, some of them did."

He sat there for a moment, pondering that. Then he turned to face me.

"You know, Coach, I never thought of you as black or white," he said. "I just thought of you as Carter."

I didn't let him see how much that comment meant to me. I just smiled and thanked him. But the truth is, his words meant more to me than I can say. All the other negative stuff washed away in that moment.

Doesn't matter where you came from. What matters is where you stand.

Every one of the lessons I mention in this book—indeed every challenge we ever face in life—leads to the same result. If we heed the lessons and meet the challenges, we become better people. We *improve.* That is the essence of our story—the idea that we must always strive to be better.

To get there, we all need a lot of help. If you are truly blessed, you will have parents like mine—strong, devoted, caring. You will have a mother like my mother, who relentlessly fought for her children and their futures. You will have a family like my family, which is noisy and loving and endlessly supportive. You will have a community like my community at Beverly Hills High, which embraced me as a skinny little kid from South Central and, a few tough times notwithstanding, embraces me today.

You will have a partner like my wife, Karen, who is simply the most loving, miraculous companion a man could ever hope to have.

And if you are blessed, you will have a friend like my friend Steven Fenton.

I've taken so many journeys in my life, as we all do: from South Central to Beverly Hills, from assistant football coach to principal, from a son to a father. And I hope that, at every step, I learned things that made me better, that helped me reach even higher.

And that I, in turn, passed those lessons along to others.

"Don't settle for just being good," my mother always told me. "Strive to be better. Strive to be great."

Hopefully, I will never stop striving to be great.

None of us ever should.

ACKNOWLEDGMENTS

CARTER:

THIS BOOK IS dedicated to my parents, Lessie and Carter Paysinger Sr. For more than fifty years, my mother and father made an unbelievable team. Their unshakable emphasis on family, integrity, and character, along with their unrelenting love, commitment, and sacrifice, will live through me and my brothers forever.

To my best friend, my confidante, and my beautiful wife, Karen, thank you! Your unwavering love and support has been the foundation of my adult life. For thirty-seven years you have been my world, my rock, and without a doubt the strength of our relationship. You made me not only the beneficiary of an incredible wife, but my mother-in-law, Bernice, and my late father-in-law, Joseph Jackson, were instrumental in my development as a young man.

Three years ago Karen and I were blessed beyond belief. We became parents to a beautiful baby boy, Chandler Brian Paysinger. Chandler is the light of our life, and he amazes us daily. We are determined to give him the opportunity to grow up with as much love and happiness as we were able to enjoy.

"It takes a village" could not have been a more accurate description of our family. Thank you to all of our aunts, uncles, and cousins. Growing up with the best brothers in the world—Carlton, Donald, and Vonzie—allowed me to learn the true meaning of loyalty, compromise, and teamwork. We grew up as best friends supporting and loving each other. The experiences we shared I will always cherish. As adults, we were joined by some extraordinary women. My wife's sisters, Deborah and Sheryl; the love of Vonzie's life, Coleen; and Donald's wife, Autumn, are all tremendous additions to the Paysinger family. I would also like to acknowledge all of their children, our talented nieces and nephews: Justin, Spencer, Cameron, Cheyenne, Sierra, Reina, and Maya.

My experiences would never have been what they were without the help and support of all of my former students, mentors, and colleagues. I've had a tremendous run from the athletic department to the main office; thank you all for your support and commitment. Also, a special thank-you goes to Chuck Kloes. I owe you more than anyone could ever imagine. Rob Wigod, thank you for enhancing my career by giving me an opportunity to be a member of the governing body of high school sports in the state of California.

Reed Aljian and Alan Jackson are two of the best attorneys in the country. I am truly grateful for your support and friendship.

Thank you to all of my childhood friends, as well as my current friends, in both Beverly Hills and South Central, Los Angeles. Your friendships were and will always be invaluable. I would like to acknowledge Lawrence Tolliver, our barber for more than forty years, for his friendship and support to so many of us in the community. Additionally, I would like to acknowledge our crew, our inner circle of friends; you know who you are. Thank you for always being there.

Frank and Judie Fenton, your love and support for the Paysinger family over the years have been very much appreciated and will never be forgotten. Finally, Steven, I am as proud of you today as I was twenty-seven years ago when you were my gutsy, determined, and hugely successful second baseman.

STEVEN:

I WANT TO thank the love of my life, Leeza Gibbons, for her unwavering and tireless support of the book. On our first date, I shared with her the story of my friendship with Carter and the very reasons why I wanted to give back to my community. Six years later, her commitment to me has been nothing short of staggering, voluminous, and irrefutable. Standing by my side, having my back at all times, and loving me in a way I had never known, Leeza is simply the best person I have ever known.

Leeza also gave me the gift of becoming a stepdad to three phenomenal children, Lexi, Troy, and Nathan, all of whom have captured my heart in such a profound way.

This transition into becoming a stepfather was seamless and due in large part to their father, Steve Meadows. He supported me from day one, and because of it my relationship with the kids flourished. I will be forever grateful to him because of it.

Thanks to my father-in-law, Carlos Gibbons, for being a true inspiration and role model. As an educational leader in the Deep South in the '50s and '60s, he was progressive, aggressive, and determined to make sure all people were treated fairly regardless of the color of their skin. He's the real hero in our family.

I also want to thank my mom for her unwavering love and guidance throughout this entire experience. In our community, my mom is loved, not so loved, respected, feared, envied. But to me, she's just Mom, and I love her unconditionally.

This book wouldn't be complete without acknowledging my ninety-eight-year-old Nana and my brother (Gary) and my sister (Jenny), all of whom have taken heat for some of my decisions but never wavered in their support of me (or Carter). I'm so fortunate to have them not only as my family but also as my best friends.

The person responsible for giving birth to this book is Lacy Lynch. From conception through inception, this young, dynamic super-agent from Dupree/Miller came up with the idea for the book, sold it, and stood by our side until the very end. Her unshakeable faith in us was more than we deserved, and she gets the sole credit for making this book happen. She wasn't just our agent; she was our partner on this entire journey.

A journey made possible because of Jessica Wong, Becky Nesbitt, Jonathan Merkh, and the entire team at Howard Books/Simon & Schuster. It was Jessica's passion and unequivocal support that became a game changer for us.

We would be remiss if we didn't thank Alex Tresniowski and Bettina Gilois for their significant contributions to the book. They helped give shape and context to our story, and we are thankful for their efforts.

To the late Ron Brown for pushing me at a young age to be the best that I could be, and to Jeff Witjas and Chuck Weingarten for continuing the tradition by pushing me at this older age to be even better.

Thank you to my former coaches Jim Barker, Bill Erickson, and Joe Sutton for their guidance and mentoring. To my former college coach, Doug Bletcher. thank you for warning me that, "Steve(er), you always straddle that line as a player between aggressiveness and stupidity." I think about that often as I catch myself drifting toward that line.

My former school district teammates, Alex Cherniss, Dick Douglas, Pat Escalante, Jerry Gross, Sylvester Harris, Dave Hoffman, Steve Kessler, Dawnalyn Murakawa-Leopard, Irene Stern, Rich Waters, and Pam Kraushaar, thank you for believing in the vision . . . and in me.

Under great pressure, my former school board teammates Brian Goldberg and Jake Manaster didn't flinch as they secured their place in history when they voted for Carter. Jake knew which side of history he wanted to be on, as he was Carter's third and final vote. He forever changed Beverly as he singlehandedly tipped the scales in Carter's favor. When people in our community look back at this historic 3-2 vote, Jake will be remembered as the man who made it happen. For that, our entire community owes him a debt of gratitude.

A special thank you to our close friend Alan Nierob who deftly navigated the public relations waters for us. Alan lived the real-life version of this book, as he was a teammate of Carter's and a longtime friend of mine. We owe him, and don't think for a second that he doesn't tell us that every single day. Ha!

Finally, to my dad's best friends, Bruce Corwin and Mikey Roberts. Thank you for always being there for my dad and for watching hundreds of Dallas Cowboy games with us over the years.